Markets from Culture

Markets from Culture

Institutional Logics and Organizational Decisions in Higher Education Publishing

PATRICIA H. THORNTON

Stanford Business Books
An imprint of Stanford University Press
Stanford, California 2004

Stanford University Press
Stanford, California

© 2004 by the Board of Trustees of the
Leland Stanford Junior University.
All rights reserved.

Printed and bound by CPI Group (UK) Ltd,
Croydon, CR0 4YY

Library of Congress Cataloging-in-Publication Data

Thornton, Patricia H.
  Markets from culture : institutional logics and organizational
decisions in higher education publishing / Patricia H. Thornton.
      p. cm.
  Includes bibliographical references and index.
  ISBN 0-8047-4021-6 (acid-free paper)
  1. Educational publishing.   2. Organizational sociology.
3. Educational publishing—United States—Management—Case studies.
4. Organizational change—United States—Case studies.   5. Decision
making—United States—Case studies.   I. Title.
Z286.E3 T47 2004
070.5'7—dc22   2003023989

Original Printing 2004

Designed by Rob Ehle
Typeset by Classic Typography in 10.5/12 Bembo

For my parents Mary Edwina Shattles and Louis Herbert Helmke

Contents

Contents

Figures and Tables

Figures

THE IMPORTANCE of understanding the cultural determinants of organizational decisions is highlighted by the many events and changes going on in our societies—globalization, corporate governance, and world conflicts based in economic and religious differences. However, scholars of organizational decision making have given little attention to the question of how cultural changes in wider institutional environments shape decision premises.

Theories of attention and decision making have emphasized how cognitive schemas at the individual level and structural routines at the organizational level shape attention and decision-making processes. Attention theory examines how individuals come to concentrate on certain characteristics to the exclusion of alternatives that would shift decision choices in other directions. This book is the first to focus on a third level by linking cultural analysis to the study of organizational decisions. While building on these earlier traditions, it presents a theory of attention showing how organizational decisions are premised on institutional logics at the societal sector level. These analyses are grounded in the case study of the changes in the higher education publishing marketplace from 1958 to the 1990s. They include extensive interviews with key publishers and investment bankers as well as historical and archival research and event-history statistical analyses.

While there has been no shortage of books and articles about the changes in publishing, this plethora lacks an examination that intertwines history and theory and systematically tests arguments with confirmatory methods of analysis. The higher education publishing marketplace has changed from a culture of independent domestic publishers in the 1950s, organized according to personal imprints and author–editor relational networks to one currently exemplified by international corporate hierarchies and corporate managers focused on building market channels and the market position of the firm. The acquisition of many independent, old-line publishing houses by major corporate and foreign buyers galvanized a new business culture. The economic conditions in the marketplace and the management culture are examined—tracing their development as the seeds of institutional change, progressing from the late 1950s through the 1960s, 1970s, and 1980s, and into the 1990s.

When personal capitalism and the editorial logic were dominant, attention was focused on the markets (for books) that were created from relational networks. When market capitalism became dominant, attention focused on the markets (for companies) that were created from hierarchies in which managers used the firm in new ways to increase financial returns. While role relations in networks and managerial relations in hierarchies have been shown to create markets, this book examines how societal-level culture influences these clique- and field-level market-making mechanisms. As the meta-analysis in Chapter 8 explains, whether in the form of markets or hierarchies, not all of these types of networks have equivalent effects because they focus attention on different governance mechanisms.

As will unfold in this book—the hard data and results of the statistical analyses defy simple economic explanations. Why do we observe differences in the predictors of organizational decisions from one historical period to the other? For example, there is no difference in the number of mergers and acquisitions between the periods 1958 to 1974, and 1975 to 1990. Why, then, is their effect in predicting organizational decisions so drastically different from one period to another? When the level of resource competition is actually higher, why is cooperation among publishers also higher? To address such questions, I examine how culture in the form of institutional logics moderates managers' interpretation of these structural differences.

Culture exists in a variety of units for empirical analysis, some of which are more researched and familiar than others. Scholars may readily intuit how cognitive schemas and organizational structures can focus attention. However, the work that links attention to the institutional sector level remains relatively undeveloped. The goal of this book is to develop and test a theory of attention that predicts the influence that institutional logics have on decision maker's attention to various problems and solutions in their arenas—in the specific case of my analysis, the firms and markets in publishing. Institutional logics are both the symbolic and material organizing principles of a societal sector, such as the professions, the market, the corporation, the family, and the religions. They shape attention by influencing mediating mechanisms such as cognitive schemas and organization structures. My theory of attention is tested in three critical decisions that organizations often face: changes in leadership, strategy, and structure. The analyses explain how a change in institutional logics in publishing, from personal to market capitalism, shifted decision makers' attention to alternative problems and solutions in their firms and markets. This change in institutional logics resulted in different determinants of the decisions on executive succession, divisionalization, and acquisition.

Culture is not typically used as an explanation for strategy because traditionally it has been used to explain continuity in action in the face of structural change. My theory of attention and the empirical analyses show how culture is also a source of strategic action. By theorizing about individuals and their ability to transpose elements of culture across institutional sectors, my theory explains how entrepreneurs mediate cultural change, relatively independent of inertial forces associated with social and economic structures. As meta-analyses across the decisions about leadership, strategy, and structure will show, some of these carriers of culture are more agentive than others in determining organizational decisions.

A rich case history of the contemporary development of higher education publishing is presented. But make no mistake, this book is not just about publishing—it shows the relationships between the cultural analyses of societies and organizational decision making in markets. The theory is applicable to explaining institutional changes and management decisions in other industrial contexts, particularly professional services industries, such as health care and financial services that are undergoing institutional transformation.

The interviews and coding of the event-history data set were conducted simultaneously during my graduate education at Stanford University. The interview experience provided me with many contacts in higher education publishing, and some publishers contributed valuable comments on drafts of papers that led to the development of this book. I coded all three dependent variables in the analyses—executive succession, acquisition, and divisionalization—at the same time, even though only one, acquisition (which provides the research for Chapter 7), was used for my dissertation. I remember Dick Scott sternly questioning the time I spent on the coding. The event history data set includes information at three levels of analysis—individuals and their positions, organizations and their relations, and market structures. My approach to the project ensured that I would only read through thirty-two years of the *Literary Marketplace* once. I hope he now understands.

What motivated me to study publishing had to do with conversations at home and at school. As a graduate student I remember Paul Lawrence visiting and giving a talk about the acquisitions in the late 1980s—how many of the transactions did not create economic value. I remember my husband Jack struggling to make sense of the changes in the industry. In retrospect it is understandable, at the time of the interview and archival data collection it was befuddling. The research of Neal Fligstein and Paul DiMaggio were central to figuring it out.

This book may be of interest to students of culture, networks, organization theory, institutional theory, management science, economic sociology, business history, and of course publishers. Students of methodology may also be interested in my integrative approach drawing on both qualitative and quantitative methods in theory building and testing. Additionally, anyone interested in publishing's inner workings will enjoy reading the many interviews and thumbnail case histories.

Acknowledgments

I AM INDEBTED TO many people for helping me develop this book. First and foremost, I owe a debt of gratitude to my husband, Jack N. Thornton who through his experience in publishing both as co-founder and as CEO of Brooks/Cole Publishing Co., and later as CEO of Wadsworth, Inc. showed me firsthand the world of higher education publishing. Without his social capital, I could not have obtained access to the heads of the major houses and the legendary editors who played a key role in developing the higher education marketplace.

I also thank Michael Brown, former CEO of the Thomson Organization, for letters of introduction to the investment bankers who work with the publishing industry. I also thank Tom McKee, formerly staff of the American Association of Publishers, for graciously sharing his data on publishing firms and for the numerous conversations in which he helped me interpret the data and historical events in higher education publishing.

I am grateful to many academic colleagues who have helped me develop my scholarship. My first thanks go to my teachers and mentors, Dick Scott, John Meyer, Jeff Pfeffer, Nancy Tuma, Buzz Zelditch, Bernie Cohen, and Don Palmer. Bill Barnett receives the credit for the idea to code the hierarchies of firms in an event-history data set. A special thank you goes to my colleague, Willie Ocasio, whose research assistant coded the variable on public/private ownership. His *Strategic Management Journal* article on attention and our many long conversations and heated debates have inspired numerous arguments presented in this book. Nancy Tuma's class notes and her availability to answer questions along the way were invaluable in developing the format of the data set and in selecting the statistical models. Bob Jackson in the Department of Sociology at Duke University was very helpful, putting up a version of RATE on the Duke UNIX system and always making time to address my many questions on data management. I very much appreciate the astute comments from many others on my related research papers and presentations: Howard Aldrich, Jeff Barden, Maura Belliveau, Nicole Biggart,

Rich Burton, Tina Dacin, Paul DiMaggio, Frank Dobbin, Neil Fligstein, Richard Florida, Roger Friedland, Heinrich Greve, Heather Haveman, Paul Hirsch, Candace Jones, Pete Kyle, Theresa Lant, Mike Lounsbury, Steve Mezias, Jim March, Will Mitchell, Mark Mizruchi, Chris Moorman, Woody Powell, Marc Schneiberg, Ida Simpson, Sim Sitkin, Ken Spenner, Joel Smith, Vanessa Tinsley, Edward Tiryakian, Marc Ventresca, and Xueguang Zhou.

I also owe a special thanks to the many publishers and investment bankers who consented to be interviewed, and whose names shall, according to human subject requirements, not be revealed. A few publishers and bankers I can thank individually for their reviews and comments on drafts of papers that have led to the development of this book. They are Lynn Lukow, former CEO of Jossey-Bass Publishing Co. and Director of Leadership Training for Stanford University Publisher's College; John Davis, former CEO of Prentice Hall; Don Shaeffer, former CEO of Prentice Hall; Henry Herschberg, head of the Higher Education Division, McGraw-Hill; Martin Levin Esq.; former head of Higher Education Division, Times Mirror; and Richard Abel, Publisher.

I thank the Fuqua School of Business for their support, in particular Debu Purohit, Rick Staelin, and Gerry DeSanctis, and the management faculty and Ph.D. student seminar participants for their helpful comments on Chapters 5 and 8. I also thank John Forsyth and the Hartman Center at Duke University for research support. I also appreciate the support of Provost Peter Lange of Duke University.

I owe a special thank you for technical assistance to John Morris of Meadowdance.

Last but not least, I thank the anonymous reviewers and the editors at Stanford University Press, Laura Comay, Bill Hicks, and Kate Wahl, for their foresight and advice in developing this book.

Markets from Culture

CHAPTER 1

Institutional Change and Organizational Decisions

The sociology of markets lacks a theory of social
institutions. . . .
—Neil Fligstein (2001, 8), *The Architecture of Markets:*
An Economic Sociology of Twenty-First-Century
Capitalist Societies

Introduction

This book is about analyzing the historical changes in the higher education publishing marketplace and using this analysis to develop organization theory and economic sociology. The central questions I address are how cultural institutions affect attention and decision making in organizations and markets. Classic and contemporary theory and research has focused on the economic, political, and social psychological dynamics of decision making in organizations. Institutional approaches suggest a different focus for the study of attention to organizational decisions—that economic and political interests and behavioral perceptions in organizations are shaped by *institutional logics* prevailing in wider environments (Friedland and Alford 1991). According to this perspective, although economic, political, and social psychological interests are pervasive in all organizations, their sources, meaning, and consequences for the focus of attention are to some extent contingent on higher-order institutional logics. Although the idea that organizational decisions are themselves conditioned by the cultural context has been explored from a historical perspective (Fligstein 1990), the role of culture in organizational decisions is relatively undeveloped in theories of strategic action.

The recent crisis in corporate organization motivates a search for new theories of the firm. The publishing industry is a research context well-suited to this goal. Publishers as content providers to global media and Internet enterprises are a central focus of the creative industries (Delaney 2000; Milliot

2000a, b). Characterized as both network and hierarchical structures that marry art and commerce, publishers are currently an analytic focus of the rapidly evolving branch of contract theory in economics (Caves 2000). Publishers are also relevant to the development of the new theories of markets in economic sociology (Fligstein 2001; White 2002).

We have an organization theory to understand how to respond to market failure: bring economic transactions in-house to be governed by the hierarchy (Williamson 1975). However, when organizations (hierarchies) fail, economists point to market solutions—the firm as a nexus of contracts (Caves 2000). As an alternative, this book brings back for examination a relatively forgotten logic of organization—cultural and attentional theories of the firm— and a third mechanism of governance—the professions (Blau and Scott 1962; Freidson 2002).

I draw on perspectives of networks and hierarchies in markets to motivate my analysis of how culture affects the strategic action of firms (Powell 1990; Fligstein 2001; White 2002). Sociological approaches to strategy and structure have emphasized explanations for the stability of firms and markets by relying on several mechanisms of transmitting cultural institutions and funneling attention—socialization, power, and organizational structure (Fligstein 1990, 1996; Palmer, Jennings, and Zhou 1993). I build on these analyses, but focus on how change in institutional logics shifts attention to alternative sources of adaptation in firms. And I also explore how culture may determine strategic action independent of social and economic structures (Swidler 1986; DiMaggio 1994).

Fligstein and Dauber (1989, 94) suggested linking the research from the Carnegie and neoinstitutional schools to the work on the strategy and structure of the corporation. The goal of this linkage is to articulate the mechanisms that connect decisions of actors inside organizations to cultural belief systems in contexts outside. This marriage promised two gains. First, the organization of cognitive attention is a pivotal process from which decisions emerge. Because this process takes place in the heads of individuals, it is potentially changeable and not inherently structurally constrained. Second, economic theory holds that decision makers are trying to achieve the most of some value under conditions of incomplete information, often called utilities or preferences. Cultural institutions establish the criteria by which individuals discover their preferences (Powell and DiMaggio 1991).[1]

In this book, through testing ideal types, I develop the concept of *institutional logics*. Institutional logics refer to the axial principles of organization and action based on cultural discourses and material practices prevalent in different institutional or societal sectors. According to Friedland and Alford (1991), the institutions that shape organizational action are embedded within higher-order societal logics. The major institutional sectors of society—the market, the state, the corporation, the professions, religion, and the family—provide a distinct set of often-contradictory logics that form the bases of political conflicts in organizations and society. Individuals, organizations, and society constitute three nested levels, where organization- and societal-level institutions specify progressively higher levels of opportunity and constraint for individual action. In Chapter 2 I explain the ideal types of institutional logics and their specific instantiations for attention to organizational decision making in publishing—the editorial and the market logics.

As the data and analyses of higher education publishing in subsequent chapters show, resource competition was actually higher in the editorial period. The number of mergers and acquisitions was not significantly different between the editorial and market periods. However, the editorial period had a culture that placed a different interpretation on these decision factors—an interpretation that resulted in decisions that placed a higher value on personal reputation and prestige of the house than on increasing profits and market share. While the economic events may have been the same in the two periods, the meaning and decision consequences of these material events varied as the business culture changed. As one former publisher, who turned boutique investment banker stated,

While it may seem rather late in coming, what happened in publishing during the 1980s was the idea of creating a pool of capital and having choices besides organic growth as to how that capital is manipulated. . . . The acceptance of this simple realization opened the door for decisions to be more profit driven than about long-term building.

Recent news reports have been filled with stories about how unethical individuals in corporations such as Enron, Arthur Anderson, and WorldCom went astray in their decision making. In the press, critical thinkers also point out an embarrassing observation—that rules already exist to control fraudulent decision making in corporations. These events and observations point to troubling questions: Why wasn't anyone paying attention? How did a set of finite accounting rules get misinterpreted? How did professional services firms in accounting and management consulting turn into hierarchies governed, not by an internal culture of professionalism or an external peer review system, but instead by the logics of market capitalism?

More than ever before, the scarcest resource isn't ideas or even talent, but attention itself (Davenport and Beck 2001). In the coming chapters, I develop and empirically test a theory of attention. Economic theories of the firm focus primarily on two perspectives. The first is the transaction-cost view, which states that organizations exist because they are efficient contractual instruments (Williamson 1975). The second perspective is the knowledge- and resource-based view, which argues that organizations exist because they are better than markets at integrating and applying valuable knowledge and resources to business activity (Penrose 1959; Nelson and Winter 1982; Wernerfelt 1984). Both views argue that organizations exist because they are superior to markets; both views also fail to provide an explanation for how the sources of identity, control, and strategy of firms may vary by culture.

I develop my argument by showing how culture shapes the attention of management and thus the strategic actions of the firm by charting the evolution of business culture through a case study of higher education publishing. Case studies on publishing document that it experienced a transformation from an industry emphasizing publishing as a *profession* to one in which leadership paid increasing attention to the influences of *market* forces (Coser, Kadushin, and Powell 1982, 179; Shatzkin 1982, 219; Powell 1985, 10; Tebbel 1981, 1987, 464; Greco 1997, 51; Schiffrin 2000, 105; Epstein 2001; Dreazen, Ip, and Kulish 2002).

I empirically demonstrate how this historical shift in the dominant institutional logic of an industry—from the logic of personal capitalism and the professions to the logic of market capitalism and the corporation—led to a change in the sources of focus of management attention in determining decisions on corporate power and leadership and strategy and structure. I integrate and build on the scholarly literatures on attention and cognition (Simon [1947] 1997; March and Olsen 1976; Ocasio 1997) and the sociology of the strategy and structure of the firm (Fligstein 1990, 1996, 2001). I expand on questions posed by scholars concerning why organizational decision makers attend to certain problems and solutions and not to others, independent of economic reality. I show how the sources of power in organizations based on rational behavior can produce decision choices and social structures that are contradictory and nonrational over the long term. By comparing the effects of the institutions of two forms of capitalism on organizational decisions, I quantitatively test principles of causality in management attention. I apply and test these arguments in three studies of higher education publishing, each of which develops a different scope condition of the theory for how a change in institutional logics (culture) affects the attention of organizational decision makers.

Change in the Institutions of Capitalism: The Case of Higher Education Publishing

The higher education publishing marketplace has changed from a culture of independent domestic publishers in the 1950s, organized according to relational network structures (Coser, Kadushin, and Powell 1982; Powell 1990) to one currently exemplified by international corporate hierarchies (Epstein 2001; Dreazen, Ip, Kulish 2002). The acquisition of many independent, old-line publishing houses by major corporate and foreign buyers galvanized a new business culture (Tebbel 1987; Greco 1997). I examine the economic conditions in the marketplace and the management culture of the late 1950s and trace their development as the seeds of institutional change, progressing through the 1960s, 1970s, 1980s, and into the 1990s. The historian John Tebbel (1981) has called this transformation the great change from the gentleman publisher, focused on establishing personal imprints and author–editor relationships, to the corporate manager, focused on building market channels and the market position of the firm.

I examine this shift in institutional logics in the industry by intertwining historical analysis with theoretical application. Economists have been skeptical of institutional analysis because its lack of formalization has prevented the development of a positive agenda of research (Stigler 1983; Williamson 1994). To capture the richness of the historical research and interviews with industry principals, but also to make the information amenable for theory construction and testing, I present the descriptive information in the stylized format of historical ideal types (Weber [1922] 1978). The ideal types are the elements of the theory that I weave together with semantic statements in subsequent chapters—grounding the theory in publisher's experiences with past and current problems and solutions. First, I review precursor studies to foreshadow my approach.

Precursor Studies

THE FIRST STEPS

Chandler's (1962) richly detailed case studies of the American corporation triggered the interest of economists who examined aspects of corporate strategy and structure, building the foundation for the modern field of business strategy. While this agenda emerged and advanced in several discrete stages—to large-sample statistical methods for studying business strategy (Wrigley 1970) and to incorporating the language and theory of economics (Rumelt 1974; Williamson 1975; Armour and Teece 1978)—it also naively portrayed senior management as faithful and rational servants to organizational goals (Donaldson 1996; Galaskiewicz and Bielefeld 1998, 9).

Unexplained and anomalous findings emerged: studies showed, for example, that corporate decisions were found to deviate from the principles of economic efficiency and converge toward collective outcomes. The initial adopters of the divisionalized organization could be explained by improved performance. As the number of adopters increased, however, the relationship between economic performance and structure disappeared (Armour and Teece 1978; Rumelt 1974). Mergers and acquisitions were shown to occur collectively in waves (Nelson 1959; Golbe and White 1988) that could not be explained by efficiency outcomes (Ravenscraft 1987, 20).

Unexplained findings continued to multiply and relate to other aspects of corporate strategy and structure, in particular to corporate governance and leadership. The effects of economic performance on executive succession were found to be small (Weisbach 1988; Frederickson, Hambrick, and Baumrin 1988) or nonexistent (Fizel, Louie, and Mentzer 1990). In some cases, the executive succession was preceded by abnormally good performance (Morck, Shleifer, and Vishny 1989).

Researchers interested in organizational decision making pursued a variety of approaches, but their work remained relatively disconnected from each other. While some researchers productively developed rational and behavioral theories (Tversky and Kahneman 1986; Payne, Bettman, and Johnson 1992), others pursued explanations of a cultural and structural origin (Fligstein 1990; Palmer et al. 1995). The anomalous economic findings in particular caught the eye of the sociologists. Fligstein (1987, 1990, 1996) developed a political–cultural theory of the firm in which corporate decision makers create stability in firms and markets by solving two problems: the creation of a set of cultural understandings and the government legitimation of those understandings. He found, for example, that chief executives in the 1960s and 1970s with corporate subunit experience in finance behaved differently from their counterparts in manufacturing and marketing, tending to see and solve problems in financial terms rather than those of manufacturing and marketing.[2] Other scholars built on Fligstein's ideas, for example in explaining the late adoption of the multidivisional form (Palmer, Jennings, and Zhou 1993) and styles of CEO decision making in the 1980s (Ocasio and Kim 1999).

While the sociological approaches were useful in explaining historically how executives used culture to create stable markets, they were less applicable to understanding the decision making of firms in rapidly changing markets characteristic of the post managerial era. The argument of imbibing culture through the socialization of values in a particular place, such as the subunit of a corporation or an elite business school, is a relatively slow structural process and one that is associated with institutional persistence, not the rapid pace of change required of corporate decision making under the pressures of market capitalism.[3] To press this issue of agency, researchers began to look elsewhere—to the Carnegie school and cognitive psychology (Powell and DiMaggio 1991; DiMaggio 1997, 267).

INTEGRATING LEVELS AND PERSPECTIVES

While the Carnegie and neoinstitutional schools focus on different levels of analysis, they share compatible metatheories. The neoinstitutional perspective accounts for the role of culture (Zucker 1977; Scott 2001), and the

Carnegie school explains the role of bounded rationality in decision making within the politics of the firm (March and Olsen 1976; Simon [1947] 1997). Simon ([1947]1957) and March and Simon (1958) laid the foundation for amending the rational assumptions of the neoclassical model of decision making. This perspective dates back to Barnard (1938), who emphasized organizational cognition and the management and coordination of knowledge within complex systems. Building on Barnard's cognitive focus, Simon ([1947] 1997, 118) defined the central concern of administrative theory as the boundary between the rational and nonrational aspects of human social behavior. The work of Simon ([1947] 1997, [1945] 1957) and March and Simon (1958) introduced the idea that decision makers may not be rational actors possessing relatively perfect information. Instead, they may have cognitive and informational constraints that explain suboptimal decision making. Organizational decisions are not necessarily the most efficient because managerial attention is boundedly rational, being shaped by the situational politics and organizational routines and structures of the firm (March and Simon 1958; Cyert and March 1963).

Similarly, the cognitive versions of institutional theory offered avenues for understanding how culture explains management decisions that diverge from the rational assumptions of the neoclassical model. For example, organizational environments are enacted (Weick 1976), they are loosely coupled systems (Weick 1976; March and Olsen 1976; Meyer and Rowan 1977), and they are highly institutionalized settings in which managers make decisions for reasons of legitimacy rather than efficiency (Meyer and Zucker 1989). However, even when these neoinstitutional perspectives have been applied to corporate settings, they lack a clear sense of interest and agency and an understanding of the historical and cultural contingency in decision styles.

The Carnegie school's concepts of attention, decision premises, routines, and firm as a political coalition open a way to theoretically frame Chandler's descriptions. However, with the exception of Amburgey and Miner (1992), who showed that managerial cognition and organizational routines drove decisions on acquisition strategy, empirical research in the strategy-and-structure paradigm that drew on the Carnegie school did not readily take hold. The link between the Carnegie school and Chandlerian contingency theory was also curiously absent from the quantitative research on the strategy and structure of the firm—even though these paradigms developed simultaneously (Lawrence and Lorsch [1967] 1986). Nelson and Winter's (1982) evolutionary theory of the firm is an exception. However, while they linked the Carnegie school to dynamic markets, their focus on selection theory and routines and capabilities embedded in organizational structure de-emphasizes change and the transformation of business institutions.[4] In sum, each perspective offers a partial explanation of the role of culture in organizational decision making. I build on and integrate these approaches in the three studies presented in subsequent chapters.

Issues That Foreshadow a New Approach

Several empirical observations and theoretical issues motivate my research questions and methods of analysis. First, the sociological research on the strategy and structure of the corporation has examined the effects of different forms of managerial capitalism and the impact of the state in determining the institutional environments of organizations and markets. However, significant social and economic changes have occurred since the managerial revolution (Chandler 1977). Market capitalism, with its image of rapidly changing competitive markets does not resonate as well with a model in which producers use government regulation to create stable markets.

Second, if power is theorized as a sole or even first-order construct in any explanation of institutional change, at least two problems need to be addressed. Stinchcombe (2002, 429) identifies these issues most clearly in arguing that power is created in the course of action; it does not occur prior to the action it explains. Therefore, any cultural theory of strategic action needs to explain how cultural influences may operate independent of power interests. Additionally, the decision to use power is a rational, strategic choice; yet it is not always possible to know the available choices in advance of action. These assumptions suggest that rational political theories of action are incomplete explanations because the necessary sequence of events may be unlikely to occur. One way to explore this problem in causal logic is to identify the mechanisms of culture and the range of expected strategic actions that is compatible with explanations derived from power (Dobbin 1994).[5]

At the same time, my argument brings to bear the sticky issue of disentangling the effects of culture from those of power and of the resource dependence on the state (Kraatz and Zajac 1996, 832; Schneiberg and Clemens forthcoming). As I show in subsequent empirical chapters, the publishing industry is a research context well-suited to partitioning the effects of the state from those of culture. It is an entrepreneurial industry largely exempt from federal subsidy (Levin 1996, 137) and state regulation (Smith 1995, 178).[6] Entrepreneurial practices were institutionalized as early as the fifteenth century with Gutenberg's development of the first printing press.[7] Tebbel (1972, 1981) points out that this spirit of independence is more than a quest for profits; its historical origins in the United States stem from colonials who used printing presses to promote political dissidence. This independent spirit is also evident in the identity and purpose of the original founders, Tebbel likens some publishers, such as Wiley, to missionaries and some to defectors from traditional education like Allyn & Bacon.

Finally, scholars have waged related versions of the agency-structure critique of organization theories (DiMaggio 1988; Stinchcombe 1997; Hirsch and Lounsbury 1997; Aldrich 1999, 50). This debate has classic roots in sociology (Weber 1904; Mayhew 1980; Sewell 1992).[8] Economists are typically interested in developing theories with assumptions of self-interest and universal powers of prediction, which may underscore their relative neglect of culture. They generally argue that cultural influences on economic decisions are only salient in less developed places, not in fully developed market spaces (DiMaggio 1994, 29–30). Traditionally, the structuralist school in sociology also has de-emphasized cultural explanations for market phenomena (Swedberg 1994). However, more recently Scott (2001, 210) has argued that markets are not culturally neutral a priori; instead all markets have institutional frameworks in which their constitutive and regulative rules vary in particular ways.[9]

In the coming chapters, I try to advance these questions through an investigation of how culture and social and economic structures shape the attention and courses of actions of organizational decision makers. I explore the scope conditions of economic and sociological theories of organizations and markets that I draw on in examining the changes in higher education publishing. Can they be applied as universals, as an objective state, or is the power of their predictions contingent on historical and cultural interpretation? I attempt to partition the locus of agency to better understand at what levels of analysis, individual, organizational, or environmental, and whether it is culture or social and economic structures that are relatively more or less agentive sources of organizational decisions in markets.

Quantitative Data and Methods

The data include continuous-time observations of the characteristics of individuals, organizations, and the environment. To my knowledge, this is the first data set to include annual observations at all three levels of analysis. These observations include five types of measures: (1) measures of the characteristics of individuals, including the individual traits of founders and executives; (2) measures of the characteristics of organizations, including size, types of structure, ownership forms, and relational linkages with other organizations; (3) measures of types of strategies, including imprint publishing and growth by acquisition; (4) measures of significant events, including leadership succession, acquisition, founding, and disbanding; and (5) measures of the characteristics and changes in the environment and the marketplace, including resource competition and supply and demand characteristics, among others. Detailed information on all of the measures and the sources of the data is included in Chapter 4 and Appendix B.

My method of drawing a population differs from most ecological studies of organizational founding and mortality that use a single organizational form to define the population boundary (Carroll and Hannan 2000, 60–65). I defined the population boundary according to a product market assuming in theory that a diversity of organizational forms compete and cooperate in markets (White 2002). I use a typology of ideal types to clarify differences in the cultural meaning and identities of organizational forms (Weber [1922] 1978; Doty and Glick 1994; Carroll and Hannan 2000). These ideal types are an abstract model of organizational forms that enable comparisons between different strategies and structures.

My event-history data have several theoretical and methodological advantages over cross-sectional, panel, and event-count data structures (Tuma and Hannan 1984, chap. 2). Cross-sectional data offer only a snapshot of a market, industry, or organizational field at a single point in time. Panel data, which focus on specific variables at two or more discrete points in time, are very dependent on the accuracy of the selected time points and cannot distinguish discontinuous from incremental change. Compared to panel data, event-count designs include more time points, but aggregate organizational events to the population level. This limits the ability to determine if changes at the population level are due to the entry of new actors, the demise of old ones, or the transformation of existing organizations (Scott et al. 2000, 38–39).

The research presented in this book improves on prior research on the effects of institutional and organizational change through the use of open-ended, in-depth interviews with industry principals and a typology to define the institutional logics, the identity of organizational forms, and the historical time periods in which they prevailed. The archival data on which the hazard-rate analyses were based were coded independently of the analysis of the historical and interview data and the development of the ideal types.

The statistical analyses make use of piecewise, exponential hazard-rate models for the simultaneous analysis of the interaction effects between the covariates and the time periods of the events. This approach addresses the critique that institutional analysis focuses on obvious period effects represented by simple dummy variables, showing instead how institutional logics moderate the effect of the causal variables rather than just changing the period intercepts. Nested models and equality constraints serve to test for time-period differences for individual covariates, an approach that improves on the use of time-period dummy variables. Detailed information on the specification of the statistical models is included in Chapter 4.

Studies that are so new and so varied as to render their findings incomparable with other studies do not advance literatures. Because I am breaking from convention in certain respects previously discussed, I have also consciously taken care to be doctrinaire in following other research design traditions. I have selected conventional dependent variables from the strategy and organization theory literatures to test my theory of attention. I also have been painstakingly consistent in the collection, presentation, and analysis of the data across the three studies. I have employed cross-validating methods such as triangulation of data sources, employing interviews, surveys, historical research, and archival data (Eisenhardt 1989; Doty and Glick 1994). I also have been deliberately consistent in the analysis of the data. I experimented with analytical strategies and found the data to be robust using a variety of modeling procedures. In the final analysis, I use the same modeling strategy across the three studies to facilitate comparison of the results. My research strategy is to replicate effects across the three studies, holding constant the typical sources of variation in meta-analytic research. I believe this strategy provides a stronger test of my cultural argument.

The Evolution of Organization Studies Paves the Way

The development of organization theory in the United States provides the foundation for my approach to a theory of attention. Studies of organizations in the 1950s and 1960s were focused on the behavior of participants within organizations, treating the organization itself as the focal context. Organizations were viewed as natural living systems that transformed themselves to keep pace with environmental change (Selznick 1949; Clark 1956; Zald and Denton 1963). It was the participants themselves who intentionally brought about organizational adaptation and change by manipulating the formal and informal processes of conflict, cooptation, and goal displacement (Merton 1949; Selznick 1957).

With the development of systems theories in the 1960s (Thompson 1967; Miller and Rice 1967; Perrow 1967; and Lawrence and Lorsch [1967] 1986), researchers focused on organizations as "open systems" to their external environments. Variations in organizational performance, for example, were attributed to differences in organizations' ability to manage the growing complexity of institutional environments in one industry system versus another (Hirsch 1972, 1975). This emphasis gave rise to a number of new theories giving primacy to influences of the external environment in determining organizational behavior (Meyer and Rowan 1977; Hannan and Freeman 1977; Pfeffer and Salancik 1978).

Organization researchers in the 1980s (DiMaggio and Powell 1983; Scott and Meyer 1983) continued to elaborate the complexities of the institutional environment. The early dichotomous view of "technical versus institutional environments," that presumed that organizations were influenced either by material technologies, resources, and market exchanges, or by the elaboration of rule making by the state and the professions, has given way to the realization that all types of organizations operate in markets of various types (Scott 2001, 210).

This evolutionary development from a focus on behavior inside organizations to one stressing the influences of the external environment changed the style and goals of research from an emphasis on concrete situational accounts of organizations to one focused on abstract and generalizable concepts across different contexts (Barley and Kunda 2001). Population ecology and neoinstitutional theories are exemplars with their abstract focus on competition and legitimacy that is rooted in the developmental structure of an industry or an organizational field.[10]

With this paradigm shift, the earlier utilitarian concepts of agency and conflict fade from researchers' view. Hence, the rational concepts of conflict, cooptation, and goal displacement, mechanisms by which both workers and management achieved goal consensus, were supplanted in the newer macro theories with a focus on expectations, rules, and cognitive limits to rationality. Organizations, for example, keep their boundaries intact not through conflict or attempts to achieve goal consensus (Selznick 1957), but by avoiding conflict (Meyer and Rowan 1977). Thus, researchers began to understand organizations as multilayered symbolic systems (Pfeffer and Salancik 1978), wherein the activities at the periphery of the organization, the area most susceptible to influences from the external environment, are loosely coupled or only ceremoniously incorporated into the activities of the organization's core (Meyer and Rowan 1977; Hannan and Freeman 1984). The focus of researchers' attention evolved from theories of organizational change to those of stasis (DiMaggio and Powell 1983), external control (Pfeffer and Salancik 1978), environmental selection (Hannan and Freeman 1977), and symbolic management (Westphal and Zajac 1994, Zajac and Westphal 2001), hence fueling the need for research on institutional change, conflict, interest, and agency.

My qualitative and interpretive analysis builds on the richness of the earlier sociology of behavior within organizations (Selznick 1957; Blau and Scott 1962). At the same time, my approach revitalizes this tradition by drawing on the recent developments in theory and methodology in economic and organizational sociology.

The Argument

The core of my theoretical argument is that institutional logics focus the attention of decision makers in organizations on issues and solutions that are consistent with the prevailing institutional logic. When a change in institutional logics occurs, the attention of decision makers shifts to alternative issues and solutions. Institutional logics, once they become dominant, affect the decisions of organizations with respect to leadership, strategy, and structure by focusing the attention of executives toward the set of issues and solutions that are consistent with the dominant logic and away from those issues and solutions that are not.

I propose four mechanisms by which institutional logics shape executive decisions in organizations with respect to power and leadership and to organization strategy and structure. First, the *meaning, appropriateness,* and *legitimacy* of various sources of executive power and of strategy and structure, are shaped by the rules of the prevailing institutional logic. For example, with respect to power, institutional logics provide the rules that determine whether positional, relational, or market factors form the basis of leadership power and authority in organizations (March and Olsen 1989). In the context of the publishing industry, institutional logics indicate how the positions of founder, editor, publisher, president, manager, and chief executive officer (CEO) are valued and understood.

Second, institutional logics determine which *issues and problems* to attend to in controlling market forces and rewarding political behavior in organizations (March and Olsen 1976; Ocasio 1997). Logics provide the rules of the game that shape the cognition of social actors in organizations (DiMaggio 1997). Given ambiguity and cognitive limitations on executive decision making, organizations cannot attend to every aspect of their environments (March and Olsen 1976; Simon [1947] 1997). Hence, organizational decision makers are constrained to focus their attention on a limited set of issues. Institutional logics comprise a set of implicit rules of the game that regulate which issues, strategic contingencies, or problems become important in the political struggle among actors in organizations (Ocasio 1997). For example, whether power is allocated to those enhancing the prestige of the publishing house or to those improving market position depends on whether the prevailing institutional logic focuses attention on prestige or, alternatively, on market competition.

Third, the assumptions, values, beliefs, and rules that constitute institutional logics determine what *answers and solutions* are available and appropriate in controlling economic forces and political activity in organizations and markets (March and Olsen 1976; Ocasio 1997). For example, with respect to organization strategy and structure, institutional logics regulate whether to control or reward publishing executives' focus on particular solutions, such as organic (internal) or acquisition growth strategies, building personal imprints or developing market channels. Consequently, the use of leadership succession, relational networks, formal hierarchy, and acquisition activity as solutions to organizational problems of market instability depends not only on economic conditions, but also on whether the prevailing institutional logics legitimate these answers and solutions as appropriate responses to market instability. One publisher commented, for example, in the 1980s under the market logic that: "Firms began to suffer internally when they let the level of organic growth go because a lot of funds were instead moved over to acquisitions."

Fourth, institutional logics affect organizations' decisions to adapt and change. Institutional logics legitimate certain business strategies, but not others, and therefore moderate the development and persistence of particular organizational structures. For example, logics focusing attention on prestige favor relational network strategies and structures; logics focusing attention on market competition favor strategies and structures characteristic of managerial hierarchies. I propose that organizations are legitimate and competitive to the extent that they are in conformity with higher-order institutional logics (Friedland and Alford 1991; Scott 2001, 43). When an organization's strategy and structure are deviant and in conflict with the prevailing institutional logic, it bears increased selection pressures to change and adapt its strategies and structures.

The fact that institutional logics manifest themselves as strategic behaviors points to two central theoretical questions. How culture manifests in people's heads (DiMaggio 1997); and how cultural schemas take on an independent existence from social and economic structures (Swidler 1986; Barley and Kunda 1992). Meeting these two requirements is necessary to construct a theoretical argument that has the flexibility to explain the sources of strategic action in firms and markets. I attempt to address these issues by showing how the ideas for strategic actions originate from different levels of analysis and institutional sectors. A multilevel approach is needed because firms, both networks and hierarchies (Fligstein 2001; White 2002), are one way markets take place. Markets also are nonfirms, and undoubtedly have preexisted firms (Hayek 1945). In Chapter 3 on a theory of attention, I develop these arguments.

The Historical Change in Institutional Logics

A number of authors have noted that there has been no shortage of books and articles about the changes in publishing (Tebbel 1981, 1987; Coser, Kadushin and Powell 1982; Powell 1985; Schiffrin 2000; Epstein 2001). However, this plethora seems to lack a review that intertwines history and theory, and that, more importantly, tests these accounts using systematic data and confirmatory methods of analysis (Caves 2000).

In Chapter 2, I chronicle the institutional transformation of the industry. Using quotations from the industry literature and excerpts from the interviews, I trace the institutional and organizational changes to a number of factors that contributed to the decline of an editorial logic and the rise of a market logic. The early 1970s saw a period of transition in logics that was first and foremost propelled by four factors: (1) rising demand and the availability of corporate capital, (2) an increase in resource competition in the product market after the mid-1970s, (3) new sources of information from trade presses that emphasized a focus on market logics, and (4) the development of investment banking practices and firms specialized to and within the industry.[11] With respect to the latter, in the period of a market logic, deal-maker networks from within the industry literally constructed a market for companies (White 2002). One publisher for example stated that: "Deal makers invent deals by calling up publishers and telling them that a company is for sale and then calling the other party and saying there is a willing buyer." Another publisher elaborated: "There is a network out there that knows about mergers. Within three hours of my contacting McGraw-Hill about the decision to sell my company, which is the only company I contacted, an investment banker called me and said 'I understand your division is on the block'!"

Using this historical research and the interviews, I present in Table 2-1 (see Chapter 2) a set of ideal types—the editorial and market logics. These institutional logics are associated with different forms of capitalism and organizational archetypes, providing a set of expectations for decisions on the strategy and structure of the firm. In Chapter 3, I present the semantic statements that link the ideal types to a theory of attention. In Chapter 4, I present detailed information on the data sources and methods of analysis used in the subsequent empirical chapters.

Three Tests of the Argument

ATTENTION TO THE SOURCES OF POWER IN LEADERSHIP SUCCESSION

In Chapter 5, I show how a shift in the prevailing institutional logic shapes executive attention and thereby moderates the sources of power that determine leadership succession. I examine three sources of power—positional, relational, and market. Positional power refers to those determinants of power that are inherent in the actor's role or position, such as founder or division executive. For relational power, I investigate those determinants of power that derive from the structure of relationships among actors and groups of actors, both intra- and interorganizationally, such as the relationships between authors and editors or producers and distributors. For market power, I assess the determinants of power related to issues that have consequences for the performance of firms in a product market. These determinants include access to public capital markets, resource competition, profitability, and the market for corporate control.

The findings show that under an editorial logic, leadership attention is directed to author–editor relationships and internal growth, and leadership succession is determined by organization size and structure. Under a market logic, executive attention is directed to issues of resource competition and growth by acquisition, and executive succession is determined by the product market and the market for corporate control. Over the observation period, there was an increase in the importance of market determinants of executive power and a decline in the effects of positional and relational sources of power in determining leadership succession in publishing firms.

ATTENTION TO THE SOURCES OF ADAPTATION
OF ORGANIZATION STRUCTURE

In Chapter 6, I extend the scope conditions of the theory to the analysis of a change in organizational structure—the decision to divisionalize. I address the theoretical puzzle of why publishing firms adopted the divisionalized organization structure given the relative lack of scale economies that are derived from standardization (Chandler 1962). I examine two alternative sources of structure, professional and market. Professional sources of structure refer to expertise embodied in individuals who derive their authority and autonomy from the social legitimacy of their missions and their exclusive ability to apply expert and esoteric knowledge to particular cases. Examples of this are editors in publishing, certified public accountants, and physicians (Hirsch 1972; Freidson 1986, 2002, Abbott 1988). Alternatively, knowledge and expertise can be embedded in routines and hierarchies, as in the cases of state bureaucracies and multidivisional corporations. I argue that when two or more institutional logics are in conflict, organizations are pressured to change. Organizations that are in conformity with the prevailing institutional logic are viewed as more legitimate, competitive, and immune from change pressures than those organizations that are not.

The findings show that under an editorial logic, the focus of attention is on professional sources of structure such as author–editor relational networks and personal imprint publishing, which decreased the transition rate of firms to corporate divisions. Under a market logic, attention is focused on market sources such as the growth of hierarchies by acquisitions and building market share, which increased the transition rate to corporate divisions. One well-known publisher recalled one of the ways that relational networks began to break down with the hiring of industry outsiders into management positions. He stated:

Many years ago I was the business and economics editor at Holt, Rinehart & Winston and they hired a new sales manager from outside the industry—I think he was, if you would believe, from a large company that manufactured plumbing fixtures. One day he came into my office with this research folder he'd spent God knows how many hours and how much money on it, and he said, "I think it would be helpful to you as an editor to know that Samuelson's book sold 125,000 copies last year."

I said, "No it didn't, it sold 176,532." He said, "For God sakes, where would you get that kind of information?" I said, "I called and asked the editor over at McGraw." He said, "What?" I said "We share this kind of information because it's useful to both sides." He said, "Well, how do you know what's backing it?" I said, "The printer will tell me if it is accurate."

Overall over the observation period there was an increase in the importance of market determinants of organization structure and a decline in the effects of professional sources of structure. More generally, these findings address the current policy question of how firms that were traditionally governed by professional sources of structure, for example, publishing, accounting, and management consulting, turn into hierarchies governed by market logics (Dreazen, Ip, and Kulish 2002).

ATTENTION TO THE SOURCES OF ADAPTATION OF ORGANIZATIONAL STRATEGY

Parallel to the format in Chapters 5 and 6, in Chapter 7, I extend the scope of the theory to examine decisions on organization strategy. I examine two sources of strategy, organizational and market. Organizational sources of strategy refer to basic relationships between strategy and structure that are important to the production and distribution of products; most particularly: Should firms vertically integrate or outsource distribution? Should they grow organically or seek acquisitions?

I examined the decision to seek an acquisition within the framework of two questions drawn from contingency theory (Lawrence and Lorsch [1967] 1986), agency theory (Manne 1965; Jensen and Ruback 1983), and economic history (Marris and Mueller 1980, 42). First, I ask, "Does capitalism select optimal organization structures?" Second, "What is an optimal fit between organization strategy and structure and the economic and cultural environment?"

I argue that different forms of capitalism, personal and market, create different selection pressures on organizations. Once again, organizations that conform to the institutional logic of the prevailing form of capitalism are more legitimate and competitive, and therefore more immune to selection pressures, such as the risk of acquisition. The findings show that under a market logic, publishers that focused their attention on organizational sources of strategy, such as relational networks in production and distribution, were at higher risk of acquisition. Interestingly, the effects of resource competition decreased the risk of acquisition under an editorial logic, but increased risk under a market logic. These findings support Powell's (1990) argument that relational network structures have a unique organizational form with their own logic of governance—one that emphasizes dampening market competition through cooperation, not by acquiring market share. However, the ability of relational network forms to flourish and to mitigate the effects of resource competition is contingent on a culture that supports norms of trust, reputation, and reciprocity—attributes inherent in the editorial logic, but not in the market logic. Over the observation period, there was an increase in the importance of market determinants of strategy and a decline in the effects of the organizational sources of strategy.

Meta-analysis: Markets from Culture

Each of the three studies presented in Chapters 5, 6, and 7 develops a theory of attention to understand how publishers used culture to make critical decisions for their organizations in changing markets. In Chapter 8, I assess the scope conditions of the theories employed in these analyses, both the locus of agency and their predictive power, by combining the findings of the independent variables across the three studies. I explore which levels of analysis or carriers of institutions were the more agentive mediators in determining how culture moderates the social and economic structural forces that influence organizational decisions (Barley and Kunda 1992).

In performing this meta-analysis, I shift the focus of this comparison to a higher level of abstraction—from the firm to the market. Markets coordinate many types of decisions and how this coordination occurs has been a subject of debate by both economists and sociologists (Williamson 1975, 1991; Granovetter 1985; Powell 1990; Fligstein 1996). From these stylized debates, I extract three ideal types of markets, each of which produces a set of assumptions and predictions on governance mechanisms with respect to the locus and logics of action and whether the predictions of the theories are expected to be universal or particular. First, I describe the three ideal types of markets: (1) markets as economic exchanges, (2) markets as relational structures, and (3) markets as political–cultural arenas. Second, I use them as a comparative yardstick to address the questions foreshadowed earlier on agency and structure and universalism or particularism.

The findings show that positional effects are universal; relational network effects are particular; and economic effects are both universal and particular across historical and cultural contexts. The findings also show that the predictive power of the economic and organizational theories employed in each of the three studies—resource dependence, managerial, and agency—was not universal, but contingent on the prevailing institutional logic. It is of interest that the economic variables have mixed effects, universal in some cases, but particular in others—indicating that some economic processes are more subject to social construction and cultural interpretation than others.

The combination of these findings has several implications for the prolific school of relational networks in structural sociology.[12] The meta-analyses discussed in Chapter 8 provide evidence that markets derive from culture; the agentive effects of both relational networks and resource competition on organizational decisions are consistently particular and culturally contingent. When the editorial logic was dominant, attention was focused on the markets (for books) that were created from relational networks among editors and authors. When the market logic was dominant, attention was focused on the markets (for companies) that were created from hierarchies in which managers used the firm to produce higher financial returns (Fligstein 1990). Overall, my findings suggest that although relational networks are ubiquitous—be they networks between book editors or investment bankers—their effects are not universal across various types of markets; the effects are particular to the type of market and the cultural context.

Conclusion

The interviews and the historical research established that the prevailing institutional logic shifted in the 1970s, from the industry-specific instantiations of the professions and networks to those of the market and the corporation. We can understand this transformation as publishers transposing and adopting elements of the institutional logics from one societal sector and applying them to another. In the editorial period, publishers' attention and sources of identity stemmed from the professions—from the cultural elite and academic communities; in the market period their attention and sources of identity came from the financial communities. Publishers repeatedly expressed this idea through a number of sentiments. For example:

The problem we created by all the mergers and acquisitions is that we have broken the relationships in the marketplace. We no longer have the same kind of bonds between the academic publishers and the professor—that link has been broken. In comparison with the early 1970s, there is a real difference in the quality of interaction among publishers at academic meetings and how publishers are now viewed by the academic community—basically commercial stuff and almost a necessary evil. . . . In the past academics liked to see us because as "travelers" we knew what was going on and carried the gossip from one campus to another.

Institutional change in modern societies is seldom abrupt and wholesale unless it is a result of the visible hand of the state or a competence destroying technology (Tushman and Anderson 1986). Of all the forces that contributed to the shift from a professional to a market logic, the need for new sources of capital to meet growing demand was the central factor. Retained earnings under the governance of family ownership could not provide sufficient capital and investment bankers had difficulty valuing publishing assets, claiming that the formula for a best-selling book defies rationality. Thus, corporate capital—through mergers and acquisitions, particularly during two waves in the late 1960s and 1980s—was used to solve publishing companies' growth-financing problem. The first wave was largely a result of industry outsiders who planted financial and corporate models; in the second wave, boutique investment banking firms developed to specialize solely in publishing. However, the central finding with respect to acquisitions is that the meaning and consequences of acquisition were quite distinct according to the different institutional logics prevailing in the two periods.

The sources of institutional change in organizational power, strategy, and structure examined in this book are a consequence of the rationalization of the institutional logics of capitalism and the extent to which an organization's strategy and structure are in conformity with the logics of the prevailing form of capitalism. Publishing houses that were driven by an editorial logic—with their author–editor relational network strategies, structures of personal imprints, and values against vertical integration (Hirsch 1972, 641)—faced new pressures to adapt and change. They risked selection pressures if they did not transform themselves as the industry shifted to a new cultural regime—a market logic.

It may appear at the population-level of analysis that the story of the consequences of the shift in logics from the professions to the markets is a monolithic process of rationalization occurring when all industries modernize. In most of the individual cases in my analyses, institutional change is relatively linear and evolutionary. Still in a few, it is contested and perhaps cyclical. This is an empirical question that requires a longer observation period for analysis.

The history of Prentice Hall (PH) until its acquisition by Gulf & Western in 1985 is an example of a relatively linear rationalization of their publishing businesses by using financial practices such as acquisitions and corporate ventures as the building blocks to develop companies.[13] The founder of PH, R. P. Ettinger was a professor of finance at New York University. In 1985 when Prentice Hall was acquired by then Gulf & Western, later named Paramount Communications, PH was the largest publisher in the world and had twenty-two divisions and subsidiaries, many of which came in as acquisitions. How did PH do this? They shrewdly planted their seeds and then let them grow.

For example, Prentice Hall acquired two old-line publishers in the 1950s, Charles E. Merrill, founded in 1842, and Allyn & Bacon (A&B), founded in 1868. I follow the case of A&B. In 1952, on the accidental death of Paul Bacon, son of one of the founders, PH acquired A&B, one of the oldest school textbook houses in the United States. Prentice Hall instilled new energy, capital, and leadership, making the company at once old-line and an innovative publisher (Tebbel 1981, 525). The connection endured long enough for PH to plant its people and its decentralized entrepreneurial practices. In

1957, less than five years after the acquisition, PH spun off A&B as a separate stock company after having established a successful college division, expanded numerous lists, and opened a warehouse and distribution center. The management team who were successful in the development of A&B then went on to found Wadsworth. Originally an internal corporate venture of PH, it was subsequently spun off as a separate stock company in 1964. Wadsworth itself carried on the practice of founding new divisions both by organic means and acquisitions, eventually being acquired by Thomson in 1978 and becoming the fifth largest higher education publisher in the United States by 1992.

In another example, the recent battle at Bertelsmann over the decision of whether to focus attention back to its roots in family capitalism or to proceed with the CEO's vision of an IPO and building a media empire is a contemporary example of institutional logics in conflict (Karnitschnig and Boudette 2002).

The analysis of institutional and organizational change through the case of higher education publishing brings to light the complex issue of distinguishing the effects of culture and cognition from the effects of economic and social structure. How much is the attention to organizational decisions attributable to a fundamental change in culture independent of shifts in the material–resource environment? How much are organizational decisions due to a rational adaptation to a change in the value of economic and social resources?

In these chapters, I empirically show that structural change did, indeed, occur. However, the findings also suggest that there is not a one-to-one correspondence between changes in social and economic structures and changes in institutional logics that have consequences for leadership power and succession and organizational strategy and structure. I propose that this relative autonomy of cultural logics stems from the fact that they operate by focusing the attention and cognition of decision makers in organizations, thereby moderating the effects of economic and social structural forces. This theoretical question has practical implications with respect to the questions posed earlier in this chapter. If we know more about how organizational decision making is influenced by culture, versus organizational design, regulation, and economic supply and demand, then we know better how to protect against faulty and fraudulent decision making in organizations.

My interviews with higher education publishers and the analyses of the archival data have led me to argue that a culture of the professions differs in fundamental ways from a culture of the market in influencing organizational decisions. As a check on the self-interest and guile of market capitalism, the professions rely on peer review mechanisms external to organization structures that are not driven by the financial markets, particularly the equities markets. Public corporations (hierarchies) bring such functions in-house under the purview of managers who are influenced by incentive systems based in the financial markets. This is not to say that professional models are not performance oriented, but that they focus attention on alternative goals and means to achieve outcomes. As the interviews showed, publishers under an editorial logic focused on sales derived from evaluation by product markets, not on the manipulation of the bottom line by various strategies and accounting procedures derived from evaluation by financial markets. The former focuses on employee incentives that instill meaning in the art of publishing, the latter on financial incentives that place higher values on the break-up price of a firm (Davis, Diekmann, and Tinsley 1994, 549). Ironically, the financial performance data from the Association of American Publishers in Appendix C show that the financial performance of the larger hierarchical publishers, developed largely from the market for companies, declined relative to that of smaller publishers as the economic system of market capitalism came to prevail.

The study of higher education publishing shows that culture is a critical factor in determining organizational decisions. Structural forces such as changes in resource competition, while also important influences, cannot completely explain or remedy the differences observed in decision making in the publishing industry between 1958 and the 1990s—differences that the front-page business press indicates are happening in many industries (Dreazen, Ip, and Kulish 2002).

Through the practices of higher education publishing, I have chronicled the changes from personal to market capitalism and have quantitatively shown these changes' consequences on organizational decisions. This empirical work has given me an opportunity to develop a general theory of attention that is applicable to other industries, historical periods, and forms of capitalism. Although the interviews and quantitative data were collected largely from the period 1958 to 1990, as the interviews and the recent quote from *Publishers Weekly* below indicate, the events chronicled in this book continue to be in the spotlight of the media.

When Holt, Rinehart & Winston was acquired by CBS in 1967, it remained intact; it was not dismembered into pieces to be sold off. However, in 1987 when CBS divested Holt, Rinehart & Winston to Harcourt Brace Jovanovich, it eventually disappeared. As one publisher stated:

A lot of acquisitions in the 1980s disappeared into Paramount and McGraw-Hill and Macmillan. . . . I've seen publishers that make essentially just a one-year big increase in earnings from buying a company. In hindsight, the later deals did not make good financial sense, so in order to make the acquisitions pay, they were going to have to plan on a lot of consolidation. Under these conditions, down the company goes as it gets older and deteriorates as nobody is there to make it grow and maintain it. So you'd think they would want to buy the creative people behind it too. We lost some great publishing imprints. It took fifty to seventy-five years to get the market identification, yet the acquiring company is like the Attila the Hun. . . . Harper ended up with ten introductory psychology books to add to their own. So they now have psych to burn because they could only publish one or two a year.

Now fast forward to the anticipated divestiture of Houghton Mifflin purchased only a year ago in 2001 by the French conglomerate Vivendi with the goal of competing in the worldwide media empire. (Houghton Mifflin was one of the last large American companies left intact besides Wiley and McGraw.) Jim Milliot (2002, 10) in a recent *Publishers Weekly* article states:

One open question is whether Houghton Mifflin is worth more sold as a unit or in pieces. There are a lot of bankers buzzing around New York now trying to figure that one out. . . . Regarding the new CEO, who took over July 1, 2002, while widely regarded as a good executive, sources said that HM executives were disappointed that a person with experience in educational publishing wasn't named to the post. It [educational publishing] has a steep learning curve, said one banker, a curve whose climb might take a lot of time. And it has become clear in the last few weeks that time is something Vivendi doesn't really have.

This book, I hope, will move the reader through an understanding of the descriptive and the particular, grounded in the institutional changes of higher education publishing to an understanding of a general cultural theory of attention applied to organizational decision making in markets. Publishing, once known as the "accidental profession" in which good books were once thought to sell themselves and editors were the gatekeepers of culture (Coser 1975), holds an analogy to other craft- and profession-based industries in which the public consequences of corporate decision making are significantly higher. One author writing about Arthur Andersen stated:

In the historical case of the "gentleman's profession" of accounting, salespeople were once unheard of and thought to be antithetical to preserving the mission and authority of the profession as the conscience of capitalism. (Dugan 2002)

CHAPTER 2

The Historical Change in Institutional Logics

The work of the American institutionalists led to nothing. . . .
Without a theory, they had nothing to pass on except a mass
of descriptive material waiting for a theory or a fire.
—Oliver Williamson (1994) paraphrasing Ronald Coase,
   "The new institutional economics." *Journal of*
   Institutional and Theoretical Economics 140: 229, 231

INSTITUTIONAL ANALYSIS in both economics and sociology has been criticized as historical description of little value to theory construction and discipline building. In this chapter, I describe the transformation of the U.S. higher education publishing market in the second half of the 20th century as an instance of profound change in the institutions of capitalism. I formalize the presentation of the historical descriptive material using the method of typologies to develop two ideal types of capitalism, personal and market. First, I discuss the benefits of formal typologies as a method of theory construction. Then I chronicle the empirical evidence that identifies and grounds the ideal types.

Typologies in Theory Construction

The historical comparative method of formal typologies stems from Weber's analysis of authority structures or systems of legitimate social control in organizations—for example, his categories of traditional, charismatic, and legal authority.[1] Typologies allow for multidimensional classification of phenomena and are composed of two parts: (1) the description of ideal types and (2) the set of assertions that relate the ideal types to the dependent variable (Doty and Glick 1994). The ideal types are a conceptual scheme that implies a set of hypotheses.

Typologies must meet three criteria for theory building: (1) constructs must be identified, (2) relationships among these constructs must be specified, and (3) these relationships must be falsifiable. The ideal types are intended to provide an abstract model that represents a combination of those attributes believed to determine the dependent variables of interest. The ideal types provide a means of clustering organizations into categorical types to measure and explain deviation from the extreme. In this way, intelligible comparisons can be made (Zelditch 1971), and the theory can be falsified by determining the degree of similarity or dissimilarity of the ideal types to the dependent variables of interest.

Typologies have a number of advantages. First, the ideal types are not specified with organizations in the sample. Organizations in the sample may or may not closely resemble the ideal types described in the theory. Therefore, the process of theory development and the range of the dependent variables are not restricted by the characteristics of the sample.

Second, typological methods of theory building are useful for specifying multiple patterns of constructs and nonlinear relationships that determine the dependent variable. Two constructs may be positively related in organizations that resemble one ideal type, negatively related in those that look like a second ideal type, and unrelated in organizations that are similar to a third or fourth ideal type (Doty and Glick 1994, 244).

This conceptual flexibility is helpful in theory construction in which countervailing and time-dependent effects are expected. Moreover, this feature is a good fit in theory testing using dynamic event-history models because it does not constrain assumptions, for example, about the reversal of a theoretically precise causal relationship (Tuma and Hannan 1984) or about multilevel effects (DiPrete and Forristal 1994). This allows, for example, the effects at the individual level of analysis to vary from the effects at the organizational and environmental levels of analysis. To understand how to conduct event-history analysis, students are first taught to draw a diagram of the state spaces for the independent and dependent variable(s) of interest and the theoretically expected transitions from one state space to another (Tuma 1990).[2] However, without at least an argument in mind, this is a confusing task for the student. Knowledge of the elements of typology can make this task clearer.[3] Last, typological methods are useful for testing a cultural argument in which the researcher is required to show, net of a change in structural positions or material conditions, how cultural effects vary within the population or across the time span studied (DiMaggio 1994, 28).

The conceptual scheme of the ideal types offer a guide for developing hypotheses about the effects of institutional change on the attributes likely to affect the dependent variables of interest. This conceptual scheme includes the following categories: economic system, organizational identity, legitimacy, authority structures, mission, focus of attention, strategy, logics of investment, and governance.

To identify the ideal types, I conducted taped, in-depth interviews with higher education publishers, investment bankers who specialize in publishing, and the staff of the Association of American Publishers (AAP). The transcripts of these interviews supplemented historical research using industry trade literature, publisher case histories written by John Tebbel, and other books and articles on publishing. Further information on the interviews is included in Appendix B. I used these sources to develop the ideal types and to associate them with the historical period in which they prevailed.

Ideal Types of Institutional Logics: Editorial and Market

In my interviews and the historical sources, publishers characterized higher education publishing in the 1950s and 1960s as dominated by small houses that were privately owned by families and individuals who engaged in publishing as a lifestyle and a profession. The dominant form of leadership was the founder–editor, whose legitimacy and authority stemmed from their personal reputations in the field, their positions in the organizational hierarchies, their relational networks with authors, and the stature of their books (Coser, Kadushin, and Powell 1982). The founder–editor's expertise was embodied in the individual person, and because of the uncertainty in the precise ingredients of a best seller, these leaders were accorded professional status (Hirsch 1972).

During this era, publishers viewed their mission as building the prestige and the sales of their publishing houses. To do so, they focused their attention on strategies of organic growth, hiring and developing editors with the best reputations to build personal imprints, develop new titles, refine backlists of existing titles, and nurture relationships with authors (Asser 1989). Editors were rewarded for their success with prestige in publisher–academic circles and in some cases by the establishment of their own personal imprints. Personal imprint publishing is an organizational form that recognizes the importance of personal and relational networks in developing new authors and manuscripts. It emphasizes the editors' professional autonomy and freedom from the influences of management and hierarchy (Powell 1990). Governance was by family ownership and independent publishers' participation in a trade association (Chandler 1962). Both practices emphasize committing capital to one's firm as a logic of investment (not necessarily seeking the highest market return on the capital). I refer to this first ideal-type attributes as the *editorial logic.*

The prevalence of an editorial logic during this time is exemplified by comments from the executive vice president in charge of strategic planning for a major higher education publisher.

In the 1960s, publishing was a different world. Most of the companies were small and private. Nobody talked about profits; sales, yes, but not profits. . . . Nobody cared that much about making a lot of money. You went into publishing because you liked books and authors. . . . A lot of the publishing companies in those days were still run by the grand old men of publishing. I used to see Mr. Knopf come in every day with his white hair and his cane and walk into his dark blue velvet office with a great mahogany desk. These were truly devoted editors, who were really into literature. . . . And so this world was really not about business, you went into publishing because you liked authors and books.

In another interview, a former president and CEO in the early 1980s of one of the largest companies with both trade and higher education divisions talked about the historical change in the salience of personal reputation and relational networks with authors. He said:

When Prentice Hall bought Allyn & Bacon from the family in the 1950s, we asked about the royalty rate paid to authors. I remember how incredulous I felt when I heard their response—they said it depended on whether they had a good year or not.

Within the period of an editorial logic, there were companies that operated as hierarchies—for example, the larger companies such as Prentice Hall, McGraw-Hill, and Macmillan. In addition, some of the venerable old-line publishers, such as Wiley and Harcourt, Brace, became hierarchies in the 1960s (Moore 1982; Morris 1994). When William Jovanovich became president of Harcourt in 1960, he took the company public and began to mold it into a diversified hierarchy. However, at the same time, he continued to run the publishing interests from an editorial logic, centered on a dominant individual, editing manuscripts himself (Tebbel 1981). The growth of publishing hierarchies added the attribute of rank in the hierarchy as a salient characteristic of organizational identity under an editorial logic.

In my interviews, publishers described a change that occurred in the identity and the organization of publishers during the 1970s, a shift from the view of publishing as a profession to that of publishing as a business. This shift is consistent with my historical research from scholarly books and the trade press. With the change to publishing as a business, the dominant form of leadership became the CEO, whose legitimacy and authority stemmed from the firm's market position and performance rank, the corporate parent firm, and public shareholders. The mission was to build the competitive position of the firm and increase profit margins. To do so, the focus of executives' attention changed to counteracting problems of resource competition using strategies such as acquisition growth and building market channels. This attention to *marketing* books is in sharp contrast to the older editorial logic where it was believed that good books sold themselves by favorable word of mouth (Powell 1985, 10). Hence, there was little point in investing in marketing a good book—people either have or lack the capacity to appreciate genius (Lane and Booth 1970, 42). Tebbel (*Microsoft Encarta 97 Encyclopedia* [CD-ROM], *s.v.* "book trade") reinforces this point by noting that in the 1960s, modern marketing methods were rare in publishing. However by the early 1980s, most publishers were emphasizing the most advanced marketing techniques. The logic of investment is to commit capital to its highest market return, and the salient rules of succession are shaped by the market for corporate control.[4] I refer to this second set of ideal type attributes as the *market logic*. Table 2.1 summarizes the two ideal types of institutional logic, the editorial and the market.

One veteran publisher summarized this new market logic as follows.

If you take it back to the 1960s, I remember seeing some things that were odd by publishing standards at the time. . . . The conglomerate phenomenon was one. It was not only the big companies outside the industry buying publishers, but there were some internal examples. . . . What sticks in my mind was the guy who put together InText. Buying up all those little companies to make one big important company. We real publishers looked at this and wondered—why was he doing this? This didn't fit publishing as we knew it. . . . All of a sudden what were really editors were now managers. The outside conglomerates gave up and divested. . . . they couldn't understand the business . . . that we don't break even until nine months into the year. . . . But the conglomerate acquisitions gave publishers a first glance at finance skills and a new business—investment banking. . . . Maybe that is why we

TABLE 2.1

Two Ideal Types of Institutional Logics in Higher Education Publishing

Characteristic	Editorial Logic	Market Logic
Economic system	Personal capitalism	Market capitalism
Organizational identity	Publishing as a profession	Publishing as a business
Legitimacy	Personal reputation	Market position of firm
Authority structures	Founder–editor	CEO
	Personal networks	Corporate parent firm
	Private ownership	Public ownership
Mission	Build prestige of house	Build competitive position
	Increase sales	Increase profits and cash flow
Focus of attention	Author–editor networks	Resource competition
Strategy	Organic growth	Acquisition growth
	Build personal imprints	Build market channels
Logic of investment	Capital committed to firm	Capital committed to market return
Governance	Family ownership	Market for corporate control
	Trade association	

now (1991) have a market for publishing companies. . . . Of course, market pressures now create a whole new problem for executive stability.

Another executive publisher described the heightened attention to marketing and building market channels and how the editorial focus became contested in his company.

In the early 1970s, when I was the executive in charge of a division, the company CEO had a serious discussion with me about how I had to get rid of all these little books. Even though my books were important in their fields and selling well, they were in small markets and required the same amount of a sales rep's time—time that could be spent selling a book for a larger market. . . . But my real recognition of how this business had changed came when the parent company asked us not for editorial talent but for management talent for their other divisions. It was the realization that our mission was to grow managers, not book editors. That really shook me.

The market logic is exemplified by comments from one higher education publisher who began in the business as a sales representative in the early 1960s and became an editor and subsequently a divisional executive.

In the 1960s, the Fortune 500 companies outside the industry started buying publishers. These acquisitions were a failed experiment because their accountants could never figure out how our business worked. . . . The Fortune 500 ended up giving up and divested their publishing properties, but they left behind the seeds for how publishing changed over the next twenty some years. For one, just look at the emphasis now on growing by acquisition. I know, I was originally trained to be an editor, but had to learn to do *due diligence* to keep in step. Sure, in the past we had mergers and acquisitions, but it wasn't considered a way to do publishing.

And one of the well-known investment bankers—who earlier had had a career in higher education publishing, beginning as a production editor and ending as the head of the higher education division for a major publisher—stated:

If you went back and looked at an organization chart for Prentice Hall's college division in 1961, the year I started, and you were to take the same organization chart this morning to Prentice Hall, . . . the major change would be the financial people, the MBAs. . . . Thirty-five years ago having anybody knowing anything about finance within an operating position of a publishing company was unheard of. In the past we were a part of the academic community. Now we are more a part of the financial community.

And, one executive publisher in a medium-size firm added:

Even the acquisition editors are now forced to become general managers to control their own destiny. In the old days editors would go out and find people they thought would make good authors. For example, I used to work for Stanford and Berkeley and went after all kinds of books—people of outstanding caliber to write even basic books. Now editors have to develop financial models to sign a book and because of the investment they don't take chances on those kinds of authors. Editors now make it clear that they are expecting a tremendous amount of cooperation and the publisher outlines the book to make sure it fits the market.

I also found support for a rise in market logic in the publishing industry literature. For example, Greco (1996, 1997) describes what he termed a "substantive reconfiguration" within publishing attributed to the direct impact of strategic planning practices on executives. Shatzkin (1982) comments on the commercialization of publishing strategies and its impact on the declining prominence of the editorial function. In reference to scholarly publishing, Powell (1985, 12) described a "shift in power within publishing houses—one in which editors are in decline and corporate managers and marketing are in ascendance." With respect to college text, scholarly, and trade publishing, Coser, Kadushin, and Powell (1982, 29) noted "a shift in the internal status order within publishing houses—a process in which the power of editors declined . . . and the influence of professional managers had risen." Last, the publishing historian Tebbel (1987, 463, 464) also describes the decline in the influence of editors and the rise of market influences on publishing. He notes, "When the giant conglomerates stretched their tentacles into the book business, the moves sometimes brought into the publishing world a kind of executive not seen before." In another book, Tebbel (1981, 511) also discusses this point by saying, "Management was now in the hands of business-oriented people, while those who had combined business with editorial creativity were out of control."

The Forces of Institutional Change

A number of factors contributed to the decline of an editorial logic and the rise of a market logic. Haveman and Rao (forthcoming) argue that when "segregating" processes occur, they create pressures that contradict the prevailing logic and give rise to a new one. These processes include changes in competition, new political processes, the atrophy of social networks, new views of legitimacy, and new technologies. A review of the industry literature and time series data indicates that several of these processes occurred. The early 1970s marked a period of transition in logics propelled by new sources of capital in the industry, an increase in resource competition in the product market after the mid-1970s, new sources of information from trade presses that emphasized a focus on market logics, and the development of investment banking practices and firms specialized to the industry.

The antecedents for the changes in logics were evidenced by changes in market demand and the need for new sources of capital. In the 1960s, market demand exploded along with the demographic expansion of postwar baby boomers en route to college and with increased state and federal investments in the construction of new colleges and universities (Coser, Kadushin, and Powell 1982; Brint and Karabel 1991). Figure 2.1 shows the continuous increase in college enrollments prior to 1975, with a tapering off of the rate of increase afterward. Similarly, the sales of college-level books, approximately $67 million in 1956, had grown to more than $531 million in 1975, indicating that publishers responded to the increased demand in the product market (*Bowker Annual of Library and Book Trade Information* [1958, 1975]). With this growth, Wall Street analysts began to tout higher education publishing as a growth industry, signaling to corporate executives outside the industry, who were engaged in the heralded diversification strategies of this time (Fligstein 1990), that publishing firms were attractive targets for acquisition (Powell 1980; Coser, Kadushin, and Powell 1982, 25). Faced with both market growth and increasing competition, publishers needed new sources of capital (Smith 1995). As a result, family-estate publishers faced two choices: go public to obtain access to public capital markets or secure corporate capital by being acquired.[5] As one publisher stated, "on the corporate capital route came the talk about synergy and economies of scale and the financial wizards pushing us to grow."

The increase in demand led to an increased number of publishing organizations and a change in the level of resource competition. Figure 2.2 depicts change in the market resource competition in the industry over time. After 1975, three factors contributed to the salience of resource competition in the product market: the decline in the rate of increase in college enrollments (see Figure 2.1), the acquisitions campaign into the American marketplace by foreign conglomerates (Graham 1994; Levin 1996), and the entry of nontraditional competitors specializing in course packs and used books (Baker and Hileman 1987, Bernstein Research 1994).

For publishing companies that were acquired, one consequence was that they became divisions and subsidiaries of corporate parent firms. Parent corporations superimposed on these publishers new performance expectations for yearly increases in profits and market share. This in turn refocused executives' logics of investment on market processes and on a new solution—the strategy of acquisition growth. For example, one publisher stated,

Instead of being able to manage your business for the value of future cash flow, you had to manage it for yearly profits transferred to the parent company. . . . Every year had to be better than the previous year. The only way to get bigger rapidly is to go outside and acquire others. Then you set up a new kind of industry competitiveness, which is: I want to buy this other company because if I don't our competitors will get it. So the attention shifts from publishing to what it is we can buy.

Executives told me that market position and reputation, which had previously taken years to establish under the editorial logic, could be obtained

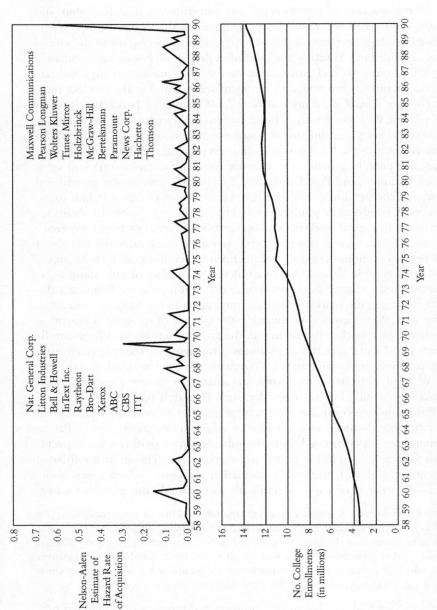

FIGURE 2.1. Time-Series Data for Higher Education Publishing, 1958–1990, Nelson–Aalen Estimates of the Hazard Rate of Acquisition and Time–Series Data on College Enrollment,[a] 1958–1990

[a] Enrollment is in millions of students. Data are from the National Center for Education Statistics *Digest*.

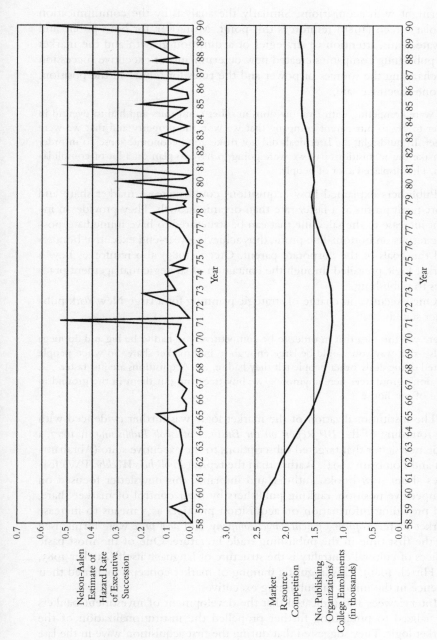

FIGURE 2.2. Time-Series Data for Higher Education Publishing, 1958–1990, Nelson–Aalen Estimates of the Hazard Rate of Executive Succession and Time-Series Data on Market Resource Competition,[a] 1958–1990

[a] Market resource competition is the number of publishing organizations divided by college enrollment, in millions of students.

overnight with acquisitions. Similarly, the analysis by the communication scholar Greco (1989) reinforces this point. Moreover, for both public and private firms, attention to strategies of acquisition growth and the market for publishing companies created new determinants of executive succession by changing the sources of power and the rules for tenure in the position. As one executive said,

We were competing with rival divisions in other companies and had to overbid in order to say to our parent company that we won the property and that we were better. In hindsight, the later deals did not make good economic sense, so in order to make the acquisitions pay, we were going to have to plan on a lot of consolidation. This displaced a lot of people.

Publishers explained how acquisitions could increase market share and short-term profits at a faster rate than organic growth. They provide an instant increase to the sales line that can be structured to have immediate, positive results on bottom-line profit, thus achieving year-end executive bonuses and the goals of the corporate parent. Greco (1989) also reinforces how a market logic prevailed through the contagion of strategic management practices to publishing.

One executive in charge of strategic planning for a large New York publisher stated:

There was this idea that in order to be competitive, you had to be big and do mega deals—that way you would be large enough to buy market share. So when people started doing deals, other people felt they had to. . . . Acquisitions are just faster. . . . We don't grow trees here anymore—we buy trees and put them in the ground in front of our house.

The institutionalization of the market logic was further evidenced with the founding of the *BP Report on the Business of Book Publishing* in 1977, a trade newsletter that targeted subscriptions to the executive suite (Abrahamson and Fombrun 1994). Rather than the typical *Publishers Weekly* (PW) features about new books, authors, and imprints, this newsletter focused on competitive position, ranking publishers by their control of market share, and providing information on acquisition practices as a means to increase market share. *Acquiring parent, target company*, and *deal price* were terms used for the first time in the publishing trade literature. One of the most basic indices of cultural centrality is the structure of language itself (Zucker 1983, 33; Hirsch 1986). This linguistic framing of market concepts increased their salience in the minds of publishing executives.

Interviewees also indicated that the development of investment bankers specialized to publishing further propelled the institutionalization of the market logic. They suggested that during the first acquisition wave in the late

1960s, *deal makers* were neither formal publishers nor tightly connected to the industry. Then, those deal makers came from Wall Street, and the acquiring firms were located in industries outside of publishing. One investment banker said, "One of the things that will come out in your interviews is that nobody in this industry in the 1960s knew what mergers and acquisitions were, much less the word investment banking!" However, in the market period, as one CEO stated, "Investment bankers are now wired into the process." And another stated, "The boutiques grew within the industry in part because the big guys, Goldman Sachs, Solomon Brothers, and others were great on finance, but didn't have a clue about how to value publishing contacts—this is a tricky business that requires industry knowledge." This practice has continued to formalize and to legitimatize acquisition growth as a strategy to accomplish the mission of building the competitive position of the firm. Investment bankers now conduct training for publishers in how to "stay ahead of the game," using acquisitions and consolidation as a business strategy (Fulcrum Information Services 1998, 2). Particularly with publishers in executive positions but also with acquisition editors who are typically called on to value book contracts in the due diligence phase of an acquisition, the shift in emphasis from organic to acquisition growth increasingly made publishers more a part of the financial community, slowly eroding publishers' connections to the academic community.

In contrasting the two industry-level logics in Table 2.1, I note evidence of how editorial and market logics are identified with and shaped by societal-level logics of the professions and markets, respectively (Friedland and Alford 1991). The professions are organized bodies of experts who derive their authority and autonomy from their legitimate social missions (Freidson 1986) and from their ability to apply esoteric knowledge to particular cases (Abbott 1988, 99–100). As indicated by my interviews and the industry literature, the traditional ideology of the industry was founded on viewing publishing as a profession.[6] The logic of the professions permeates the editorial logic, with editorial reputation and author–editor networks as key foci of attention in implementing the mission and strategy of the firm. However, a closer examination of the editorial logic also reveals the impact of another societal logic: the logic of the corporation. Both rank in the organizational hierarchy and the personal reputation of editors are key sources of legitimacy in the industry. The logic of the corporation is also revealed in the commitment of capital to the firm, rather than to the individual editors.[7] Publishing houses under the editorial logic were perhaps best described as quasi-professional firms, where the ideology of the profession is intermixed with a formal hierarchy. Unlike pure professional practice firms—such as traditional law, public accounting, and architecture firms—publishing firms required no formal certification for gaining entrance to the profession. This may be one reason publishing came to be labeled "the accidental profession" (Coser, Kadushin, and Powell 1982, 100). With the shift to a market logic, the professional orientation of the publishing industry declined and was replaced by the logic of Wall Street investment bankers and the increasing concern with profitability and market orientation common to other U.S. industries (Davis and Stout 1992; Useem 1996).

The ideal types developed from the interview data and historical research are a simplified method to group the problems and the related solutions that publishers faced over the period in which they were observed. However, the ideal types are not a theory, but instead are elements in need of a set of assertions that relate the attributes of the ideal types to one another and to the dependent variables to form a coherent argument. In the next chapter, I link the elements of the ideal types to a theory of attention and institutional change.

CHAPTER 3

A Theory of Attention

It is no news to sociologists that culture exists, *sui generis*,
at the collective level. The positions taken here—that
culture is also manifest in people's heads—is probably
more controversial.
—Paul DiMaggio (1997), *Annual Review of Sociology*

CHAPTER 2 DESCRIBED the attributes of two ideal type patterns of strategy
and structure of higher education publishing firms. However, the ideal types
are only elements of a theory. A theory of how culture may affect strategic
actions must state the logical relationships that exist between the definitions
of the ideal types and the behaviors to which the definitions refer. In this
chapter, I develop a theory of how and why publishers shifted their *attention*
from an editorial to a market logic in managing their firms. Attention is how
individuals come to concentrate on certain characteristics to the exclusion
of alternatives that would shift decision choices in other directions (Ocasio
1997).[1] Psychological research suggests that individuals readily shift into deliber-
ate modes of thought when their attention is attracted to a problem (DiMaggio
1997). The questions, then, are how actors organize their attention and what
causes actors to change their focus of attention from one set of problems to
another.[2]

Understanding how actors organize and change the focus of their attention
requires the identification of mediating mechanisms that position individuals
and organizations in society and explains how culture has supra-individual influences (Friedland and Alford 1991). I draw on classic and current research in
cognitive science, social psychology, administrative theory, and the sociology
of organizations and culture to identify the mediating mechanisms and develop my arguments on how attention is influenced by both cultural and
structural mechanisms. Research is rapidly developing in a number of quar-
ters that lends insights into how cognitive processes are focused for example
by cognitive schemas, organization structures, and institutional logics (Cerulo

2002). Scholars working in these areas of study or *cultural units of analysis* show how culture, both internal and external to the firm, influences the content of cognition and therefore the attention of decision makers (DiMaggio 1997).

Culture is an argument typically invoked to explain continuity in action in the face of structural change (Swidler 1986). However, to explain the changes in strategies and structures of publishing firms requires a theory of how different groups behave differently in the same structural situation. Newer concepts have shifted emphasis away from the idea of culture as a force of continuity—a latent variable influencing in common such manifestations as media images, responses to attitude questionnaires, and values and practices acquired in the course of socialization. Instead, recent research finds culture to be fragmented across groups and inconsistent in its manifestations (Martin 1992); it is a variable that can exist independently of persons and of social and economic structures (DiMaggio 1997, 273). Culture comes packaged in units that can be coupled and decoupled in different iterations. As I argue in subsequent discussions, particularly in Chapter 8, this modularity of cultural units of analysis enables me to theorize the agentive role of culture in strategic action and the identification of the locus of agency.

Understanding the mechanisms of imbibing culture and how it affects strategic action requires specifying the *carriers of culture* and identifying the level of analysis at which these causal mechanisms operate. Where is culture located: in individuals' cognitive schemas, the structural positions, relational networks, and routines of organizational hierarchies, or in the larger context of the institutional logics of societal sectors? We can draw on several approaches to address these questions, such as examining how attention is influenced by socialization, cognitive schemas, organizational structures, and institutional logics. In addressing these questions and areas of cultural units of analysis, I focus on two central issues: how cognitive processes are influenced by cultural sources at different levels of analysis and how institutional logics reproduce and change.

Socialization

According to the latent-variable view, individuals act based on their socialization to cultural norms and values within particular domains such as families, schools, and corporations (Parsons 1951).[3] Socialization is a mechanism that explains how decision-making practices become institutionalized. Empirical research, for example, has shown how executives were socialized to different decision-making practices depending on their training and location in subunits of corporations or their schooling and cohort in elite universities (Fligstein 1987, 1990; Palmer, Jennings, and Zhou 1993). This research has also shown how powerful actors use these practices to create stability in firms and markets (Fligstein 1996).[4] However, socialization as a mechanism of institutionalization also means that it is a source of inertia. DiMaggio (1997) and Swidler (1986) for example argue that socialization as a mechanism complicates a cultural theory of action because it obscures an understanding of how period effects change.[5] To be strategic, individual and organizational behaviors have to be readily changeable; if culture is a part of the cause, then other mechanisms are likely to explain the relationship between culture and strategic action.

ORGANIZATION STRUCTURES

Attention is not only socialized, it is a result of organizational strategies and structures.[6] Network structures for example invoke cognitive schemas (Fuchs 2001) and hierarchical structures distribute attention (March and Simon 1958). Scholars of the Carnegie school developed a theory of decision choices by the structural allocation of managerial cognition in which the firm's economic and social structures act to channel and distribute the scarce resource of attention in organizations (Simon [1947] 1997; March and Simon 1958; March and Olsen 1976; Cyert and March 1963). According to this school, socialization and learning are mechanisms to make attention routine, but organizational structures themselves also allocate attention. This latter idea clears the way for an understanding of bounded rationality, the limited capacity of humans for rational decision making. Additionally, this idea reveals that what may appear to be passive habit may indeed be active behavior under the conditions of selective attention (DiMaggio and Powell 1991). Finally, while socialization implies a lengthy process and one likely to result in relatively enduring personal traits and expertise, attention can easily be reallocated by the managerial act of changing organizational structures.

For example, organizational hierarchies, as nearly decomposable systems, are easily rearranged to change the focus of attention (Simon 1962).[7] The various structural configurations, such as departmental versus multidivisional forms, carry different consequences for information impactedness, the transfer of knowledge, and thus the allocation of attention (Williamson 1975). Network structures call up cognitive schemas that focus attention from related and different meanings. Fuchs (2001, 167) makes this point clearly in his comparison of art networks. He states,

Meaning is a relation within a network, not an intention in the head. . . . Meaning changes go along with changes in connectivity. It matters to a piece of art, and its meaning, whether it circulates primarily among commodities and markets, or along networks of cutting-edge galleries.

However, the Carnegie school's focus is internal to the organization, leaving the connection to the larger market and society relatively undeveloped—in White's (2002) words, linking "memory and nation," and in Fligstein's (2001) words, linking firms and markets to societal level frameworks. (See

Ocasio 1997 for a review of the research on attention and a formulation of an attention-based theory of the firm in which organizational structure is the mechanism to mediate internal and external cultural stimuli.) Moreover, the dual emphasis that ties structure to cognition, in which the firm is the central mediator of attention, in theory also favors the expectation of stability over change, thus under-representing the variety of strategic decision choices actually observed in corporate settings. This leads me to search for additional avenues to understand the agentive role of culture in decision making, one that can be decoupled from inertial effects of structure.[8]

TOOL KITS

Swidler (1986) uses the metaphor of a *tool kit* to argue the causal role of culture in shaping strategies of action. Rejecting the view of culture as socialization to values, she theorizes culture as a cognitive process of scripts and schemas that can be decoupled from structure, enabling the insight about how culture shapes strategic action and change.[9] While strategies of action are products of socialization to cultural values, individuals and organizations also develop "cultural competences" and engage in "cultural retooling" by manipulating the contents of their tool kits—containing symbols, stories, rituals, and world-views. Swidler (1986, 274, 277) argues for example, "Culture shapes action by defining what people want. . . . A culture is not a unified system that pushes action in a consistent direction. Rather, it is more like a tool kit or repertoire from which actors select differing pieces for constructing lines of action." Accordingly, actors are not "cultural dopes" that are products of socialization to values (Parsons 1951), or post hoc rationalizations based in the reproduction of social structures that are culturally legitimate accounts (Garfinkel 1967). Instead, actors use culture to strategically act in ways that are independent of social structure. In theory, actors have more culture in their tool kits than they need, making use of only those pieces of culture necessary to accurately read and respond to the cues of other actors and to environmental events. Swidler's view of culture as action prompts two questions: What is the origin and persistence of the contents of an actor's tool kit? What is the empirical evidence?

COGNITIVE SCHEMAS

Experimental research lends insight to the origin question with the development of a related concept, cognitive schemas.[10] Schemas are scripts that simplify cognition, telling us how culture shapes and biases thought (Abelson 1982; Garfinkel 1967). Schemas organize and focus attention; they are both information processing mechanisms and representations of new and old knowledge (Fiske and Linville 1980). As information processing mechanisms, they help individuals make sense of the information that is distributed across them. As representations, schemas entail images of objects and the relations among them. They can refer to highly abstract concepts, to concrete activity, and to complex social phenomena (DiMaggio 1997, 269). Research has shown that an individual is more likely to perceive, to recall, to more accurately interpret, and to falsely identify events that did not occur if that individual's information is embedded in schemas (von Hippel et al. 1993). Fleck ([1935] 1979) found for example that outdated models constrained medical scientists' interpretations of new evidence. (See DiMaggio 1997 for a review.) Recent research has found that schemas stem from prior knowledge and that variations in cognitive schemas are historically and culturally contingent. Social organization appears to affect cognitive processes in two basic ways: first, indirectly by focusing attention on different parts of the environment, and second, by making some kinds of social communication patterns more acceptable than others (Morris and Peng 1994; Nisbett et al. 2001, 294).[11]

Similar to Swidler's tool kit, cognitive schemas are a means for imbibing and using culture in a changeable fashion, making schemas a useful concept for understanding the agentive role of culture in organizational decision making. Here I draw on Sewell's (1992, 19) definition of agency as the actor's ability to use cultural schemas to reinterpret and mobilize an array of resources other than those that initially constituted the array. Schemas enable the random access of multiple ideas or images from social and economic environments (DiMaggio 1997, 267). Accordingly, when schemas are carried in individuals' heads, the effects of culture are transposable across situations. However, except in historical and cross-cultural studies (such as ancient Greek, Chinese, and Anglo-American cultures), in which differences are quite dramatic, it is not clear how cognitive schemas are related to larger cultural and economic constructs, such as different societal sectors and systems of capitalism.

While theories of attention explain how the firm mediates selective attention, if culture is part of a dynamic explanation for strategy, then we need to better understand not only how culture is encoded and subject to manipulation inside individuals' heads, but also how individual-level cognition is cued by social and economic systems (Carley 1989; Lant 2002). Developing these ideas requires a discussion of how micro-level cognitive processes are related to macro-level cultural and economic structures and an explanation of cultural change and persistence (DiMaggio 1997, 278). Linking the concepts of cognitive schemas and institutional logics of action to a theory of attention is a promising approach.

INSTITUTIONAL LOGICS

Institutional logics link internal mental cognitions to external rituals and stimuli. They refer to taxonomies of institutions that represent the influences of culture on action in a domain or societal sector (DiMaggio 1997). Institutional logics are an analytic advance in cultural analysis over latent variable and organizational field approaches. They specify a priori ideal type models of cultural practices and symbol systems within specific contexts, illustrating how culture is anchored in a set of elemental building blocks, not just as critics muse, "floating out there in thin air."[12] These primary categories are useful for comparative analysis within and across societal sectors to reveal consistency or fragmentation exposed by various elements of culture, helping to classify the underlying meaning of points of conflict and conformity in decision making. As subsequent discussion will elaborate, these attributes facilitate the articulation of a theory of cultural conflict and change (DiMaggio 1997, 277).

Western society is comprised of multiple institutional orders or societal sectors, each of which has a central logic—both material practices and symbols that comprise its organizing principles and that are available to individuals and organizations to elaborate. These organizing principles spell out the vocabularies of motives, the logics of action, and the sense of self in specific societal sectors, such as the market, the corporation, the professions, the family, the religions, and the state. An underlying assumption is that both the practical and the symbolic—are mutually constitutive of one another (Ventresca and Mohr 2002). Table 3.1 shows an example of the key elements of ideal-type taxonomies for each of these societal sectors. As discussed in Chapter 2, the pure ideal types approximate to a greater or lesser extent hybrid types that are observable in the real world. Note also that Table 2.1 in Chapter 2 illustrates a testable subset, particular to the publishing industry, of these more general institutional logics. In theory, hybrid types occur because institutional entrepreneurs, who "live across institutions," act as agents of institutional change when they access different elements of the institutional logics from various societal sectors (Friedland and Alford 1991, 248, 255).[13]

For example, the control mechanisms characteristic of the professions are a code of ethics and peer surveillance organized by external voluntary associations. This allows workers to have a much greater degree of personal control over their expert knowledge. In contrast, the logic of the corporation assumes that expertise is encoded in the routines and capabilities of the firm (Freidson 2001) and is under the administrative control of managers in the hierarchy (Blau and Scott 1962). A scandal from the turn of this century provides an illustration. Writers have noted how Arthur Andersen adopted the mechanisms of control from one societal sector and transposed them onto another—from the professions to the corporation. Dugan (2002) notes,

It was a gentleman's profession . . . full-time salespeople were unheard of . . . computers were making auditing services less valuable, so accounting firms began developing new sources of revenue. . . . Mr. Rider says that after Ernst & Young set sales goals for partners and put them through sales training in 1995, he spent one-third of his time on "practice development." I sold professional services. . . . Once, he says, a client barked at him: "Are you my auditor or a salesperson?"

The transposition of elements of institutional logics from different societal sectors also occurs when structures overlap, for example between or within organizations. The former is evident with the acquisitions by the Fortune 500 firms in the publishing industry in the late 1960s and early 1970s. Organizations merged that had cultures supported by the elements of different societal sectors—the family and the professions and the corporation and the market. With respect to the latter, when accounting firms incorporated management consultants into their organizations, they incorporated the elements of conflicting institutional logics from two distinct societal sectors—shifting the basis of attention from overseeing the accuracy of clients' books to that of using exposure to accounting ledgers (auditing function) as an opportunity to identify consulting clients.

CULTURAL CHANGE AND PERSISTENCE

Two arguments bear on an explanation for cultural change and persistence. First, contradictions in the institutional logics of societal sectors precipitate innovation and change (Clemens and Cook 1999). Actors who are entrepreneurial, and perceive these contradictions, can serve as change agents by borrowing and manipulating new combinations of the elements of the various taxonomies across institutional sectors. Sewell (1992, 17) argues that such actors are capable of carrying a wide range of even incompatible schematic elements to a variety of circumstances outside the context in which they were initially learned, presenting new solutions to similar problems.[14] With respect to publishing and corporate decision making, the retrenching at Bertelsmann in 2002 is a current example in which there was tension between institutional logics—those of family versus market driven strategies (Peers, Rose, and Karnitschnig 2002). The family took control back after releasing the CEO who was hell-bent on using acquisitions to remake the firm into a global media empire. In sum, returning to Swidler's (1986) metaphor of a cultural tool kit, entrepreneurs can act as Johnny Appleseeds, transporting institutional logics from one sector to another and creating new avenues for institutional change.[15]

CULTURAL ANALOGY

Second, Douglas (1986) argues that the legitimacy and persistence of an institution is contingent on the association of the institution with an analogy to the natural world.[16] According to Douglas, an analogy serves to obscure the purely human origins of the institution, making it appear as a part of the cosmos and order of the universe. The association with an analogy serves to match precedence with an authority structure—turning a convention into an ongoing institution (DiMaggio and Powell 1991, 24–25).

TABLE 3.1

Institutional Logics of Societal Sectors

Key Characteristics	Markets	Corporations	Professions	States	Families	Christian Religions
Economic System	Market capitalism	Managerial capitalism	Personal capitalism	Welfare capitalism	Personal capitalism	Occidental capitalism
Natural Effect of Symbolic Analogy	Market as transaction	Corporation as hierarchy	Profession as relational network	State as redistribution mechanism	Family as firm	Temple as bank
Sources of Identity	Faceless	Bureaucratic roles Quantity of production	Personal reputation Quality of innovation	Social class Political ideology	Family reputation Father–son relations	Occupational and vocational Association with deities
Sources of Legitimacy	Share price	Market position of firm	Personal expertise	Democratic participation	Unconditional loyalty	Importance of magic in economy
Sources of Authority	Shareholder activism	Board of directors Management	Professional association	Bureaucratic domination Political parties	Patriarchal domination	Personal charisma of prophet power and status of priesthood
Basis of Norms	Self-interest	Employment in firm	Membership in guild	Citizenship in nation	Membership in household	Membership in congregation
Basis of Attention	Status position in market	Status position in hierarchy	Status position in network	Status position of interest group	Communism of household	Relation of individual to supernatural forces
Basis of Strategy	Increase efficiency of transactions	Increase size and diversification of firm	Increase personal reputation and quality of craft	Increase community good	Increase family honor, security, and solidarity	Increase magical symbolism of natural events

Learning Mechanisms	Competition prices	Competition training and routines subunit of firm	Cooperation apprenticing relational network	Popular opinion leadership	Sponsorship	Analogy and parable formulae of prayer; Routinization of preaching
Informal Control Mechanisms	Industry analysts	Organization culture	Celebrity professional	Backroom politics	Family politics	Worship of calling
Formal Control Mechanisms	Enforcement of regulation	Board and management authority	Internal and external peer review	Enforcement of legislation	Rules of inheritance and succession	Rationalization of usury and norms of taboos
Forms of Ownership	Public	Public	Private	Public	Private	Private
Organization Form	Marketplace	M-Form organization	Network organization	Legal bureaucracy	Family partnership	Religious congregation office hierarchy
Logic of Exchange	Immediate best bargain	Personal career advancement	Indebtedness and reciprocity	Political power	Family power	As sign of God's grace
Logic of Investment	Capital committed to market returns	Capital committed to firm	Capital committed to nexus of relationships	Capital committed to public policy	Capital committed to household	Capital committed to enterprise of salvation

TABLE 3.2

Theoretical Questions, Causal Mechanisms, and Dependent Variables

Chapter	Theoretical Question	Causal Mechanism	Dependent Variable	
			Concept	Measure
Five: Attention to the sources of power	(1) Are the determinants of power in organizations universal or historically and culturally contingent?	(1) Management cognition and attention **mediate** the identification and meaning of organizational problems and solutions.	Decisions on leadership in organizations	D Executive Succession
	(2) Which sources of power in organizations are more or less universal or historically and culturally contingent—**positional, relational, and economic**?	(2) Institutional logics shape management attention and cognition and thereby **moderate** which structural and economic forces have consequences for decisions on power and leadership in organizations.		
	(3) How does institutional change modify the sources of power in organizations that determine leadership succession?	(3) Institutional logics prevail by **analogy**. The editorial and market logics are identified with and shaped by societal-level logics of the professions and the market		
		(4) Institutional logics in conflict create **countervailing determinants** of power. A shift from one logic to another can change the sources of power that determine leadership succession.		
Six: Attention to the sources of structure	(1) Are the determinants of organization structure universal or historically and culturally contingent?	(1) Management cognition and attention **mediate** the identification and meaning of organizational problems and solutions.	Decisions on structure in organizations	D Divisionalization
	(2) Which sources of organization structure are more or less universal or historically and culturally contingent—**professional and market?**	(2) Institutional logics shape management attention and thereby **moderate** which structural and economic forces have consequences for decisions on organizational structure.		
	(3) How does institutional change modify the sources of strategy that determine organization structure?	(3) Institutional logics prevail by **analogy**. The editorial and market logics are identified with and shaped by societal-level logics of the professions and the market.		
	(4) Why would craft firms adopt the divisionalized organization structure given the lack of scale economies in such firms?	(4) Institutional logics in conflict create **countervailing determinants** of structure. A shift from		

TABLE 3.2 (continued)

Theoretical Questions, Causal Mechanisms, and Dependent Variables

Chapter	Theoretical Question	Causal Mechanism	Dependent Variable	
			Concept	Measure
	(5) At what levels of analysis are institutions carried: individuals, social structures and routines?	one logic to another can change the sources of strategy that determine organization structure.		
		(5) Institutional logics in conflict create pressures on organizations to adapt and change their structures. Organizations that are in **conformity** with the prevailing institutional logic are more legitimate, competitive, and **immune from pressures to change** structures.		
Seven: Attention to the sources of strategy	(1) Are the determinants of organization strategy universal or historically and culturally contingent?	(1) Management cognition and attention **mediate** the identification and meaning of organizational problems and solutions.	Decisions on strategy in organizations and populations	D Acquired firm
	(2) Which sources of strategy are more or less universal or historically and culturally contingent—**organizational and market?**	(2) Institutional logics shape management attention and thereby **moderate** which structural and economic forces have consequences for decisions on acquisition.		
	(3) How does institutional change modify the sources of organization strategy that determine the risk of acquisition?	(3) Institutional logics prevail by **analogy**. The editorial and market logics are identified with and shaped by societal-level logics of personal capitalism and market capitalism.		
	(4) How does capitalism select "optimal" organization structures?	(4) Institutional logics in conflict create **countervailing determinants** of strategy. A shift from one logic to another can change the sources of strategy that determine the risk of acquisition.		
	(5) What are the determinants of an optimal fit between organization strategy and structure and the economic and cultural environment?	(5) Institutional logics in conflict create pressures on organizations to change their strategy. Organization strategies that are in **conformity** with the prevailing form of capitalism are more legitimate, competitive, and **immune from selection pressures** of acquisition.		

This argument is illustrated with respect to the imprint organizational structure in publishing that has persisted by transposing into a form compatible with the prevailing market logic. Although the public corporation displaced the reign of the institutional logics of the family firm and the professions, the viability of the imprint structure has persisted over and above its original and functional purpose—the professional (originally guild) control of work (Freidson 2001). For example, Coser, Kadushin, and Powell (1982) describe how imprint structures survived in modern publishing by morphing into hybrid forms located inside corporate hierarchies.

If we apply Douglas's argument, the imprint bears an analogy to both the natural and supernatural worlds in that it stems from the printer's mark, originally associated with a character in ancient Greek mythology that symbolized the printer's (early publisher's) identity and reputation.[17] Transposing the analogy to the natural world in modern times, imprints signal the relationship between the published material and professional reputation and recognition of a particular editor or the brand equity of a publishing "house" (firm). Hence, imprint structures embedded in corporate hierarchies have transposed meanings and functions that are compatible with a market logic— that of employee retention, compensation, and direct cost accounting of employee performance.[18]

In sum, linking the multilevel concepts of cognitive schemas and institutional logics suggests a mechanism of cultural change through the ability of individual and organizational actors to sample a variety of logics of action at the intersection of societal sectors.[19] At the individual level, actors' tool kits contain multiple schemas to shape the focus of attention. These schemas may or may not be consistent with the organizing principles of the sector, whether that be of the profession or the market, the family or the corporation (Friedland and Alford 1991). The transformation of the higher education publishing industry illustrates how actors switched their attention from one set of logics to another and how the model of the family firm and the professions was displaced by that of the corporation and market. We see this in the shift of attention from the founder–editor viewing his mission through a professional logic to publish high-prestige books to the corporate parent viewing its mission through a market logic to publish high-profit books.

My arguments are an explanation not only for the origin, but also the heterogeneity of the contents of tool kits. Axial principles of organization from different institutional sectors can be connected and disconnected by individual and organizational actors who have the ability to act as change agents by borrowing logics from one sector and implementing them to interpret and solve resource problems in another.

SYNTHESIS

In this chapter, I have identified the units of cultural analysis and the relationships among them to develop a theory of attention that argues how culture shapes strategic action. My review of the literature indicates that we perhaps know more about how socialization, cognitive schemas, and institutional logics structure attention than we do about how various organization strategies and structures may focus attention. The two ideal types of institutional logics in higher education publishing that were developed in Chapter 2 make specific predictions about how organizations' strategies and structures focus attention and how they themselves link to larger systems of culture. For example, network structures supported by the editorial logic focused attention on author–editor relations. Alternatively, corporate hierarchies supported by a market logic focused attention on resource competition. Both networks and hierarchies are crucial environments for the activation of cognitive schemas and logics of action.[20] However, networks and hierarchies are mediating mechanisms that cannot be specified independently of the institutional arenas in which they are located. I tend to agree with DiMaggio (1997, 274) that culture is a result of the interaction among information, mental structures, and symbolic systems, making the test of a cultural argument a daunting challenge. In the following analyses, I hypothesize about, and control for, structural change, but vary the institutional logics of action, for example, culture. In the final chapter, the meta-analyses summarize which effects on strategic decision making are more attributable to the influences of culture and which are more attributable to the influences of social and market structure. I further examine which of these influences are more agentive than others in the firm and in the market.

A Theory of Attention

I draw primarily from the Carnegie and neoinstitutional schools to state a theory of organizational decisions that articulates the mechanisms of how the decisions of actors inside organizations are connected to the cultural beliefs in contexts outside organizations (Fligstein and Dauber 1989, 94). To develop this historical and cultural contingency perspective, I build on Friedland and Alford's (1991) argument: The institutions that shape organizational actions are embedded within higher-order societal logics. Individuals, organizations, and society constitute three nested levels, wherein organization- and society-level institutions specify progressively higher levels of opportunity for and constraint on individual action. The main institutional sectors of society—the family, the religions, the professions, the state, the corporation, and the market—provide a distinct set of often conflicting or complementary logics that form the basis of institutional conflict and conformity.

The society-level logics of the professions and the markets have parallel cognitive conventions in lower-order logics: the editorial and the market logics in publishing (Douglas 1986). The professions embody organizing logics that conflict with corporations, and markets embody logics that are complementary to corporations. Therefore, the logics of the professions and the markets imply countervailing determinants of organizational decision making.

As was discussed in Chapter 1, at the level of the organization, ambiguity and cognitive limitations keep individuals and organizations from attending to all aspects of their environments (March and Olsen 1976, 1989; Simon, [1947] 1997). Institutional logics help to remedy this problem by focusing the attention of actors in organizations on a limited set of issues and solutions that are consistent with the prevailing logic. For example, in the context of the publishing industry, the meaning and legitimacy of various sources of organizational identity and of strategy and structure are shaped by a prevailing institutional logic. Publishers may identify with publishing as a profession by building their personal reputations in the industry, or publishers may identify with publishing as a business by improving the market positions of their firms. Additionally, institutional logics determine which issues and problems are salient and the focus of management's attention. Publishers may focus on increasing sales by concentrating on author–editor networks in product development, or publishers may focus on increasing profits by emphasizing control of resource competition in the product-market. Finally, institutional logics determine which answers and solutions are the focus of management's attention. Publishers may adopt strategies of growth by focusing on organic growth and building personal imprints, or publishers may concentrate on acquisition growth and building market channels.

At the level of the industry, a product market is a relevant boundary for identifying institutional logics because market producers develop identities and *valuation orders* that structure the decision making and the practices of the players (White 1981a, 1981b, 1992). Social comparisons among firms, particularly under conditions of resource and status competition, help reveal valuation orders and common and differentiated identities. These identities and valuation orders may be considered institutionalized when they are analogous with culturally legitimate accounts (Douglas 1986; Strang and Meyer 1994). For example, Davis and Greve (1997) found that network linkages alone did not explain the diffusion of poison-pill practices. Network ties must also be accompanied by an account that was perceived as legitimate because it was supported by the values of the local culture. In sum, institutional logics provide actors with a commonly understood language and rules of the game to interpret and give meaning to the social and economic structures in a market (Porac et al. 1995).

At the level of the economy, different economic systems lend legitimacy to certain business practices, moderating the development and persistence of particular organizational strategies and structures but not others (Lewin, Long, and Carroll 1999). These different systems, such as personal, managerial, and market capitalism, represent different environments for organizational adaptation and selection (Aldrich 1999).

In this chapter I have emphasized the mechanisms in which individuals can carry institutions in their heads and use them in formulating the strategic behavior of firms in markets.[21] This has required drawing on the work of scholars who theorize culture and cognition as distinct from social structure (Swidler 1986). However, institutions embedded in social structure are also an important source of agency in firms and markets. According to Scott (2001, 52–54) institutions are located in *carriers*, not only in cultures, but also in social structures and routines. Cultures are defined as rule systems that allow individuals and groups to interpret the meanings of patterns of social and economic structures. Social structures are defined as expectations embodied, for example, in individual roles, formal positions in an organization, and social networks determined by the relations between actors or groups of actors. Routines are the habitualized behaviors, competencies, capabilities, and technologies stored in *organizational memory* (Nelson and Winter 1982). By definition, carriers of institutions cut across different sectors of society and levels of analysis. This interconnection provides opportunities for institutions to come into conflict and analogy, creating pressures and prospects for organizational change and stability.

I propose that an organization's strategy and structure are legitimate and competitive to the extent that they are in conformity with the higher-order institutional logics of societal sectors. This general theory can be applied to specific areas of organizational decision making. Executives seek solutions to the problems of how leaders are chosen, the source of that leader's power, and when a leader should be replaced. Executives also seek solutions to problems and questions concerning organizational strategy and structure in various types of markets. For example, whether their enterprises should be developed as a publicly held corporations or a privately held firms, or be organized as a relational network structure or as a multidivisional hierarchy. Strategy emphasizes such questions as whether a company seeks to expand by internal growth or by merger and what companies are likely targets for acquisition.

In the coming chapters, I apply and test the theory of attention in three separate studies of organizational decision making in a product market. Table 3.2 summarizes the causal mechanisms of the theory and the research questions addressed in each of the three applications, showing the extensions of the scope conditions of the theory.

First, however, in the next chapter I describe the sources and characteristics of the data and methods of analysis.

CHAPTER 4

Quantitative Data and Methods

By a model we mean an abstract image of reality whose
construction has been guided by theory, empirical general-
izations from past research, and perhaps hunches. . . . Still,
as an image of reality, a model should mirror the way
changes can occur, not the way data are collected. The
relative rarity of phenomena that can change only at
discrete time points, coupled with our belief that models
should attempt to fit reality and not be dictated by the
observation plan used to collect data, led us to concentrate
on a framework that is continuous-time models.

—Nancy Brandon Tuma and Michael T. Hannan (1984),
  Social Dynamics: Models and Methods

THE QUANTITATIVE data set was constructed from archival data and from
the results of a telephone survey of commercial publishing firms operating
in the U.S. higher education market. I drew extensively on the collections
of the R.R. Bowker and the American Booksellers Association (ABA) libraries, which archive the most comprehensive sources of information on
the publishing industry. I used four well-known publications—*Literary Market Place (LMP)*, *Publishers Weekly (PW)*, *Educational Marketeer (EM)*, and *BP
Report on the Business of Book Publishing (BP)*—as primary data sources to
construct an organizational life history of a random sample of 230 publishing firms. I also relied on Tebbel's four-volume series of publishing-firm
case histories as well as other books and articles on the publishing industry
(Coser, Kadushin, and Powell 1982; Tebbel 1987; Greco 1997; Schiffrin
2000). As described in Chapter 2, the quantitative data were complemented
with interviews with higher education publishers, investment bankers who
specialize in publishing, and staff of the Association of American Publishers
(AAP). It should be emphasized that all variables are coded *annually*, allowing the values of the variables to move up or down to capture any transition
that has occurred within a twelve-month period.

Definitions

INDUSTRY AND MARKET

The U.S. book publishing industry consists of single-unit and multiunit organizations that publish and sell to several distinct types of markets including trade, higher education, elementary and high school, children's, and religious books. At any given point in time, the higher education market is defined as the set of firms that report in the *LMP* that they produce for and sell books to bookstores, students, and professors for use in colleges and universities. Higher education publishing as a market has a national scope and is characterized by intermediation. Publishing firms serve as intermediaries between buyers and suppliers, managing and coordinating market transactions between book authors, college and university professors, printers, large and small firms (such as Donnelly, Kingsport, and Edwards Bros.), and wholesale or retail marketing channels. These marketing channels are most often independent, chain, and college bookstores, but also include direct sales to libraries, students, and professors. My market definition is consistent with both Spulber's (1999) concept of intermediary markets and White's (1997) concept of market interfaces, wherein a set of producers is recognized by their identity in a product market.

Some publishers that sell books in the college and university market also publish books for other markets. During the observation period, some organizations in the sample moved into and out of different publishing product markets. On average over the observation period, approximately 33 percent of the publishing firms in the sample published only one type of book, 40 percent published two types, 18 percent three types, and 9 percent four types of books. On average, approximately 8 percent of the firms in the sample publish only college texts, and 4 percent publish only scholarly books. Diversification also occurs within lists. As one editor who publishes for the college market stated, "We publish all manner of excellent books, including advanced texts, reference books, and monographs" (Dougherty 1998). In 1976, books classified as general and mass market made up 34.8 percent of the higher education market (Compaine 1978, 171).

The industry and the market are an appropriate context to examine the research questions of interest for a number of reasons. The publishing industry is entrepreneurial, not state regulated, and legally exempt from government subsidy (Levin 1996). This makes it an ideal setting to partition economic from cultural and political influences (Schneiberg and Clemens forthcoming). Moreover, this type of industry is of interest for its difference from U.S. manufacturing. Large, hierarchical corporations have dominated the U.S. manufacturing industries for the entire postwar period (Chandler 1977). Higher education publishing, on the other hand, includes diverse organizational forms, both corporate hierarchies and independent unitary-form firms (Powell 1985, 2). The market and firm characteristics of higher education publishing generalize to other industries characterized by inter-mediation such as financial services, wholesale trade, and business services. Finally, this type of industry is of interest because it has emerged as an im-portant driver of market outcomes in new-economy industries traditionally driven by craft producers and professional firms with network structures (Powell 1990).

ORGANIZATION

Each publishing organization is defined as either an independent firm or a division or subsidiary of a larger multiunit parent firm. For example, Wadsworth is a division of the Thomson Corporation, but it is counted as a separate case in the population of firms (risk set) because it has a separate listing in the *LMP*, a separate organizational structure, a division president, and a geographical location distinguishable from the parent firm.

POPULATION AND SAMPLE

The sample was randomly drawn from the 766 commercial publishing organizations that reported publishing for the college and university market in the *LMP* from 1958 to 1990. One-third of this population (230 pub-lishing organizations) was selected as a sample, using the SPSS–X random-sample generator. First published in 1940 by a commercial publisher, the *LMP* remains the directory used by publishers, suppliers, distributors, writ-ers, literary agents, bookstores, and librarians to identify whom to contact in conducting business in the publishing industry. Because the *LMP* lists the names, positions, and phone numbers of key personnel, the data in the *LMP* are kept current by the annual distribution of questionnaires to all organi-zations that publish a minimum of three titles a year. To be included in the population of 766, each publishing organization must have a separate listing under its own name in the *LMP*.

The population of organizations is defined on the basis of a product mar-ket as distinct from an organizational form, as is characteristic of ecological analyses, or an organizational field as is distinctive of institutional analyses. My argument is to sample the full universe of organizational forms in a mar-ket, and to let forms vary because they are the centers of action of diverse and dynamic events, such as divisionalization and acquisition, which change the structure of firms and markets. The need to vary organizational forms stems from the argument that in most markets a diversity of organizational forms compete and cooperate. Moreover, evolutionary forces in a population of organizations operate at multiple levels (Aldrich 1999)—for example as direct competition in product markets and more diffuse competition in corporate hierarchies, particularly in the case of competition among subunits of the parent firm for the reallocation of corporate resources (Burgelman 1991).

Although my research design includes population-level variables, my focus is not on the theoretical variables of interest in traditional ecological studies, such as organization founding, mortality, age, and size. Instead, I have selected variables that allow me to address questions about how diversity in organizational forms (which are argued to represent different institutional logics and organizational routines) influences the decisions that organizations make. For example, how do relational networks and corporate hierarchies, which imply different types of governance mechanisms for economic exchange (Powell 1990), differentially affect how organizations make decisions about strategy and structure? Different governance mechanisms should imply different pressures on organizational stakeholders and therefore different decision outcomes for organizations.

Population ecologists (Hannan and Carroll 1992) argue that studies of organizational populations are more rigorous if the observation period includes the period when the population was first founded. Given the age of the publishing industry, this is a Herculean requirement. In the United States, organized publishing dates back to the mid-1800s. In Europe, it is older; indeed Oxford University Press lists its founding date as 1478. Such an early origin point requires a tradeoff—the exclusion of fine-grained observations of the characteristics of individuals and organizations, a unique feature of my data and analyses.

Nonetheless, Tuma and Hannan (1984) argue that the left truncation of observations is not a serious problem. The piecewise exponential models used here lead to consistent estimates when neither the age clock for each firm nor the tenure clock for each executive is restarted in 1958, the beginning of the observation period. In this analysis, I have started the clocks for each firm at the founding date and for each executive at the first year of tenure. I also have selected the earliest observation point at which fine-grained observations are available—a starting point that captures significant variation. The observation period includes two merger waves that coincide with the general trends in other industries. The first occurred in the late 1960s to the early 1970s, and the second in the late 1980s (Thornton 1995). It also includes two different forms of capitalism—smaller and medium-size firms under family ownership and global, publicly traded conglomerates.

A feature of this historical design and sampling method is that firms in which the logic of the professions is prevalent are likely to be privately held and unlikely to publicly disclose performance data. The majority of firms in the risk set were smaller, privately held companies until approximately 1975. For example, I cannot distinguish if, in the editorial period, firms were relatively immune to the pressures to change their leadership and strategy and structure because they could afford to sacrifice profits for prestige, or if, in the market period, firms were resistant to such changes because they focused on profits and had the advantages of scale economies.

The sample includes three different organizational forms competing in the same product market: independent firms, divisions or subsidiaries, and corporate parent firms, the latter may or may not publish their own titles and thus compete with their divisions and subsidiaries. In 1958 at the beginning of the observation period, 12.9 percent of the records in the sample were for firms identified as divisions and subsidiaries; by 1990 this proportion had risen to 41 percent. These data support the observations made by many authors that during the period from 1958 to 1990, higher education publishing in the United States gradually transformed itself from a market of independent publishers to one influenced considerably by managerial hierarchies (Coser, Kadushin, and Powell 1982; Tebbel 1987).

Given the definition of organizational form, some organizations in the sample were subunits of larger corporate entities. To examine the potential for nonindependence effects, I conducted diagnostic analyses with a subsample that kept only one division from each corporation. The subsample results for the theoretical variables were the same as those for the full-sample analyses.

Organizations are in the sample from the date (year) that they first appear in the *LMP* until the date they are delisted because they no longer report information on the company and its employees. To ensure that my coding of delisted firms was accurate and not an artifact of a firm's missing one or two years' listings in the *LMP*, all firms in the sample were traced through 1995, five years beyond the end of the observation period.

It is noteworthy that the higher education market is a very dynamic ecology. Over the 32-year observation period, 84 firms in the sample were dissolved, 159 firms were founded, 106 were acquired, and 13 were absorbed by their parent firms. Ocasio and Thornton (2002) present an analysis of organizational exit from this data set that examines exit rates by different organizational forms and strategic capabilities, such as acquisition, vertical integration, and diversification.

To elaborate, there are more acquisition events than there are dissolutions. While an acquisition event will, in all likelihood, alter the firm's political coalition, it cannot be assumed, a priori, that an acquisition will be an automatic source of demise that dissolves the organizational structure of the acquired firm. Instead, mergers and acquisitions may signal entrepreneurial opportunities for continued growth and survival of the firm that is acquired or merged (Thornton 1999a). A firm may seek to be acquired to obtain financing and other resources to propel its growth at a more rapid pace. This was certainly the case in the higher education market in the 1960s with the rapid increase in college enrollments and public financial support of universities. In other cases, high-performing firms might be acquired when some of their organizational capabilities are valued more highly by another firm than by its owners. This is often the case with firms operating outside the market seeking entry. This occurred in the 1970s with the invasion by foreign-owned firms in the higher education market—a market entry that foreign publishers tried and failed by organic strategies a decade earlier. In still other cases a firm may seek a merger partner to strengthen its market share. For example in telling how mergers and acquisitions were central to entrepreneurship, one publisher recounted the history of the very active acquisitions program of Paramount Communications. This source noted its surprising origins in 1934 as the Michigan Bumper Company, and how it subsequently transformed its capabilities from Gulf & Western Industries to a media company. Examples range from its acquisition of Prentice Hall, the largest publisher in the world in 1985, to its eventual absorption through acquisition by Viacom.

In examining all cases of organizational dissolution, I found that five publishers exited the risk set by acquisition, 66 exited by dissolution, and 13 publishers exited by absorption to the parent firm. Dissolution, the liquidation and involuntary bankruptcy of a publisher, is distinct from absorption, in which the structure of the publishing unit is dissolved, but it may retain business capabilities and routines in the marketplace. For example, while a publisher may lose its autonomous structure, its brand identity may live on in the market by transfer to a new owner, another division or subsidiary, or to a parent firm (Mitchell 1994). For example, when Richard D. Irwin was acquired by McGraw-Hill, Irwin's separate organization structure was dissolved and absorbed into one of McGraw's subunits, reducing Irwin's autonomy, and retaining only its brand in the marketplace as an imprint of the McGraw-Hill higher education division.

The data file is organized by case (publishing organization) and within case by year. There is a new record for each year that indicates if a change in any variable occurred or did not occur for each year the organization exists in the risk set. All theoretical variables, except college enrollments, and all control variables, except ownership and interest rates, were coded from the *LMP*. All variables are coded annually. The format of these data conforms to the specifications of the RATE computer program (Tuma 1993).

Variables

DEPENDENT

How organizations select their leader; how they organize their business; and how they engage strategies of acquisition—these are some of the most critical economic decisions organizations make. These decisions are represented by the classic variables of interest in the literature of such fields as sociology, economics, organization theory, and strategy. In the analyses of the subsequent chapters, I examine three dependent variables: the hazard rates of executive succession, divisionalization, and acquisition. In the following, I define the independent and dependent variables used in these analyses. Before each variable name, a D denotes a dummy variable, and N indicates cumulate number. Additionally, the integer in parentheses is a unique identifier to facilitate comparisons of the values and effects of the variables across models. These numbers appear after the variable names in the tables with the descriptive statistics and the hazard rate models.

Executive Succession was coded as a dichotomous variable, D Executive Succession (1), set equal to 1 if the executive listed in the *LMP* as the top person with line responsibility for the organization was succeeded, and set equal to 0 if the chief executive did not change. To determine when executives were succeeded, executive names were compared across consecutive years for each organization for each year that the organization was listed in the *LMP*. Executive succession in the year after acquisition is coded as a succession event, whether or not the acquired firm was integrated into the parent firm or remained as a separate organization. In the case of succession due to acquisition, my interviews with industry principals indicate that there is generally a three- to six-month period where executives of acquired firms are given incentives to remain in their position in order to smooth the transition to the new owners.

Given that executive turnover, even when not explicitly forced, typically entails a "push" factor associated with the loss of executive power, the distinction between "voluntary" and "forced" successions is difficult to establish. Political pressures on CEOs that result in executive succession need not imply a forced dismissal. CEOs may choose to depart and seek employment in other organizations when they have lost control over the firm's political coalition. Furthermore, research indicates that the information available for distinguishing between voluntary and forced succession is not reliable for publicly held firms (Beatty and Zajac 1987) and is almost nonexistent for privately held firms, which constitute approximately three-fourths of my sample. In support of this research, publishing executives I interviewed indicated that the release of information to employees and the business press is euphemized for a number of reasons. It is important to the stakeholders to protect the firm from disruption, to maintain the market power of executives so that they may find other positions, to prevent lawsuits, and, at least for the executives, to ensure the payout of their financial incentive plans. Therefore, I cannot distinguish between "voluntary" and "forced" successions. Instead, I control for retirement effects by controlling for retirement age and by estimating models for a subsample that includes only executives sixty-three years old or less (Puffer and Weintrop 1991; Ocasio 1994).

Note that I use the variable, D Executive Succession (1), also as a control variable in the analysis and the models of the rate of divisionalization. Both Fligstein (1987) and Mezias (1990) have shown that new executives are likely to bring new models of management to the organization and therefore leadership succession may affect the rate of divisionalization.

Divisionalization was coded as a dichotomous variable, D Divisionalization (2), set equal to 1 if the organization switched its structure to a divisionalized form and set equal to 0 if it did not. I applied the organization structure coding scheme used by Fligstein (1985, 383), drawing on Chandler (1962) and Rumelt (1974), to the specific instances of the publishing industry. This coding scheme is elaborated in the appendix of Fligstein (1990).

Acquisition was coded as a dichotomous variable, D Acquired Firm (3), set equal to 1 in every year that an organization was acquired. Organizations were coded 1 only in the year of acquisition and 0 for every subsequent year in which acquisition did not occur. The acquisition variable was coded from all transactions listed in the *LMP* section on mergers and acquisitions. The *LMP* section on mergers and acquisitions also references the industry- and business-press articles that describe the transactions in detail. All primary source articles were reviewed to verify the identity of the acquired and acquiring firms.

Note that I use the variable, D Acquired Firm (3), as a control in the models examining the rate of divisionalization. Acquisition may increase the rate of divisionalization because when a firm is acquired it can become a separate division of an M-form organization (Coser, Kadushin, and Powell 1982, 179; Levin 1996).

INDEPENDENT

The independent variables were selected to examine the determinants of the three organizational decisions—executive succession, divisionalization, and acquisition. While the logic of my research design argues that organizations make decisions in the context of market institutions, scholars have developed different views of how institutions create marketplaces. For example, product markets can be investigated from the perspective of faceless economic exchanges (Smith [1776] 1976; Williamson 1975); they can be analyzed as relational social structures (Granovetter 1985; Powell 1990); and they can be examined from the standpoints of political–cultural arenas (Dobbin 1994; Fligstein 1996). Each of these views locates the sources of agency at different levels of analysis and identifies distinct mechanisms that coordinate decisions on economic exchanges, such as the positional (individuals), relational (network organizations), and economic (markets) determinants.

Positional variables refer to concepts that involve an individual actor's role, reputation, or status position, such as founder or chief executive officer. *Relational* variables refer to the structure of relationships among actors or groups of actors, such as author–editor relational networks in production or publisher–contractual relational networks in distribution. *Economic* variables refer to concepts that have consequences for firms in markets, such as resource competition in a product market, access to capital markets, or vulnerability to the market for corporate control. In the following sections, I organize and define the independent variables in the subsequent analyses according to each of these different views of marketplaces.

Positional

The variable, D Founder (4), was coded as a dichotomous variable set equal to 1 in every year that the executive in office also was the founder of the organization. A chief executive listed in the *LMP* at the date of the company founding was assumed to be the founder. When the name of the founder was not available from published sources, I gathered this information by telephone.

Relational

The variable, ln N Imprints (5), is the natural logarithm of the number of publishing imprints per firm as listed in the *LMP*. I used the logarithmic transformation because the distribution of the number of imprints is skewed. An example of an imprint in higher education publishing would be an advanced mathematics series or a list of books on the sociology of culture. The variable, ln N Imprints (5), is a measure of publisher–author relational networks in production and is an indicator of editorial control in the organization. It also is a measure of organization size and differentiation.

The variable, D Distribution Contract (6), is a measure of publisher–distributor relational networks in distribution and was coded as a dichotomous variable set equal to 1 if a publishing organization (supplier) had a contract for distribution of its books by another, separately owned, distributor or publisher. This variable was set equal to 0 if there were no such contracts. These contracts do not involve equity ownership sharing arrangements between firms, but simply represent the outsourcing of expenses for services such as advertising, selling, and fulfillment that are payable as a percent of sales.

The variable, D Division/Subsidiary (7), was coded as a dichotomous variable set equal to 1 in every year that the organization was listed in the *LMP* as a division or subsidiary of a larger parent firm. The division/subsidiary variable was reset to 0 or to 1 if the organization's status in this regard changed in any given year.

Economic

The variable, D Public/Private Ownership (8), was coded as a dichotomous variable set equal to 1 in every year that the subject organization was publicly traded. Data on ownership were obtained from the Standard and Poor's and Moody's industry directories, *Ward's Business Directory of Major U.S. Private Companies*, and *Ward's Business Directory of U.S. Private and Public Companies*.

Publicly owned firms may have a higher rate of divisionalization because they tend to be professionally managed and have access to public capital markets. Moreover, family or private ownership is associated with centralized control and a reluctance to fund diversification strategies (Palmer et al. 1987). Additionally, different ownership forms imply different sources of power that may affect the likelihood of acquisition. Davis and Stout (1992) and Palmer et al. (1995) found that the risk of acquisition is lower for privately held and family-owned firms. Private investors and family members are often involved in running the firm or have the power to monitor management, making these firms less likely to be administered with excessive organizational slack and less likely to be acquired. When private ownership is concentrated, owners have veto power over unwanted offers.

The variable, *D* Acquiring Firm (9), a measure of acquisition growth, was coded as a dichotomous variable set equal to 1 in each year a firm acquired another publishing firm and set equal to 0 in those years it did not. The *LMP* also references the business press articles that described all the transactions noted in the directory. I reviewed the primary source articles to distinguish the acquired firm from the acquiring firms.

The variable, Resource Competition (10), was computed as the total number of publishing organizations divided by the total number of college enrollments for each year. This ratio measures an annual count of potential competitors (all publishing organizations) and available resources (college and university enrollments).[1] College and university enrollment data were obtained from the *Digest of Education Statistics*, published by the National Center for Education Statistics (1993). The Resource Competition (10) variable is consistent with the ecological research that compares measures of population density to resource availability (Barron, West, and Hannan 1994).

CONTROL

The advanced age of the chief executive may create both individual- and industry-level cohort retirement effects. To control for the effect of executive age on the rate of executive succession, I computed the variable, Executive Age Post-63 (11). Executive age was coded in actual years and then transformed as the number of years over age sixty-three. I conducted a telephone survey to obtain the ages of executives. Two organizations in the sample refused to provide information about the ages of their chief executives. I obtained age information for executives of the eighty-four organizations that were disbanded during the observation period in one of two ways. If these individuals continued to be employed in the industry, I contacted them at the organizations in which they were subsequently employed. For retired or deceased individuals, five key leaders with long histories in the industry helped me identify missing age data. Using these methods, I was able to obtain the ages of over 60 percent of the chief executives of firms in the sample. I estimated values for missing age data based on the mean value of actual age data, using a dichotomous flag variable, *D* Estimated Age (12), set equal to 1 for age values that were estimated.

Longer executive tenure may explain succession, either in the case of the executive becoming "stale in the saddle" or having entrenched power (Ocasio 1994). To control for the effects of executive tenure on the rate of executive succession, I computed a cumulative count variable, Executive Tenure (13), which is the number of years an executive is in office. Each executive begins with a value of 1, which is incremented by 1 for each additional year the executive remains in office.

Founders and investors wishing to retire may use acquisition as an exit strategy to cash out (Lazonick 1992, Tebbel 1981). To control for retirement effects on the rate of acquisition, I calculated the product of two variables, *D* Founder (4) and Executive Age Post-63 (11), described earlier. This new variable is called Founder Age Post-63 (14).

The relationship between organizational age and the rates of divisionalization and acquisition is not clear. Fligstein (1985) found that older firms were more likely to adopt the M-form structure. Palmer and his colleagues (1987, 1993) found no effect for organization age. Hannan and Freeman (1984) argued that older firms' imprinting and inertia make them less likely to change. Therefore, one can argue that this inability to change in the face of changes in the environment will make an older firm more vulnerable to acquisition. In fact, Davis and Stout (1992) found that older firms had a higher risk of hostile takeover attempts in the 1980s.

I very briefly summarize an extensive literature in population ecology theory on the effects of organization age on the hazard rates of founding and mortality events because it may be applicable to the dependent variables of interest in this study. The effects of organization age on mortality have been examined as a liability of newness (Stinchcombe 1965), a liability of adolescence (Fichman and Levinthal 1991; Brudderl and Schussler 1990; Carroll and Delacroix 1982; Freeman, Carroll, and Hannan 1983), and a liability of senescence and obsolescence (Barron, West, and Hannan 1994). Hannan (1998) reviews and summarizes the age literature into five processes that drive the theoretical arguments—endowment, imprinting, inertia, capability, and position. The interplay of these five processes leads to variation in mortality rates of organizations as they age. To control for organization age, I coded the variable, Organization Age (15), as the number of years since a publishing organization's founding date as listed in the *LMP*. The age range for firms is from 1 to 205 years.

The amount of capital needed to purchase a larger firm may create a barrier to acquisition. To control for the effects of organization size and differentiation, I calculated the variable, *N* Division/Subsidiary (16), which is a count of the number of divisions and subsidiaries per firm as listed in the *LMP*. Organizations have a value of zero if they have a unitary form without divisions and subsidiaries. For example, Prentice Hall had a value of 22 in 1985. Note also that the independent variable, ln *N* Imprints (5), is also a measure of size and differentiation. The two size variables fluctuate annually based on changes in the number of divisions and subsidiaries and imprints.

Coser, Kadushin, and Powell (1982, 38–41) explain that alternative measures of organization size, such as the number of titles and the number of employees, are not reliable measures in the publishing industry. This is because some publishers make extensive use of freelance workers and because the size of the market of individual titles can vary greatly by the type of book, making the number of titles within and across publishing organizations incomparable units.

I also considered the use of firm assets as a measure of organization size. However, because the sampling procedure used here required temporal variation in forms of ownership (public and private) and organizational structure (independent and divisional or subsidiary), it was not possible to obtain data on assets for all organizations in the sample for the entire observation period.[2] For similar reasons, I was unable to examine the effects of the structure of the boards of directors.[3]

Organizational strategies and structures themselves can be a mechanism to both embody institutional logics and to propel the spread of logics within a market, industry, or organizational field (Nelson and Winter 1982; Haveman and Rao 1997). For example, Fligstein's (1987) work showed CEOs with marketing and finance backgrounds were favored in their rise to the top of multidivisional form, M-form, organizations but not in unitary form, U-form, organizations. His argument is that power struggles and the sources of change in power are located in organizational structure because structure locates resources available to actors: both information and authority (p. 46). In Fligstein's research, the particular source of agency stems from differences in the type of socialization and background of executives from various subunits of the corporation, for example manufacturing as distinct from finance. The popularity of types of executives manifests itself in cohort or style effects that create, to some extent, a dominant conception of strategy and structure within a market for a period of time, creating "mimetic isomorphism" (DiMaggio and Powell 1983).[4]

To control for changes in the market prevalence of organizational strategy and structure, I computed three industry-level variables: the proportion of acquisition activity, Industry Acquisition Activity (17); the proportion of organizations that are divisions and subsidiaries of parent firms, Industry Proportion Div/Sub (18); and the proportion of organizations that are of multidivisional form, Industry Proportion MDF (19). The proportion of acquisition activity is the yearly hazard rate of acquisition of firms. The proportion of divisions and subsidiaries and the proportion of MDF is the percentage of these types of organizations in the sample in any given year.

Changes in other subfields of publishing can also drive the rates of adoption, particularly acquisition. To control for cross-field effects, I computed a 0/1 dummy variable, Entryage, to distinguish time since the firm was founded from time since the firm's operation in the higher education product market. Diagnostic analyses showed that this variable is not significant in the models and that the two age variables are proxies for each other. The correlation between Organization Age (15) and Entryage is 0.97. For parsimony, I used only Organization Age (15) in the final models.

Related diversification of product lines, as an indicator of an increase in scope, may increase the rate of acquisition and divisionalization (Fligstein 1985, 387; Palmer et al. 1987; Palmer, Jennings, and Zhou 1993). Fligstein and Markowitz (1993) found that diversified firms were more likely to engage in strategies of financial reorganizations because they signal the basis of their profitability. To control for the effects of related diversification, I calculated two variables, Related Diversification (20), the number of different book markets per firm, and D Diversified Publisher (21), a dummy variable set to one in each year an organization produces for multiple markets, for example trade and college.

Fluctuations in demand may also affect the results of the models. To control for this, I computed a variable, Percent Change in College Enrollments (22), as the total change in student enrollments from the year $t-1$ to the year t divided by enrollments in the year $t-1$.

Changes in the availability of finance capital may also affect the rate of acquisition and divisionalization. When interest rates are lower, corporate expansion costs are lower and thus the rate of acquisition and divisionalization is likely to increase. To control for the availability of finance capital and more generally economic uncertainty, I calculated the variable Percent Change in Interest Rates (23) as year $(t-1)$ to the year (t) divided by the prime interest rate in the year $(t-1)$.

Financial performance may account for my findings, however I do not have financial data at the firm level of analysis. To test my hypotheses, I needed a longitudinal research design to examine the effects of differences in forms of capitalism, personal and market, on organization strategy and structure. As I mentioned earlier in the chapter, the lack of firm-level financial data makes it impossible to determine if a firm's financial success has made it relatively immune to pressures to change its leadership, strategy or structure.

However, instead of financial performance at the firm level, I evaluate how market competition and other selection pressures at the organization and population levels affected firms with respect to leadership succession, the strategy of acquisition, and the change to the divisionalized organization structure. I also examine the effects of a number of control variables that proxy for economic factors, such as organization size and ownership form. In addition, I review the empirical findings on the performance of economic organizations with respect to the dependent variables of interest and discuss the lack of consistency and convergence in these findings (Meyer 1994).

Selection of Historical Time Periods

My interviews and literature reviews suggest that the transition between the editorial logic and the market logic occurred during the 1970s (Tebbel 1981; Shatzkin 1982; Coser, Kadushin, and Powell 1982; Powell 1985). Coser, Kadushin, and Powell (1982) and Powell (1985) captured this transition because their sample was drawn from the 1975 *LMP*, and the interview and survey data were collected from 1976 to 1978. This is slightly later than the cut point I have selected for the change, but is well within the period of cultural turmoil that surrounded the transition. To select the exact time periods for the hazard rate models, I relied on graph analysis of time series data of indicators associated with the changes in institutional logics. I also conducted sensitivity analyses to determine whether the results were sensitive to the specific cutoff period. Based on comparisons of these interview and literature review accounts, the graphical analyses, and the model specifications, I divided the observations for empirical analysis into two historical periods that approximate 1958–75 and 1976–90. These two periods correspond with the two ideal types of institutional logics shown in Table 2.1 in Chapter 2. As further validation that the institutional logics and their periodization are consistent with the publishers' own understanding, the ideal types are used at a well-known university publisher's college in their executive education program.

More specifically, I performed a sensitivity analysis to empirically examine the selection of the time-period cut point. Using an exponential model including all covariates, I estimated half-year time intervals on both sides of the cutoff years for each of the three dependent variables. For example for executive succession, I estimated twenty-two models for three years before 1975 and eight years after 1975. While 1975 is the best fit, the statistically significant differences between the two time periods remain if I select the cut point at any time between 1972 and 1983.[5] Similarly, for acquisition, I estimated twenty-one time periods set at half-year intervals from 1967 to 1977. While 1973 is the best fit, the statistically significant differences between the two time periods remain if I select the cut point at any time between 1968.5 and 1976. I obtained similar results for divisionalization, in which the best fit is the year 1974. This indicates a transition period during which cut points are not very sensitive. This is quantitative support for two distinct periods or institutional logics that manifest their most significant effects earlier and later in the observation period.

As noted above, the time-period cutoff points vary by a few years to reflect the models' best fit to each of the three dependent variables. The overall models do remain statistically significant, though not the best fit, if I use the exact same cutoff period in modeling each of the dependent variables. Also because the cutoff points vary, comparison of the descriptive statistics across periods may reveal some differences; most notable is the case with changes in the control variable for interest rates. These results suggest that there is some order or sequencing in the strategic decisions that organizations made and in the effects of the shift in institutional logics. Although the focus of this analysis is on the consequences, not the causes of the shift in institutional logics, the comparison across the three studies suggests an order of causation of change events with acquisition occurring first, divisionalization second, and leadership succession last. Chapter 2 described a number of factors that led to and explained the change in institutional logics. This ordering supports the argument that acquisition was one of the pivotal change events. Acquisition is consistent with the publishing firms' inability to meet the increased demand in the marketplace by using retained earnings to capitalize growth. In many respects, corporate capital was the best solution to the problem of growth because, in general, the growth rate of publishing firms was below that expected with bringing a private firm public to access the public capital markets. At the same time, the solution of marrying a wealthier, probably public, firm through acquisition brought new models of organization and leadership to the industry. Moreover, this explanation is consistent with the empirical observation that of the 106 acquisition events, only 5 resulted in mortality for the acquired firm (Barron, West, and Hannan 1994; Carroll and Hannan 2000, 43–45).

Figure 2.1 on page 32 shows graphs of two indicator variables: the Nelson-Aalen estimates of the hazard rate of acquisition and a market demand measure, the number of student enrollments in higher education for each year in the observation period. Figure 2.2 on page 33 shows the hazard rate of the variable, D Executive Succession (1), and a measure of the covariate,

Resource Competition (10) (the ratio of the number of publishing organizations divided by the number of student enrollments in higher education).

The measures of market demand, Resource Competition (10), and acquisition activity suggest the early to mid-1970s as a cutoff point. Note in Figure 2.1 that market demand, as measured by the number of student enrollments, begins to level off after 1975. Note in Figure 2.2 that, before 1975, resource competition is decreasing and it begins to level and increase after 1975, signaling intensifying competition in the marketplace. With respect to the influences of acquisition activity, interview and literature reviews established that there were two periods of acquisition activity, and the hazard plot in Figure 2.1 supports these observations for my sample of firms (Thornton 1995). In the first wave, in the late 1960s and early 1970s, most acquired publishers were privately owned and were acquired by Fortune 500 firms outside the industry that were diversifying into higher-growth markets (Powell 1980). In the second wave, in the 1980s and onward, acquirers were conglomerate publishers attempting to increase market share by horizontal integration under conditions of rising resource competition (Greco 1997). The hazard rate graph of acquisition in Figure 2.1 identifies the main acquiring firms in the two time periods. The time series data on market demand and resource competition appear to be consistent with the characteristics of acquisition activity in the two time periods.

Selection of Statistical Models

I am not aware of prior analyses that have incorporated individual-, organizational-, and environmental-level data into population-level hazard-rate analyses. The difficulty of collecting such fine-grained data on organizations in a population over its history, with records available on an annual basis, has hampered this research. Given the relative lack of a modeling convention and the newness of my approach, I have selected the flexible piecewise exponential model to examine the hazard rate of all three transitions: executive succession, divisionalization, and acquisition (Barron, West, and Hannan 1994). Piecewise exponential models have been used to study such diverse topics as the rates of job shifts across time periods in China (Zhou, Tuma, and Moen 1997) and the political and cultural effects of women's suffrage across time periods (Ramirez, Soysal, and Shanahan 1997). However, they have not been used before in instances with data at three different levels of analysis.

In Chapter 8, I compare the estimates for the independent variables across the three studies presented in Chapters 5, 6, and 7. This meta-analysis requires that several elements of the research design be held relatively constant across the three studies—industry, data set, observation period, several of the independent and control variables, and the statistical modeling procedures. Therefore, for each of the three studies, I use the same statistical model while varying the dependent variables.

For each dependent variable, my arguments about change in the effects of institutional logics require a model that allows effects to vary freely, rising and falling, across historical time periods. For example, they must be free to vary not only with the characteristics of individuals at risk of a succession event and but also with the characteristics of organizations at risk of an acquisition and a divisionalization event. Piecewise exponential models, which allow the intercepts and the effects of covariates to vary in an unconstrained way across historical (calendar) time periods, are well suited to these requirements.

The equation below summarizes the functional form of this model.

$$\log r_{jk_p}(t) = x(t)' \beta_{jk_p}$$

The subscript p denotes a given historical period (e.g., 1958–1975, 1976–1990) and $x(t)$ refers to the set of explanatory and control variables used in the analysis. Models were estimated by maximum likelihood (ML) using RATE software (Tuma 1993).

CHAPTER 5

Attention to the Sources of Power

with William Ocasio[1]

The environment comprised of organizations transacting with the focal organization is, however, not the environment that determines organizational action, for this environment, in order to affect action, must be observed and registered. Observation, attention, and perception are active processes which must occur for events to exist in the experience of any social actor. Thus, the third level of the organization's environment can be characterized as the level of the organization's perception and representation of the environment—its enacted environment.

—Jeffrey Pfeffer and Gerald Salancik (1978), *The External Control of Organizations: A Resource Dependence Perspective*

ACCORDING TO political theories (Perrow 1986; Pfeffer and Salancik 1978/2003; Pfeffer 1981, 1992), leaders derive their power and authority from their formal position in the organization, their social relationships, the organization's reputation and status, and their ability to manage the organization's strategic contingencies and resource dependencies. We build on existing power and politics perspectives by examining how these determinants of power in organizations are historically and culturally contingent (Thornton and Ocasio 1999). The theory and analysis, while consistent with resource-dependence theory and structural contingency perspectives, emphasizes how the determinants of power are moderated by the prevailing institutional logic.

We define institutional logics as the socially constructed, historical pattern of material practices, assumptions, values, beliefs, and rules by which individuals produce and reproduce their material subsistence, organize time and space, and provide meaning to their social reality. Institutional logics are both material and symbolic—they provide the formal and informal rules of action, interaction, and interpretation that guide and constrain decision makers in accomplishing the organization's tasks and in obtaining social status, credits, penalties, and rewards in the process. These rules constitute a set of assumptions and values, usually implicit, about how to interpret organizational reality, what constitutes appropriate behavior, and how to succeed (Jackall 1988, 112; Friedland and Alford 1991, 243).

Several scholars have developed work on both private and public sector organizations that emphasizes how the historical patterns of institutional change are important in understanding power and control in organizations (Brint and Karabel 1991; Fligstein 1987, 1990). This idea stems back to Weber ([1922] 1978) and his identification of historically situated ideal types: control by individual charisma, by tradition, and by legal bureaucracy. Similarly, Grusky recounts how the problem of succession went through several historical stages that accompanied institutional change in the governance of American business: (1) control by the charismatic leader—the entrepreneur–founder, (2) transfer of control on the basis of kinship, and (3) change in control on the bureaucratic basis of professional competence. He noted that "the particular sequence of stages should influence the nature of the succession problem" (Grusky 1960, 110). More recently, Fligstein (1987) and Ocasio and Kim (1999) found that the functional backgrounds of those who rose to power in large U.S. corporations were determined by historical shifts in conceptions of control. Similarly, Brint and Karabel (1991) showed how administrators' ability to promote change and to advance their managerial interests in U.S. community colleges was shaped by new institutions for student testing and placement and the adoption of the guiding ideology of vocationalization.

In this chapter, we explore how industry-level institutional logics shape the positional, relational, and economic determinants of leadership power and succession across different historical periods representing two different forms of capitalism. Positional power refers to those determinants of power that are inherent in the actor's role or position, such as founder or division executive. Relational power is derived from the structure of relationships among actors, and groups of actors both intra- and interorganizationally. Economic determinants of power refer to those issues that have consequences for the performance of firms in a product market, such as access to public capital markets, resource competition, and the market for corporate control.

We apply part of the theory of attention developed in Chapters 2 and 3 by proposing three mechanisms by which industry-level institutional logics shape leadership power in organizations (Ocasio 1997). To restate, the meaning, appropriateness, and legitimacy of sources of power are shaped by the rules of the prevailing institutional logics. Institutional logics provide the rules that legitimate whether positional, relational, or economic factors form the basis of leadership power and authority in organizations (March and Olsen 1989). For example, in the context of the publishing industry, institutional logics indicate how the positions of the founder, editor, publisher, president, manager, and chief executive officer (CEO) are valued and understood.

Second, institutional logics determine what issues to attend to in controlling and rewarding political behavior (Ocasio 1997). Logics provide the rules of the game that shape the cognition of social actors in organizations (Powell and DiMaggio 1991; DiMaggio 1997). Given ambiguity and cognitive limitations on executive decision making, organizations are limited in their ability to attend to all aspects of their environments (March and Olsen 1976; Simon [1947] 1997). Hence, organizational decision makers are constrained to focus their attention on a limited set of issues. Institutional logics comprise a set of implicit rules of the game that regulate which issues, strategies contingencies, or problems become important in the political struggle among actors in organizations. For example, whether power is allocated to those enhancing the prestige of the publishing house or to those improving market position depends on whether the prevailing institutional logic in the industry focuses attention on prestige or, alternatively, on market competition.

Third, the assumptions, values, beliefs, and rules that comprise institutional logics determine what answers and solutions are available and appropriate in controlling economic and political activity in organizations (Ocasio 1997). For example, institutional logics regulate whether to control or reward publishing executives' focus on particular solutions, such as organic (i.e., internal) or acquisition growth strategies, building personal imprints, or developing market channels. Applying the theory of attention to the utilization of succession as a strategy implies that in addition to economic conditions, institutional logics also determine the likelihood and appropriateness of leadership succession as a solution to the problems of organizational performance and market instability.

Classic and contemporary theory and research in sociology have emphasized the importance of leadership succession in demarcating changes in power and authority in organizations and in society (Fligstein 1987, 1990). Among the early studies in the sociology of organizations, Gouldner (1954) and Grusky (1960, 1963) defined succession, the replacement of key officials, as a critical process in the transition from personal to bureaucratic patterns of control in organizations. Contemporary research on succession has continued to focus on the sources of executive power and authority, with an emphasis on the internal political dynamics in organizations. For example, recent studies examine the social psychology of CEO relationships, the demographic and structural characteristics of boards of directors, and the political dynamics among board members and top management (Boeker 1992; Ocasio 1994; Zajac and Westphal 1996).

Institutional approaches suggest a different focus for studies of leadership power in organizations—that interests, power, and politics in organizations are shaped by institutional logics prevailing in wider environments (Fligstein 1990; Friedland and Alford 1991; Davis and Greve 1997). According to this view while power and politics are present in all organizations, the sources of power, its meaning, and its consequences are contingent on higher-order institutional logics. Institutional logics define the rules of the game by which executive power is gained, maintained, and lost in organizations (Jackall 1988). Moreover, institutional logics are historically variant and are shaped by economic and social structural changes (Fligstein 1985, 1987; Fligstein and Brantley 1992; Barley and Kunda 1992). However, the effects of institutional logics on the determination of power in organizations are not emphasized in most empirical analyses of intraorganizational power or in recent studies of succession. While a general theme of both classic and contemporary studies on leadership succession is that organizational politics shape executive change, the idea that the political determinants of succession are themselves conditioned by the historical and cultural context has been relatively unexplored, with the exception of Fligstein (1987).

We explore how a historical shift in the dominant institutional logic in an industry from the logic of professions to the logic of markets led to a transformation in the political dynamics in organizations. We use the attributes of the two ideal types developed in Chapter 2, an editorial and a market logic, to hypothesize how the transformation from one logic to another shifts the focus of attention in organizations with consequences for a change in the importance of the positional, relational, and economic determinants of leadership power and succession. In particular, we examine how the salience of the sources of power, both internal and external to the organization—formal position and rank in the hierarchy, organization size and differentiation, ownership form, resource competition, and the market for corporate control—are historically contingent on the prevailing institutional logics. We test these expectations using hazard rate models of leadership succession events in the industry from 1958 to 1990. In sum, we show for the higher education publishing industry a historical increase in the importance of economic determinants and a decline in the effects of positional and relational sources of power on leadership succession.

Hypotheses

POSITIONAL AND RELATIONAL DETERMINANTS OF SUCCESSION

Research indicates that the position of founder is associated with lower rates of executive succession (McEachern 1975; Ocasio 1994). McEachern (1975) argues that founders have lower rates of succession because they have greater economic and political power relative to other executives. Carroll (1984) notes that founders have persistence in their positions because they have personal characteristics that distinguish them from nonfounders— they are more likely to be owners, to have higher commitment to the organization, and to possess special expertise and knowledge. Ocasio (1999) found that founders have lower rates of succession because founder-led firms have not experienced succession and therefore lack organizational-level rules and routines that guide executive succession. Because of the lack of rules, succession is less likely to be an available solution to the problems of the organization.

According to the theory of attention, both the legitimacy of potential sources of leadership power and the salience of the rules of succession are likely to be modified by the prevailing institutional logics. First, the attributes of the ideal types in Table 2.1 (see Chapter 2) indicate that the personal and positional sources of power have greater legitimacy during the period of an editorial logic than during the period of a market logic. This implies that the effects of founders, which embody the attributes of personal and positional power, will be greater under an editorial logic. Second, the appropriateness of succession as a control mechanism for firms' actions and outcomes is likely to be greater in period 2 because attention to firm performance is more salient under a market logic. Extending this argument to the effects of founders, when a market logic prevails, firms without organization-level experience with succession are likely to rely on industry-level rules for succession as an organizational solution. The combination of these two factors leads to the expectation that:

HYPOTHESIS I
The negative effect of founder on the rate of leadership succession will be greater in the historical period when an editorial logic prevails.

Early research focused on the effects of bureaucratization, measured by organization size, on the frequency of executive succession (Grusky 1961). Grusky (1963) argued that bureaucratization increases the existence of rules and routinization and therefore the likelihood of succession of executives. Comparing the largest 26 and the smaller 27 Fortune 500 companies, he found a positive relationship between organization size and executive succession. Reexamination of early studies reveals that findings are mixed and that there is not a simple and direct relationship between organization size and succession (Gordon and Becker 1964). In subsequent studies, Salancik and Pfeffer (1980), Allen and Panian (1982), and Harrison, Torres, and Kukalis (1988) found a significant positive relationship, but Puffer and Weintrop (1991), Boeker (1992), and Ocasio (1994) found no effect of organization size on succession. Pfeffer and Salancik (1978) point out one reason for the mixed findings on organization size and succession is that size may be confounded with the relational and political dynamics of an organization. They argue that the larger the organization, the greater the number of departments and the greater the subunit basis of power, and therefore the greater the potential for contests for control.

According to the theory of attention, the effects of organization size on succession may be conditional on whether the prevailing institutional logics focus leaders' attention on the subunit basis of power associated with increased organizational size. The number of imprints in a publishing firm is a parallel measure of organization size and differentiation to the number of departments in an industrial firm. This measure is also an indicator of editorial control and editors' relational dynamics with authors. Publishing imprints represent a list of books that have identity and cohesiveness determined by an editor's professional expertise and author networks. According to the attributes of the ideal types in Table 2.1, under an editorial logic, the focus of attention is on author–editor relationships. In such a climate, executives focused on the strategy of organic growth—ensuring the development of both new titles and a backlist of titles of personal imprints. Under a market logic, other subunits of the firm not controlled by editors—such as sales, marketing, and finance—which empower alternative strategies of growth—such as acquisitions and building market channels—should gain in importance. Therefore, the importance of imprints is likely to decline under a market logic where editor–author networks, inherently associated with the development of imprints, become less salient. Therefore:

HYPOTHESIS 2

The positive effect of the number of imprints on the rate of leadership succession will be greater in the historical period when an editorial logic prevails.

Structural position in the organizational hierarchy, derived from formal authority, is an important but relatively unexplored determinant of leadership succession. This effect remains understudied because most empirical analyses of succession focus on executives at the same level of the organizational hierarchy, typically the CEO of independent firms. An exception is Boeker's (1992) study of semiconductor firms, which found that chief executive officers were less apt to experience succession than lower ranked executives, who were more likely to be used as scapegoats when the performance of the firm was poor. In this chapter, we compare the succession rate of CEOs of division and subsidiary publishing firms with CEOs of independent publishers. Based on Table 2.1, the effects of rank in the hierarchy should be moderated by the prevailing institutional logic. In particular, the interviews and historical analysis suggest that the legitimacy of rank and position in the organizational hierarchy as a determinant of executive power is likely to be greater in the period of an editorial logic than under a market logic. Given that divisional executives are of lower rank and status than executives of independent firms:

HYPOTHESIS 3

The positive effects of divisional executives on the rate of succession will be greater in the historical period when an editorial logic prevails.

ECONOMIC DETERMINANTS OF SUCCESSION

According to the theory of attention, with a change in the prevailing institutional logic from an editorial to a market focus, the determinants of leadership succession are expected to shift from those based on positional and relational power to those based on economic power. We examine the effects of public versus private ownership as a determinant of succession. Research indicates that different forms of ownership imply different mechanisms for institutionalizing power in a firm (Pfeffer and Salancik 1978). McEachern (1975) found that owner-managed firms have increased executive tenure, and Allen and Panian (1982) found the same for family-owned firms. However, Boeker (1992) found that public versus private ownership had no effect on executive succession. Given the increased salience of economic forces under the market logic and the shift from private to public ownership, as theorized in Table 2.1.

HYPOTHESIS 4

The positive effects of public ownership on the rate of leadership succession will be greater in the historical period when a market logic prevails.

Research indicates that changes in corporate control through acquisitions are likely to be followed by above-normal levels of executive succession in target firms (Walsh 1998). According to the theory of attention and historical analysis of the development of the market for corporate control (Lazonick 1992), the effects of the market for corporate control should vary historically with a shift in the prevailing institutional logics. Moreover, the interview and historical analysis of the industry indicate that the practice of acquiring firms to replace executives of target firms was more commonly accepted in the period when a market logic was dominant. Therefore:

HYPOTHESIS 5
The positive effects of acquisition on the rate of leadership succession will be greater in the historical period when a market logic prevails.

Last, we examine the effects of product market competition on succession. Given data limitations in the sample, we cannot directly measure firm-level performance for most firms. Instead, we evaluate how resource competition affects leadership succession. Previous research on succession has not investigated the effects of competition on succession within a population of firms. According to the theory of attention, the focus of executive attention shifted from author–editor networks to resource competition in the product market. Thus, performance in the product market is likely to gain salience in determining executive power in the period when a market logic prevails. Because of this, higher education publishing firms under a market logic will more likely view succession as a legitimate and appropriate remedy to issues of resource competition in the product market. Consequently:

HYPOTHESIS 6
The positive effects of resource competition on the rate of leadership succession will be greater in the historical period when a market logic prevailed.

Results

Table 5.1 presents the mean values and the correlation coefficients for all variables in the models. Table 5.2 presents the maximum likelihood (ML) estimates of piecewise exponential models on the rate of leadership succession. To test for time variation in the effects of the variables, we compared two effects models: a time-invariant model (model A) and a time-varying model (model B). Model A has time-varying intercepts, which are listed under the historical period for which they apply, and time invariant effects of covariates, which are listed under the column labeled All Years. The pattern of effects in the All Years model is analogous to an average effect for the 1958–1990 period. For model B, time-varying parameter estimates are located under the historical period for which they apply. The coefficients give the effect of the covariate on the log of the rate of executive succession. A relative comparison of the scale of effects can be determined by taking the antilogs of the coefficients to provide the multiplier of the base rate. Two-tailed tests are used to interpret significance levels for the models as a whole. One-tailed tests are used to compare whether individual parameter estimates

TABLE 5.1

Means, Pearson Correlations, and F-tests for Covariates of Higher Education Publishing Firms

Covariate Means	Time Period 1958–1975 Editorial	Time Period 1976–1990 Market	F-value	p-level	1	2	3	4	5	6	7	8	9	10	11	12	13
1 D Executive Succession (1)	0.05	0.06	1.59	0.207													
2 Executive Age Post 63 (11)	0.35	0.96	56.59	0.000	0.03*												
3 D Estimated Age (12)	0.35	0.34	0.83	0.361	0.00	-0.12***											
4 Executive Tenure (13)	10.25	11.05	6.77	0.009	-0.02	0.51***	-0.12***										
5 Organization Age (15)	34.13	28.37	24.97	0.000	0.04*	0.19***	-0.18***	0.14***									
6 Percent Change in College Enrollments (22)	6.92	1.53	6086.15	0.000	-0.02	-0.08**	0.00	-0.02	0.07***								
7 Industry Proportion Div/Sub (18)	0.21	0.29	2366.47	0.000	0.05**	0.15***	-0.03*	0.06***	-0.05**	-0.50***							
8 Industry Acquisition Activity (17)	0.02	0.04	197.99	0.000	0.05**	0.09***	-0.04**	0.05**	0.03	-0.02	0.43***						
9 D Founder (4)	0.55	0.54	0.48	0.487	-0.11***	0.09***	0.10***	0.36***	-0.47***	0.00	-0.04**	-0.06***					
10 ln N Imprints (5)	0.15	0.26	55.30	0.000	0.07***	0.03	-0.12***	-0.06***	0.09***	-0.09***	0.18***	0.08***	-0.20***				
11 D Division/Subsidiary (7)	0.28	0.35	21.36	0.000	0.12***	-0.06***	-0.05**	-0.13***	0.16***	-0.06***	-0.12***	0.05**	-0.34***	0.10***			
12 D Public/Private Ownership (8)	0.22	0.27	9.40	0.002	0.14***	-0.06***	-0.14***	-0.13***	0.24***	-0.03*	0.00	0.05**	-0.37***	0.23***	0.50***		
13 D Acquired Firm (3)	0.02	0.03	1.05	0.305	0.09***	0.01	0.02	0.01	0.02	-0.01	-0.01	0.03*	-0.05**	0.02	0.17***	0.13***	
14 Resource Competition (10)	1.58	1.63	32.85	0.000	-0.02	0.00	-0.03	0.01	0.04**	-0.06***	-0.06***	0.11***	-0.06***	-0.03	-0.06***	-0.06***	-0.06***

NOTES: N = number; D = dummy variable
* $p \leq 0.05$, two-tailed tests.
** $p \leq 0.01$
*** $p \leq 0.001$

TABLE 5.2

Maximum Likelihood Estimates of
Piecewise Exponential Models of the Rate of Leadership Succession

Covariates	All Years	Time Period		χ^2 Test of Constraint
		1958–1975 Editorial	1976–1990 Market	
Intercept (model A)[a]		−3.036***	−3.435***	
Intercept (model B)[b]		−3.402	−4.646***	
Control Variables				
Executive Age Post 63 (11)	0.068**	0.144*	0.075**	
D Estimated Age (12)	0.226	0.423+	0.116	
Executive Tenure (13)	0.018*	0.046***	−0.000	
Organization Age (15)	−0.003+	−0.005	−0.003	
Industry Proportion Div/Sub (18)	0.013	−0.002	−0.014	
Industry Acquisition Activity (19)	4.087	5.596	4.403	
Percent Change in College Enrollments (22)	−0.060*	−0.030	−0.084*	
Theoretical Variables[c]				
D Acquired Firm (3)	0.534	−0.855	0.945**	4.02
D Founder (4)	−0.870***	−1.125***	−0.650**	1.55
ln N Imprints (5)	0.301**	0.701**	0.227+	2.69*
D Division/Subsidiary (7)	0.364*	1.027***	0.175	6.03**
D Public/Private Ownership (8)	0.671***	0.422	0.714***	0.68
Resource Competition (10)	−0.012	−0.083	1.334**	2.74

NOTES: N = number, D = dummy variable, N of firms = 230, N of succession events = 237. Likelihood ratio χ^2 for model A = 145.24* (df = 13). For model B, χ^2 = 172.57** (df = 26). For the difference between the models, χ^2 = 27.33*** (df = 13). Reported significance levels are two-tailed tests.

[a] Model A has time-varying intercepts and time-invariant effects of covariates. Time-varying intercepts are shown under the historical period for which they apply. Time-invariant effects of covariates are listed under All Years.

[b] Model B has time-varying intercepts and time-varying effects of covariates. Time-varying effects of covariates are shown under the period for which they apply.

[c] Model B theoretical variables cannot be constrained to be equal across historical periods without significantly degrading its fit (χ^2 = 17.27; df = 6; $p \leq 0.01$). Constraining the control variables to be equal across periods marginally degrades the fit of the model (χ^2 = 11.92; df = 7; p = 0.10).

+ $p \leq 0.10$, two-tailed tests.
* $p \leq 0.05$
** $p \leq 0.01$
*** $p \leq 0.001$.

are significantly different between the two time periods, because the hypotheses are unidirectional.

The nesting of model A within model B allows the use of a likelihood ratio χ^2 statistic to test the comparative fit of model A with model B. The likelihood ratio χ^2 test comparing model A against model B indicates that model B, with both time-varying intercepts and effects, significantly improves the fit of the model ($\chi^2 = 27.33$; $df = 13$; $p = 0.01$). Thus, we can reject the model of time-invariant effects on the rate of executive succession when all covariates are considered simultaneously.

On the whole, the results support the overall hypothesis that with a shift from an editorial to a market logic, the determinants of succession changed from a basis of positional and relational authority to a basis of authority derived from economic and market forces. A χ^2 contrast shows that the parameter estimates for the theoretical variables as an entire group cannot be constrained to be equal across the two time periods without significantly degrading the fit of the model ($\chi^2 = 17.27$; $df = 6$; $p = 0.01$).

With respect to the positional and relational basis of power, first, we found that the effect of founders lowers the rate of executive succession. While this effect is as hypothesized—greater under an editorial logic than under a market logic—note that the χ^2 contrast of the effect of founder between the periods is not strong, and we cannot reject the null hypothesis of no statistically significant differences ($\chi^2 = 1.55$; $df = 1$; $p = 0.11$).

Second, increased organization size, as measured by the number of publishing imprints per firm, significantly increases the rate of leadership succession in the editorial period ($p = 0.01$). The effect on organization size also is marginally significant in the period of a market logic. This effect on the base rate of executive succession is more than one and one-half times higher in the period of an editorial logic than in the period of a market logic ($0.701 - 0.227 = 0.474$) ($e^{0.474} = 1.61$). We found support for the hypothesis of a difference in the effects of the number of imprints between the two periods. A χ^2 contrast shows that the parameter estimates cannot be constrained to be equal across the two time periods without significantly degrading the fit of the model ($\chi^2 = 2.69$; $df = 1$, $p = 0.05$).

Third, we found support for the expectation about position in the hierarchy. That is, executives in charge of a division or subsidiary of a parent firm are at a significantly higher risk of succession in the period of an editorial logic, but not in the period of a market logic. This variable is significant in the editorial period, at $p = 0.000$ and not significant in the market period. This effect on the base rate of succession is more than two times higher in the period of an editorial logic than in the period of a market logic ($1.027 - 0.175 = 0.852$) ($e^{0.852} = 2.34$). Moreover, the parameter estimates for this positional effect cannot be constrained to be equal across the two time periods without significantly degrading the fit of the model ($\chi^2 = 6.03$; $df = 1$; $p = 0.01$).

With respect to the economic bases of power, first you can see that the effects of form of ownership, public versus private, are equivocal. The size and significance of the coefficients in the two periods is consistent with the expectations—not significant under the period of an editorial logic but positive and significant under the period of a market logic. However, note that the contrast in the effect of ownership between the periods is not strong, and we cannot reject the null hypothesis of no statistically significant difference ($\chi^2 = 0.68$; $df = 1$; $p = 0.20$).

Second, the effect of acquisition of the firm on the rate of leadership succession is consistent with a market logic, emphasizing growth by acquisition. The parameter estimates are positive and significant for the period of a market logic but not for the period of an editorial logic. Consistent with the hypothesis, the two parameter estimates for acquisition cannot be constrained to be equal across periods without significantly degrading the fit of the model ($\chi^2 = 4.02$; $df = 1$; $p = 0.02$). The effect of acquisition on the base rate of succession is strong, being six times higher in the period of a market logic than in the period of an editorial logic ($0.945 - (-)0.855 = 1.800$) ($e^{1.800} = 6.05$).

Third, the findings support the expectation that the fate of leaders was tied to the issues of scarcer resources and higher competition in the product market during the period of a market logic. The parameter estimate for the effect of resource competition is positive and significant during the period of a market logic but not during the period of an editorial logic. The effect of resource competition on the base rate of leadership succession is four times higher in the period of a market logic than in the period of an editorial logic ($1.334 - (-)0.083 = 1.417$) ($e^{1.417} = 4.12$). Consistent with the hypothesis of there being a greater effect of resource competition under a market logic, the estimates for resource competition cannot be constrained to be equal across the two time periods without significantly degrading the fit of the model ($\chi^2 = 2.74$; $df = 1$; $p = 0.05$). This finding, while suggestive, is subject to potential bias given that firm-level performance data are unavailable for the study.

CONTROL VARIABLES

The estimate for executive age is positive and significant in both time periods, indicating that, independent of the effects of different institutional logics, executives due to retire because of age have a higher rate of succession. The estimate for the effect of executive tenure is positive and significant in the period of an editorial logic and negative and not significant in the period of a market logic. A positive and significant tenure effect suggests that increasing tenure may lead to obsolescent strategies that in turn trigger adversity among political coalitions in the firm and executive succession (Ocasio 1994). This finding also may suggest one mechanism by which an editorial logic was displaced with a market logic over time.

The control variable for market demand, Percent Change in College En-rollments (22), is negative and significant in the All Years model, indicating that, on average, greater demand in the product market decreases succession. Note this effect is significant in the period of a market logic but not in the period of an editorial logic. The period difference provides some support for the arguments that during the period of a market logic, market forces influenced attention to the political processes of leadership succession. The parameter estimates for the proportion of firms that are divisions and sub-sidiaries of parent firms and the rate of acquisition activity in the industry are not significant in either the all-years or the piecewise models. While graph analyses of these variables show that their proportion is increasing over time in the sample, the results from the models suggest that the effects of a change in institutional logics on leadership succession was not due to these industry-level changes in strategy and organizational form.

To test whether type of publisher and degree of market diversification might possibly affect my findings, I computed a 0/1 dummy variable set equal to "1" if a firm in the sample published books for more than one type of mar-ket. I also computed a 0/1 dummy variable set equal to "1" if a firm in the sample published only textbooks. These variables were not statistically signifi-cant in any of the models, nor did they change any of the effects of the con-trol and theoretical variables.

SUBSAMPLE ANALYSIS: SUCCESSION PRIOR TO RETIREMENT AGE

To further examine if the results can be affected by forced versus volun-tary succession, we control for voluntary retirement (Puffer and Weintrop 1991; Ocasio 1994) by estimating separate models for the effects of succes-sion of executives prior to retirement age (63 years or younger). Note that in the sample approximately 85 percent of the successions are for executives 63 years or younger. As shown in Table 5.3, the results of this diagnostic test are consistent with the theory and show that the statistically significant ef-fects of the theoretical variables on the rate of succession hold for executives prior to retirement age. A χ^2 contrast shows that the parameter estimates for the theoretical variables as an entire group cannot be constrained to be equal across the two time periods without significantly degrading the fit of the model ($\chi^2 = 14.74$; $df = 6$; $p = 0.02$).

More specifically for this subsample, the positional and the relational bases of power, as measured by the number of organizational imprints and divisional versus independent executives, significantly increased the rate of succession in the period of an editorial logic but not in the period of a market logic. The economic bases of power as measured by acquisition of the firm and resource competition significantly increased the rate of leadership succession in the period of a market logic but not in the period of an editorial logic. The χ^2 contrast of the effects of these variables between the two

TABLE 5.3

Maximum Likelihood Estimates of Piecewise Exponential Models of the Rate of Executive Succession for the Subsample, Executives Under Age 63

Covariates	All Years	Time Period	
		1958–1975 Editorial	1976–1990 Market
Intercept (model A)[a]		3.447***	−3.805***
Intercept (model B)[b]		2.146	4.761***
Control Variables			
D Estimated Age (12)	0.260+	0.458+	0.110
Executive Tenure (13)	0.021+	0.039*	0.002
Organization Age (15)	−0.004	−0.004	−0.003
Percent Change in College Enrollments (22)	−0.063*	−0.042	−0.083+
Industry Proportion Div/Sub (18)	0.023	0.028	−0.011
Industry Acquisition Activity (17)	3.280	2.513	4.251
Theoretical Variables[c]			
D Founder (4)	−0.947***	−1.063***	−0.786**
ln N Imprints (5)	0.202	0.596*	0.116
D Division/Subsidiary (7)	0.407*	0.972**	0.212
D Public/Private Ownership (8)	0.570***	0.506+	0.536**
Acquired Firm (3)	0.658+	−0.602	1.093**
Resource Competition (10)	0.065	−0.471	1.228*

NOTES: N = number, D = dummy variable, N of firms = 226, N of divisionalization events = 199. Likelihood ratio χ^2 for model A = 120.65*** (df = 12). For model B χ^2 = 139.01*** (df = 24). For the difference between the models χ^2 = 18.36+ (df = 12).

[a] Model A has time-varying intercepts and time-invariant effects of covariates. Time-varying intercepts are listed under the historical period for which they apply. Time-invariant effects of covariates are listed under All Years.

[b] Model B has time-varying intercepts and time-varying effects of covariates. Time-varying effects of covariates are listed under the period for which they apply.

[c] Model B theoretical variables cannot be constrained to be equal across time periods without significantly degrading its fit (χ^2 = 14.74; df = 6; p = 0.02). Control variables can be constrained to be equal across periods (χ^2 = 4.48; df = 6; p = 0.61).

+ $p \leq$ 0.10, two-tailed tests.
* $p \leq$ 0.05
** $p \leq$ 0.01
*** $p \leq$ 0.001

periods is strong, and we can reject the null hypothesis of no statistically significant differences. The effects of founder and public versus private ownership, while in the expected direction, are not strong enough to reject the null hypothesis of no statistically significant differences between the two periods.

Discussion and Conclusion

This work extends the research on leadership succession by providing a new set of findings on the historical and cultural contingency of the determinants of leadership power and succession. The interviews and historical research established that the prevailing institutional logic shifted in the 1970s from an editorial to a market focus. The event history models suggest that this historical change in logics led to different determinants of leadership succession. The findings support the general argument—that when, whether, and how leaders deploy their power to affect succession in organizations is conditional on the prevailing institutional logic in an industry.

In particular, the findings suggest how the salience of positional, relational, and economic determinants of power varies by industry culture. The quantitative analysis implies that changes in logics result not in an overall increase in the rate of leadership succession, but in countervailing determinants of succession in the two periods. With the transition from an editorial logic to a market logic, the effects on the rate of succession of organizational size and position in the hierarchy declined, while those of acquisition and resource competition increased.

The effects of organization size and rank and position in the hierarchy were significantly stronger in the period when an editorial logic prevailed, even though, as indicated in Tables 5.1 and 5.2, organization size and the proportion of multidivisional organizations were significantly lower in this period. In the market period, neither organization size nor the executive's position as division head or independent CEO were strong predictors of succession. Organization size was a strong predictor in the editorial period when executives focused their attention on strategies of organic (internal) growth. However, size loses significance when internal growth strategies waned in favor of an alternative strategy in the market period—growth by acquisition. The effects of divisionalization are particularly revealing. Under an editorial logic, the power of independent CEOs relative to division heads led to higher rates of succession for the latter group. Under a market logic, rank and position in the hierarchy is less important, so that the difference in rates of succession between CEOs at the top of the hierarchy and for divisions is not statistically significant.

With respect to economic determinants, the effects for firm acquisition and resource competition were significantly stronger when the market logic became dominant, even though acquisitions and resource competition were noteworthy during both periods. Both the historical analysis and interviews shed light on how to interpret these findings. The publishing historian John Tebbel (1981, 724) noted, "It was true that publishers had been surviving since the beginning of the nineteenth century through mergers and acquisitions—but the changes were mostly shifts in partnerships and within the family, so to speak." Tebbel's historical observation suggests that in period 1, when "family governance" of acquisitions was commonplace, executives were not displaced during acquisition as they were in period 2, when the "market governance" of acquisitions became commonplace. Moreover, we went back to a few of the publishers that we interviewed to discuss these findings. They indicated that many of the acquisitions in the late 1960s were made by product-unrelated conglomerate firms outside the industry. These acquiring firms had neither the incentive nor the structural means to consolidate publishers into existing operations. Instead, the acquiring firms were dependent on extant publishing leaders to run their acquired properties as relatively autonomous divisions—allowing for the prevalence of an editorial logic even upon acquisition. In contrast, the second acquisition wave, in the late 1980s, took place among product-related publishing conglomerates in a period when a market logic had taken hold. This made executives susceptible to a market logic, where attention was focused on improving market position by strategies of acquisition and integrating operations—suggesting why acquisition led to succession.

Resource competition had no effect on succession during the editorial period, although the level of resource competition—the number of publishing organizations per thousands of college enrollment—was actually higher in the early 1960s than at any time during the period when the market logic prevailed. This finding may suggest that attention to economic forces depends on the prevalence of a market logic rather than on the level of competition experienced in the industry.

The findings support the overall hypothesis that the sources of power that affect leadership succession are not universal constraints but are historically contingent. However, for two of the original six hypotheses, the null hypothesis of historically invariant effects could not be rejected. These null findings suggest that some of the determinants of executive power and succession may be less historically contingent than others. For example, we found lower rates of succession for founders in both periods. This might be explained in two ways. First, the staying power of founders may be due to their personal characteristics, such as having higher commitment and expertise, which may be more stable across time and situation than is true of organizational and environmental characteristics (Scott 2001, 137). Second, it may also be that founder-led firms, which lack experience with succession, do not rely on industry-level rules, but they instead rely on organization-level rules (Ocasio and Kim 1999).

A null finding was also uncovered for the differential effects of public and private ownership between the two periods. The strength of the main effect indicates that some sources of power are less historically and culturally contingent than others and reveals a limitation or scope condition of the theory. Note in Table 5.1 the effect of public ownership is statistically significant in the market period but not in the editorial period. However, the contrast between the findings in Tables 5.1 and 5.2 indicates that this apparent contingency may be due to a retirement effect, not to involuntary succession. The lack of historical contingency for ownership form suggests that any effects of the rise of a market logic affected both privately and publicly held firms, even though privately held firms are thought to be less susceptible to direct market pressures.

The results of both the interviews and quantitative analysis are consistent with the view that institutional logics are both material and symbolic (Friedland and Alford 1991). A shift from an editorial logic to a market logic in higher education publishing was marked by an increase in the size of publishing organizations, public ownership, and resource competition—all structural characteristics consistent with the increased importance of market forces in the industry. These structural changes in market conditions attracted new and powerful actors with different goals and tactics that comparatively deemphasized intrinsic editorial accomplishment and elevated financial pursuit. However, after controlling for structural and economic forces at the industry level, the effects of the theoretical variables remain. This suggests that without an accompanying change in the understandings that comprise an institutional logic, economic and structural changes may not be sufficient to explain the determinants of executive succession.

Generally, we found that there is not a one-to-one correspondence between changes in structural and economic forces and changes in executive power and succession. The changing determinants of executive succession held independent of the following control variables: Percent Change in College Enrollments (22), Industry Proportion MDF (19), and Industry Acquisition Activity (17). This evidence suggests that institutional logics moderate the effects of economic and structural forces affecting succession. This implies that the effects of institutional logics cannot be reduced to purely social structural and economic forces (Barley and Kunda 1992; DiMaggio 1994).

Our interpretation of the findings does not imply that logics and meanings are completely independent of changes in the social structure or in the economy. In the example, the rise of a market logic in higher education publishing—articulated with observed changes in public ownership, acquisition activity, and resource competition—allowed publishers to understand these changes and develop suitable responses. The editorial logic—with its emphasis on publishing as a profession rather than business, its emphasis on author–editor networks, and its emphasis on personal reputation and rank in the hierarchy—could not easily explain or account for the changes in the marketplace nor the rise of acquisition activity after 1975.

The findings suggest that changes in institutional logics, while serving to articulate changes in economic and social structures, are not epiphenomenal but lead to changes in the determinants of executive power and succession. We propose the view that the relative autonomy of institutional logics operates via the logic's structuring the attention of organizational decision makers. The findings suggest that institutional logics, once they become dominant, affect succession by structuring the attention of executives toward the set of issues that are consistent with the logic dominant within an industry, whether editorial or market, and away from issues that are not. While changes in key variables—such a organizational size, position in the hierarchy, acquisitions, and resource competition—may occur independent of institutional logics, whether these changes are attended to and whether or not they are consequential for decisions on executive power or succession is contingent on whether the prevailing logic makes these variables salient.

The higher education publishing industry provides evidence of the historical contingency of executive power. Future research should examine whether and how these effects change if firm-level performance measures are available. Other data limitations, particularly on firm size and CEO age may also affect the interpretation of the results. While the specific findings of this study may not be generalizable to other industries, the *theory* that is tested on the historical contingency of power in organizations is generalizable across different settings. Future research should investigate how power and succession are affected in other industrial settings that have experienced significant transformation. One example for future study is the health care sector, which has also experienced a transformation away from professional logics (Starr 1982) toward managerial and market logics (Ruef and Scott 1998; Scott 2001). We also see parallel transformations with privately held firms in accounting, consulting, investment banking, and law, each shifting from a professional logic to a market logic. In addition, the furniture and funeral home industries, originally craft-based, were subject to rationalization in the 1980s by the market for corporate control and therefore are interesting sites for comparative industry studies of the consequences of institutional change on power in organizations.

The rise of the market logic in higher education publishing and in other professional and craft industries parallels higher-order transformations in the United States (Useem 1996). Since the 1970s, managerial capitalism in the United States has been increasingly subject to pressures of the marketplace, the financial community, and the market for corporate control (Jensen 1993). The owners of capital have gained increasing control over corporate managers. While these macro-level changes have been observed primarily in settings traditionally dominated by corporate logics, such as Fortune 500 industrial firms (Davis and Stout 1992), parallel changes are observed in higher education publishing, although there the transition developed from a professional logic to the dominance of a market logic.

The historical contingency of power in organizations and the decline of the logics of the professions relative to those of the markets as mechanisms through which power is constituted implies that a different set of values determines the production of products and the distribution of resources in organizations and in society.

CHAPTER 6

Attention to the Sources of Structure

Administrative considerations tend to conflict with
technical professional considerations. Hence the
judgement of superiors, who are concerned with
administrative problems, will recurrently differ from
the judgement of their professional subordinates, who
are concerned with technical problems. . . . Conflicts
created by the merger of the two institutional forms are
resolved by the bureaucratic professional in different ways.
Some retain their identification with their professional
group, are highly committed to their professional skills,
and look for social support to professional colleagues
outside the organization as well as within. . . . Others
have less commitment to their specialized skills, come to
identify with the particular organization by which they
are employed and its program and procedures, and are
more concerned with gaining approval of administrative
superiors inside the organization than that of professional
colleagues outside.
—Peter M. Blau and W. Richard Scott (1962/2003),
  Formal Organizations

EARLY STUDIES of corporate organization examined the economic determinants of the shift from the unitary to the multidivisional form (M-form) in
the largest industrial firms (Armour and Teece 1978; Chandler 1962; Rumelt
1974). Subsequent research has focused on the political, cultural, and ecological determinants of this shift (Palmer et al. 1987; Fligstein 1985; Roy
1997). More recently, researchers have investigated a variety of conundrums:
late adoptions of the multidivisional form (Palmer, Jennings, and Zhou 1993);
which proceeds first, a change in strategy or a change in structure (Amburgey
and Dacin 1994); and the deinstitutionalization of the conglomerate form
(Davis, Diekmann, and Tinsley 1994).

Theories of the sources of organization structure can be grouped by governance mechanisms—the umbrella explanation for the forces that may suppress or give rise to the development of the firm in economic exchange. Williamson (1975) is most well known for his simplification of the question of why organizations exist with his ideal types of governance mechanisms—markets and hierarchies. Business history bears out that families are another form of governance of the firm (Chandler 1962). Indeed families and hierarchies, or their central actors—managers—are the opposing forces that form the control struggles that underscore political and power elite theories of the corporation (Mizruchi 1982; Palmer et al. 1987; Fligstein 1990).

However, there is another important governance mechanism that has been relatively unexamined by academics in their research to understand the origin and working of the profit-making organization—that is the logic of the professions (Freidson 2001). It is the contrast of the professions and the markets as governance mechanisms that I wish to draw on to understand the fundamental structural changes that took place in higher education publishing. Here, the key question is: How did corporate hierarchies grow in publishing when, by all assessments of the academics and business historians, it was a craft- and profession-based business with minimal scale economies to be achieved? While Coser, Kadushin, and Powell (1982) signaled the corporate creep into publishing, their analysis was relatively early in the process when the patterns were not fully realized and their consequences could not be observed.

In this chapter I again apply the theory of attention. I show how a historical shift in the prevailing institutional logic in higher education publishing led to an increase in the importance of market determinants of organization structure and a decline in the salience of professional sources of organization structure. With the shift in focus from author–editor relational networks to formal hierarchies that paid increasing attention to market forces, the accidental profession shifted to one in which the participants are employees in one of a handful of global media empires.

Again, using the ideal types developed in Chapters 2 and 3, I formulate hypotheses that relate those attributes to the dependent variable, the rate at which firms become divisions of M-form organizations. I report estimates of hazard rate models to analyze how the historical shift from an editorial to a market logic shaped the relative importance of pressures for change in organization structure from 1958 to 1990. I also argue that the shift from a professional to a market logic is a general phenomenon that may explain part of the corporate crisis in which financial services and accounting firms moved from control by the ethics of the professions to control by the corporate hierarchy.

Economic theories that explain the sources of organization structure focus on multiple aspects of controlling change in a firm's market environment.

Contingency theories (Chandler 1962, 1977; Lawrence and Lorsch [1967] 1986; Thompson 1967), for example, examine the sources of organization structure stemming from the rate of change in technologies and markets for suppliers and consumers. Transaction-cost perspectives shift attention from technologies and production costs to transaction costs, arguing that the sources of organization structure, that is hierarchy, stem from the need for control in highly complex and uncertain market environments (Williamson 1975). The central problem for theorizing the role of the corporation in creating wealth is to understand how to get individuals to cooperate and abide by the terms of contract agreements (Scott 2003).

In addition to markets and hierarchies, Freidson (2001) argues for a third logic: how the professions affect formal organization structure. While classic studies of organizations recognized clearly that the professions and administrative hierarchies impose different forms of control, most of this discussion was based on studies operating in the nonprofit realm such as hospitals, schools, and government-funded projects, rather than such profit-making areas as financial service and accounting firms (Blau and Scott 1962). Similarly, studies of the professional sources of structure have stemmed from the neoinstitutional school (DiMaggio 1991; Edelman 1992). However this research has focused on charitable, nonprofit organizations or on personnel systems and human resources departments, not decisions makers in corporations with line responsibility for profit and loss statements.

In this chapter, I explore how institutional logics shape the professional and market determinants of formal organization structure. Case studies illustrate that the goals and means of control of the professions are often in conflict with those of the market and the corporation (Friedland and Alford 1991). Brint and Karabel (1991, 344) and Scott (2001, 95) noted how the professions are organized bodies of individual members who create knowledge and belief systems that define arenas of interest and jurisdiction. From studies of medical professions, Freidson (1986) and Abbott (1988, 99–10) traced professional authority and autonomy to the social legitimacy of a mission and the exclusive ability to apply expert and esoteric knowledge to particular cases. In publishing, Altbach (1975), Coser (1975), and Lane (1975) described publishers as having a mission that moderates the singular quest for profits, characterizing editors as gatekeepers of knowledge and shapers of culture. Similarly, Lane and Booth (1970) and Hirsch (1972) classified publishers as professionals because the ingredients of a successful book are uncertain and represent a mysterious mix of individual expertise and entrepreneurship.

Professional sources of organization structure are embodied in individual relations, not hierarchies. For example, Coser, Kadushin, and Powell (1982) showed how competencies in traditional publishing firms were embedded more in the editor's relational networks with authors than in the routines of

formal hierarchy. Hirsch characterized traditional publishing firms as antihier-
archical, exhibiting "boundary-spanning role occupants and value constraints
against vertical integration" (1972, 641). Stinchcombe (1959) described craft-
and profession-based firms as favoring professional training and mentoring as
the means of control, unlike hierarchical corporations, in which the means of
control stem from the central administration.

In contrast, other case studies have illustrated how the institutional logics
of markets are complementary to the goals of corporations. Chandler (1962)
developed two ideal-typical descriptions to classify corporations: the unitary
form (U-form) and the multidivisional form (M-form). The U-form organization is divided into separate departments, such as manufacturing, sales,
and finance. When firms grew in complexity, executives needed an organization structure that provided greater control both of their firms and of
competition in their product market. These needs for control gave rise to the
M-form, organized by separate product and geographic divisions, with each
division approximating a U-form.

Corporate divisions are the central building blocks of the M-form. In
the U-form, the focus of management's attention is on operational decision
making: how to produce products and sell them in the market. The M-form
differs in that it separates the functions of operational decision making from
those of strategic decision making. This strategic change frees a firm's senior
management to focus on the rationalization of profits by divisional units.
Staff in the firm's central office monitor the progress of operating divisions
toward efficiency criteria and overall corporate goals (Williamson 1975).
This structural change also requires management to make decisions to redis-
tribute divisional profits—for example, in the form of expansion capital—to
those divisions with the highest potential and the best performance, thereby
decreasing the M-form's dependence on external capital markets. The M-form
also enables senior management to shed those divisions that "underperform the
market" or do not show potential for future returns. In this sense, the M-form
firm functions as an internal capital market and investment bank, providing a
means to increase the rate of growth and control market competition through
scale- and scope-expanding strategies.

The individual divisions within the M-form structure are an interesting
example of strategic business units that operate on the interface between
market and hierarchy. In a sense, they have dual selection environments, being subject to both the authority structure of the parent organization as well
as being expected to effectively compete against other divisions and organizations operating in the same market (Scott 2003).

In reality, a firm's growth into an M-form is not a dichotomous shift
from a U-form, as is implied by Chandler's ideal types. Instead, corporate
divisions are built in several ways—by organic growth (Galunic 1996) and

through strategic acquisition (Capron and Mitchell 1998), in which either a corporation acquires other firms and designates them as divisions or it is, itself, acquired and turned into a division of an existing M-form organization (Levin 1996).

Scholars taking economic perspectives have argued that the M-form readily developed in mass production industries because technology innovations and mass markets made possible standardization and economies of scale and scope. In publishing, however, neither technology nor organization innovation substantially increases minimum efficient scale (Chandler 1962). Instead, editors drive the production of books, and they can neither be standardized nor worked in assembly-line fashion around the clock. Thus, although managerial hierarchies have proven to be an effective means of control in mass production industries (Chandler 1977), as Powell (1990, 302, 307) pointed out, the network structures characteristic of the crafts and the professions have been favored over managerial hierarchies as a means of control in publishing. These fundamental differences highlight the question of how the M-form organization has displaced craft- and profession-based forms of organization in publishing.

Institutional perspectives suggest an additional explanation: actors' interpretations of economic conditions are moderated by institutional logics from wider environments (Friedland and Alford 1991). According to this approach, although economic forces impinge on organization, how actors interpret the meaning and the consequences of those economic forces is contingent on higher-order institutional logics. Institutional logics define the norms, values, and beliefs that structure the cognition of actors in organizations and provide a collective understanding of how strategic interests and decisions are formulated (DiMaggio 1997; Jackall 1988). Shifts in institutional logics can affect which economic conditions are viewed as problematic and how they can be addressed by a change in the strategy and structure of an organization (Fligstein 1990; Thornton 2002).

My findings show how institutional pressures moderate how firms define problems, making them sensitive to different market conditions. This, in turn, determines which organizational strategies and structures they are likely to adopt to solve their problems (Goodstein 1994; Oliver 1991). Firms that embody old organizational forms under old institutional logics are relatively immune from change pressures until the prevailing institutional logic changes. When a shift to a new logic occurs, firms that continue to embody old organizational forms become deviants that are particularly vulnerable to change pressures.

Prior research has examined the effects of different variants of managerial capitalism on the development of the M-form (Fligstein 1985; Palmer, Jennings, and Zhou 1993). These studies have examined the link between individual-level decisions of executives attributed to their socialization in a particular subunit of the firm or an elite business school (Fligstein; Palmer, Jennings, and Zhou). In this chapter I build on this work by drawing on Scott's (2001, 52–54) typology of *carriers* of institutions to examine the relationship between industry-level culture and organization-level social structures and routines. I show how two different forms of capitalism—personal and market—which embody the logics of the profession and the logic of the market, determine different organization structures.

Hypotheses

PROFESSIONAL DETERMINANTS OF ORGANIZATION STRUCTURE

Studies of the professions indicate that the determinants of organization structure are embodied in individuals' expertise and relational networks—their human and social capital (Burt 2000; Stinchcombe 1959). Although Abbott's (1988) case analyses illustrate how the mental health professions competed for jurisdiction over arenas of knowledge, previous research has not examined the effects of professional models of organization on divisionalization.

In his research on publishing in the mid-1970s, Powell (1990) described how personal networks competed with formal hierarchies as a governance structure.

Under these arrangements [personal imprints], successful editors enjoy freedom from corporate constraints, and authors enjoy the intimacy and closeness associated with a small company. . . . These personal relationships are vital to economic success. While competition among firms does, to some extent, influence the success or failure of particular publishing houses, these selection pressures are dampened by the dense associational ties and personal relations.

The ideal-type attributes in Table 2.1 indicate that, under an editorial logic, publishers' attention was focused on the problem of developing author–editor networks by the strategies of organic growth and building personal imprints. The number of personal imprints was a measure of the editorial control of the firm and the market. However, as the historical research indicates, from the mid-1970s on, executives with backgrounds in marketing and finance gained power and control relative to editors and executives with editorial backgrounds (Powell 1985; Schiffrin 2000).

According to the theory of attention, personal imprint publishing is an organization structure in conformity with an editorial logic. When an editorial logic prevails, personal imprint publishers should be immune to change pressures and suppress the rate of transition to a divisionalized structure. However, when a market logic prevails, the focus of publishers' attention should shift to the problem of controlling resource competition in the product-market by the strategies of building market channels and acquisition growth—strategies that require a divisionalized structure. Therefore, when a market logic prevails, to maintain their legitimacy and competitiveness, personal imprint publishers should respond to the pressure of a shift in institutional logics by changing to a divisionalized structure.

HYPOTHESIS I

The negative effect of the strategy and structure of product development via personal imprint publishing on the rate at which a firm becomes a division of an M-form organization will be greater in the historical period when an editorial logic prevailed.

According to theories of market control, the vertical integration of marketing within a unitary structure may offer benefits that contractual relationships do not, because vertical integration reduces a firm's resource dependence on powerful organizations, particularly limited-source distributors (Pfeffer and Salancik 1978). Vertical integration within an M-form, rather than a U-form, should lead to even greater power for firms because economies of throughput are likely to increase the flow of products across many market channels if firms have managerial control over many markets (Chandler 1977; Thompson 1967). M-form structures also support larger sales and marketing programs because costs can be shared or transferred across a number of operating divisions.

How marketing and distribution are managed can determine economic and power differences among firms that are likely to affect a decision to change to a divisionalized structure. For publishers, there are several strategic choices: they can vertically integrate these functions by developing their own marketing and sales departments within the unitary structure; they can contract with other publishers and distributors that have established marketing and distribution resources; or they can utilize such resources as a vertically integrated function of an M-form organization.

Contract marketing, although ensuring broad distribution of current products, can inhibit the development of future products. Publishers that lack in-house marketing and sales capabilities may find it difficult to keep in touch with market trends, to acquire cutting-edge new authors, and to develop best-selling titles (Hirsch 1972). Over the longer term, this can weaken the acquisition editorial functions of distribution-dependent publishers relative to other publishers who choose to vertically integrate marketing and distribution.

The ideal-type attributes in Table 2.1 indicate that, under a market logic, the focus of publishers' attention shifted to the problem of resource competition and the strategy of building market channels—emphasizing the marketing and distribution of books as one of the key uncertainties (Asser 1989,

57). This shift in attention to the *marketing* of books sharply contrasts with the earlier belief that if an editor developed good books, they would sell themselves (Powell 1985, 10). Under the editorial logic, little was invested in marketing because it was believed that people either have or lack the capacity to appreciate a good book (Lane and Booth 1970, 42). Tebbel (1996), for example, noted that in the 1960s, the modern marketing methods used in other industries were rare in publishing. However, by the early 1980s, many publishers were emphasizing the most advanced marketing techniques.

An executive publisher described this heightened focus on building market channels:

In the 1970s, there was this new focus on building in-house marketing and sales staff. . . . I remember going to the company management meetings and it seemed like now the national sales manager had all this new power—in the past, those executives with stellar editorial backgrounds who had started their own imprints were the ones in control. The sales manager proposed building a mega sales and marketing operation, and justified it in the sense that various editorial companies, which I guess were becoming divisions, could use it. The old idea of the editor selling or the "college traveler" was out—who needed to travel with a 100-person sales force. But, what I kept thinking was who was going to control and pay for this? It would be the revenue from my books and the books of the editors that report to me—but he (the sales manager) would have the power.

Empirical findings on resource dependence and structural change indicate that firms that control scarce and important resources and that have ties to other firms lacking such resources may encourage dependent firms to change and adopt similar strategies and structures (Pfeffer and Salancik 1978/2003). However, according to my theory, the universal effects predicted under economic and resource-dependence theories of market control should be moderated by a historical shift in institutional logics. During the editorial period, distribution was not a strategic focus of executives' attention, and other resource conditions had not yet consolidated. Although firms with distribution contracts existed, these contracts were typically with independent and self-employed sales representatives (Reid 1969). Moreover, publishing firms were less likely to have sales and marketing executives who were seeking to increase their power and the size of their operations by taking on distributees (McCormick 1998).

During the market period, publishers with distribution contracts, though in conformity with the strategy of building market channels, were nonetheless hybrids, and therefore less competitive and less legitimate than those publishers who divisionalized and vertically integrated marketing and distribution. Therefore, according to the theory of attention when a market logic prevails, publishers with distribution contracts should respond to a shift in institutional logics by changing to a divisionalized structure.

The negative effect of the strategy and structure of product distribution via contractual relationship on the rate at which a firm becomes a division of an M-form organization will be greater in the historical period when an editorial logic prevailed.

MARKET DETERMINANTS OF ORGANIZATION STRUCTURE

Economic contingency and managerial theories have argued that firms in which there is managerial discretion to expand their scale and scope through acquisitions should experience pressure to decentralize decision making and adopt the divisionalized form (Chandler 1977; Marris 1964). The empirical studies of large industrial corporations by Fligstein (1985) and Palmer, Jennings, and Zhou (1993) support these expectations, but they also reveal political and institutional explanations for the adoption of the M-form. For example, Fligstein's (1985, 1990) research indicates that firms whose CEO had a background in finance were more likely to grow by acquisition than firms whose CEO had a background in manufacturing. Additionally, firms are more likely to have a CEO with a background in finance during the historical period that favored the finance conception of managerial capitalism.

The ideal-type attributes in Table 2.1 suggest that, under a market logic, the focus of publishers' attention would shift to the strategy of acquisition growth. This change in institutional logics was reinforced by a transformation in governance from family ownership to the market for corporate control. At the same time, there was a change from a belief in committing capital to the firm to a belief in committing capital to the highest market return (Lazonick 1992; Useem 1996). According to the theory of attention, the universal effects predicted by economic contingency and managerialist theories should be moderated by a historical shift in institutional logics. Therefore, acquiring firms should be more likely to divisionalize in the market period than in the editorial period.

The positive effect of the strategy of acquisition growth on the rate at which a firm becomes a division of an M-form organization will be greater in the historical period when a market logic prevailed.

According to organization theories, market competition is a universal constraint on the behavior of firms that determines their strategies and structures (Burton and Obel 1998). The attributes in Table 2.1 suggest that, under an editorial logic, the attention of publishers would be focused on building the prestige of the house and increasing sales—missions well tuned to publishers who derived their legitimacy from their personal reputations and their relationship networks. Powell (1990, 307) argued that relational networks dampen the negative effects of competition, because they embody the logics of trust, reciprocity, and cooperation. However, with the leveling of college enrollments, competition from foreign publishers, and the development of used book and course pack companies, publishers could no longer stem the tide of competition with professional modes of organization. They refocused their mission so that the sources of legitimacy stemmed from building the market position of the firm and increasing profits. These organization strategies require a divisionalized structure and imply a different impact on the effects of resource competition.

As noted above, according to the theory, a historical shift in institutional logics should moderate universal effects of resource competition. Relational network forms of organization should have lost their immunity to the effects of competition, and publishers should have been likely to conform to institutional pressures to solve their problems of resource competition with a change to the divisionalized structure as the market logic prevailed.

HYPOTHESIS 4
The positive effect of resource competition on the rate at which a firm becomes a division of an M-form organization will be greater in the historical period when a market logic prevailed.

Results

Table 6.1 presents the mean values and the correlation coefficients for all variables in the models. Table 6.2 presents the maximum likelihood (ML) estimates of the piecewise exponential models of the rate at which a firm becomes a division of an M-form. To test for time variation in the *effects* of the variables, I compared two effects models: a time-invariant model (model A) and a time-varying model (model B). As I described in Chapter 5, model A has time-varying intercepts, listed under the historical period for which they apply, and time-invariant effects of covariates, listed under the column labeled All Years. The pattern of effects in the All Years model is analogous to the average effects for the 1958–1990 period. Model B has time-varying intercepts and time-varying effects of covariates, listed under the historical period for which they apply. The coefficients give the effect of the covariates on the log of the rate of divisionalization. A relative interpretation of the scale of effects can be determined by taking the antilogs of the coefficients to provide the multiplier of the base rate. Two-tailed tests were used to interpret significance levels for the models as a whole. One-tailed tests were used to interpret the chi-square tests of constraints that compare individual parameter estimates between the two time periods because the hypotheses are unidirectional. The nesting of model A within model B allowed the use of a likelihood ratio chi-square statistic to test the comparative fit of model A with that of model B. The last column of Table 6.2 shows the results of the chi-square test of equality constraints across periods for individual coefficients.

TABLE 6.1

Means, Pearson Correlations, and F-tests for Covariates of Higher Education Publishing Firms

Covariate Means	1958–1974 Editorial	1975–1990 Market	F-value	p-level	1	2	3	4	5	6	7	8	9	10	11
1. D Divisionalization (2)	0.28	0.35	19.69	0.000											
2. Organization Age (15)	34.65	28.35	28.92	0.000	0.16***										
3. D Public/Private Ownership (8)	0.22	0.26	8.81	0.003	0.50***	0.24***									
4. D Executive Succession (1)	0.06	0.06	0.69	0.406	0.12***	0.04*	0.14***								
5. Related Diversification (20)	2.02	2.02	0.01	0.921	0.01	0.10***	−0.01	0.04**							
6. D Acquired Firm (3)	0.03	0.03	0.15	0.703	0.17***	0.02	0.13***	0.09***	0.01						
7. Percent Change in Interest Rates (23)	9.53	1.64	137.90	0.000	−0.03	0.01	−0.01	0.01	0.00	0.01					
8. Industry Proportion MDF (19)	0.05	0.06	196.82	0.000	0.10***	−0.05***	0.09***	0.04**	−0.01	0.00	0.07***				
9. ln N Imprints (5)	0.15	0.26	48.72	0.000	0.10***	0.09***	0.23***	0.07***	0.25***	0.02	−0.04*	0.11***			
10. D Distribution Contract (6)	0.28	0.33	11.76	0.001	0.00	0.02	−0.06***	−0.00	0.03*	0.07***	0.00	0.07***	0.01		
11. D Acquiring Firm (9)	0.01	0.01	0.59	0.441	0.04**	0.03	0.07***	0.05**	0.06***	−0.02	−0.01	0.01	0.14***	−0.06	
12. Resource Competition (10)	1.61	1.62	0.68	0.408	−0.06***	0.04**	−0.06***	−0.02	0.02	0.01	−0.07***	−0.76***	−0.03	−0.05***	0.01

NOTES: N = number; D = dummy variable
* p ≤ 0.05, two-tailed tests.
** p ≤ 0.01
*** p ≤ 0.001

TABLE 6.2

Maximum Likelihood Estimates of
Piecewise Exponential Models of the Rate of Corporate Divisionalization

| Covariates | All Years | Time Period | | χ^2 Test of Constraint |
		1958–1974 Editorial	1975–1990 Market	
Intercept (model A)[a]		−3.309***	−3.143***	
Intercept (model B)[b]		−1.820**	−3.482***	
Control Variables				
Organization Age (15)	0.004***	0.003**	0.004***	
D Public/Private Ownership (8)	1.319***	1.607***	1.198***	
D Executive Succession (1)	0.179	0.362*	0.103	
Related Diversification (20)	0.035	0.158***	−0.033	
D Acquired Firm (3)	1.097***	1.241***	1.028***	
Percent Change in Interest Rates (23)	−0.002	−0.000	−0.002	
Industry Proportion MDF (19)	11.980***	2.620	6.968+	
Theoretical Variables[c]				
ln N Imprints (5)	0.055	−0.329*	0.169**	12.03***
D Distribution Contract (6)	0.088	−0.164	0.193**	6.08**
D Acquiring Firm (9)	0.854***	0.815	0.898***	0.01
Resource Competition (10)	0.344*	−0.465	0.831***	11.37***

NOTES: N = number, D = dummy variable, N of firms = 230, N of divisionalization events = 91. Likelihood ratio χ^2 for model A = 41.22*** (df = 11). For model B χ^2 = 91.78*** (df = 22). For the difference between the models χ^2 = 50.56*** (df = 11).

[a] Model A has time-varying intercepts and time-invariant effects of covariates. Time-varying intercepts are shown under the historical period for which they apply. Time-invariant effects are listed under All Years.

[b] Model B has time-varying intercepts and time-varying effects of covariates. Time-varying effects of covariates are shown under the period for which they apply.

[c] Model B theoretical variables cannot be constrained to be equal across historical periods without significantly degrading its fit (χ^2 = 29; df = 4; $p \leq 0.000$).

$+ \, p \leq 0.10$, two-tailed tests.
$* \, p \leq 0.05$
$** \, p \leq 0.01$
$*** \, p \leq 0.001$

On the whole, the results support the overall hypothesis that, with a shift from an editorial to a market logic, the determinants of a firm becoming a division of an M-form changed. The chi-square contrast comparing model A against model B indicates that model B, with both time-varying intercepts, and time-varying effects, significantly improves the fit of the model (χ^2 = 50.56; df = 11; p = 0.001). A chi-square contrast shows that the parameter estimates for the theoretical variables as a group cannot be constrained to be equal over the two time periods without significantly degrading the fit of the model ($\chi^2 = 28.81$; $df = 4$; $p = 0.001$). Thus, the model of time-invariant effects can be rejected when all covariates are considered simultaneously. A chi-square contrast comparing the likelihood for constants-only models— the All Years model and the model with intercepts for the two time periods— shows that the base rate of divisionalization is significantly higher in period 2 than in period 1 ($\chi^2 = 27.92$; $df = 1$; $p = 0.001$).

The results support Hypothesis 1, stating that the negative effect of the strategy and structure of personal imprint publishing will be greater in the editorial period than in the market period. The estimate for the covariate imprints is positive and nonsignificant in the All Years model; it is negative and significant in the editorial period at the 0.05 level; and it is positive and significant in the market period, at the 0.01 level. A chi-square contrast indicates that the two parameter estimates for imprints cannot be constrained to be equal over the two time periods without significantly degrading the fit of the model ($\chi^2 = 12.03$; $df = 1$; $p = 0.001$). The effect of imprints on the base rate at which a firm becomes a division of an M-form is more than 1.5 times higher in the market period ($0.17 - [-0.33] = 0.50$) ($e^{0.50} = 1.65$).

The results also support Hypothesis 2, stating that the negative effect of the strategy of product distribution via contractual relationships will be greater in the editorial period than in the market period. The estimate for D Distribution Contract (6) is positive and nonsignificant in the All Years model; it is negative and nonsignificant in the editorial period; and it is positive and significant in the market period, at the 0.01 level. The two parameter estimates for D Distribution Contract (6) cannot be constrained to be equal over the two time periods without significantly degrading the fit of the model. The effect of D Distribution Contract (6) on the base rate is approximately 1.0 times higher in the market period than in the editorial period.

There is some support for Hypothesis 3, stating that the positive effect of the strategy of acquisition growth will be greater in the market period than in the editorial period. The estimate for D Acquiring Firm (9) is positive and significant ($p = 0.001$) in the All Years model; it is positive and nonsignificant in the editorial period; and it is positive and significant ($p = 0.001$) in the market period. However, the two estimates can be constrained to be equal over time periods. The effect of D Acquiring Firm (9) on the base rate is 1.0 times higher in the market period.

The results support Hypothesis 4, stating that the positive effect of resource competition will be greater in the market period than in the editorial period. The estimate for resource competition will be greater in the market period than in the editorial period. The estimate for resource competition is positive and significant ($p = 0.05$) in the All Years model; it is negative and nonsignificant in the editorial period; and it is positive and significant

(p = 0.001) in the market period. These two parameter estimates cannot be constrained to be equal across the two time periods without significantly degrading the fit of the model. The effect of resource competition on the base rate is more than 3.5 times higher in the market period than in the editorial period.

CONTROL VARIABLES

The effects of three control variables—Organization Age (15), D Public/ Private Ownership (8), and D Acquired Firm (3)—are positive and significant, independent of the effects of a shift in institutional logics. Consistent with Fligstein's (1985) findings, older firms were more likely to divisionalize than younger firms. Firms with access to public capital markets were more likely to divisionalize than privately held firms. Acquired firms were more likely to become corporate divisions.

Although the effect of executive succession is not significant in the All Years model, it is positive and significant in the editorial period, but not in the market period. This finding suggests that leadership succession may account for the introduction of divisionalized organization (Fligstein 1987; Mezias 1990). The results for the theoretical variables support the argument that, with institutionalization, the locus of agency came to reside less in the effects of individual leaders and more in social structures and routines (Selznick 1957; Nelson and Winter 1982). Note that the actual level of executive succession is not significantly different between the two periods, and also that the results of a chi-square contrast test for coefficient equality are not significantly different (χ^2 = 1.44, df = 1, p = 0.23).

Related diversification had a positive *effect* on divisionalization in the editorial period, but not in the market period. Note that Table 6.1 shows that there is no significant difference in the *value* of the variable Related Diversification (20) for the two periods. This effect is consistent with large-sample studies offering evidence that economic sources of change in organization structure dissipate over time (Armour and Teece 1978; Rumelt 1974). Note also, in Table 6.1, that the value of the variable Percent Change in Interest Rates (23) is significantly higher in the editorial period than in the market period.

The effect of the variable Industry Proportion Div/Sub (18) is lower in both of the time-period equations in model B than in the All Years equation in model A. Although Industry Proportion Div/Sub (18) is only a control variable, this result is methodologically interesting and demonstrates an important point in the institutional analysis of organizations with regard to the meaning and measurement of mimetic isomorphism (Mizruchi and Fein 1999). Although used in previous research on the M-form, *percent adopters* variables can easily generate misspecification bias, because they reflect trends—they tend to go up, but not down. My modeling approach reveals such a spuriously captured mimetic effect by comparing results from the piecewise and All Years models.

Discussion and Conclusion

In this chapter I asked why craft- and profession-based firms, such as publishing, should adopt the divisionalized organization form, given their relative lack of scale economies. To examine this question, I identified two ideal-type logics, an editorial and a market logic, which lead to different organization strategies and structures for growing firms. Historical research and interviews with publishing-industry experts established the meaning of the two institutional logics and that a change occurred in the logic prevailing in publishing in the mid-1970s. Applying event history models to the data revealed support for the general argument that the determinants of whether or not a publishing firm became a corporate division were contingent on the firm's seeking strategic and structural conformity with the prevailing institutional logic.

With respect to the professional determinants, imprint publishing had a negative effect in the editorial period and a positive effect in the market period on the rate of divisionalization. The strategy and structure of relational network forms of organization, measured here by variables such as personal imprints and distribution contracts, was based on small, stable businesses in which personal connections and reputation were important. In stable environments, getting better at doing old things may aid survival. However, under conditions of environmental change, basing a publishing business on the attributes of personal capitalism was no longer perceived as an effective solution to growth and resource competition.

Distribution contracts had a positive effect on divisionalization in the market period, but not in the editorial period. Although distribution contracts are consistent with the shift in publishers' attention to building market channels, they are a strategy that emphasizes a network structure, which conforms less to a market logic than does the vertical integration of sales and marketing in a hierarchy. Alternatively, it could be argued that firms that used distribution contracts were weakened relative to other publishers that were vertically integrated and therefore sought to remedy their weakness by changing their organizational structures. However, if this were the case, one would expect a universal effect across all periods. Moreover, my finding for distribution contracts held after I controlled for firm acquisition (an exit strategy typically indicating a firm's weakness) and for other economic factors, such as related diversification and the supply of capital. The marketing executive seeking to remedy excess distribution capacity through contracts with outside publishers had not yet come of age in the editorial period. However, as my informants described, in the market period in publishing, sales and marketing executives—who were often without editorial backgrounds—used the changing conditions in the marketplace to advance new policies beneficial to their own subunit power by implementing growth strategies that pressured firms to adopt divisionalized structures (Fligstein 1985).

With respect to the market determinants, growth by acquisition had a positive effect on divisionalization in the market period, but not in the editorial period. There is no statistically significant difference between the two periods in the number or value of the variable D Acquiring Firm (9). These results suggest that the implications of growth through acquisition for a change to a divisionalized structure may be contingent on the prevalence of a market logic. However, it is important to note that the null hypothesis cannot be rejected. The chi-square contrast is not significant, and the effect in the All Years model is highly significant, indicating that this market determinant of organization structure is more universal and less culturally contingent than the others.

Resource competition had no effect on divisionalization in the editorial period and a strong, positive effect in the market period, even though resource competition was higher in the early 1960s than at any time during the period when the market logic prevailed. Note also that there is no statistically significant difference in the mean value of resource competition for the two periods. This suggests that attention to resource competition is not universal, but culturally contingent, depending on the prevalence of a market logic rather than on the actual level of competition experienced in a marketplace. This finding also supports Powell's (1990, 307) arguments that the relational network structures typical of traditional publishing in the editorial period were an alternative to hierarchies as a means of dampening the effects of competition.

In this chapter, I have attempted to advance an understanding of agency in institutional theory (DiMaggio 1988). Prior studies have shown how the decisions of organizations are linked with organizational fields through resource dependence on the state, for example, when organizations obtain resources, certification, and legitimacy via government contracts and state regulation (Baum and Oliver 1992; Schneiberg and Bartley 2001). My findings illustrate how the decisions of organizations are linked to markets through culture by showing how institutional logics moderate vulnerability to resource dependence and resource competition. Prior studies have shown that individuals are carriers of logics in that the corporate backgrounds and professional schooling of CEOs predict the adoption of the M-form (Fligstein

1985; Palmer, Jennings, and Zhou 1993). My results show that, after CEO succession was controlled for, organization-level social structures and routines such as acquisition growth were carriers of institutional logics.

Other limitations in the data may affect the interpretation of the results. First, according to arguments based on economic contingency and managerial perspectives, firms that divisionalized are those that simply became larger over time. However, previous studies conducted from a political cultural perspective have shown that organization size is not a significant factor in adoption of the M-form (Fligstein 1985, 385–387; Palmer et al. 1987, 37; Palmer, Jennings, and Zhou 1993, 118), though as previously indicated, their samples were already of relatively large firms. Note also that my findings hold after I controlled for organization age and diversification, both of which may be proxies for organization size. In addition, the independent variable, the number of publishing imprints, is also a measure of organization size and differentiation. Given this, if size is the main driver of divisionalization, imprints should be positive and significant in both periods, rather than suppressing divisionalization in the editorial period and propelling it in the market period.

Second, firms that divisionalized may have been those that were just more profitable over time. However, Palmer and colleagues (1993) found no significant relationship, and Fligstein (1985) did not examine profitability. Later analyses by Fligstein (2001, 136) do not support transaction cost arguments, finding little or no effects of the multidivisional form on the financial performance of firms. Recall that I could not obtain firm-level financial data because many of the publishing organizations in the sample were privately owned in the editorial period and were divisions of multidivisional firms in the market period. A separate analysis of a subsample of higher education publishing firms voluntarily reporting to the Association of America Publishers showed that profits were unrelated to organization size and that, with respect to larger firms, profits decreased with increased organization size (Thornton 1999a), see Appendix C.

The results point to several avenues for future research. Chief among them is research on how products that have consequences for culture and society are affected by a shift in governance and organizational forms from the crafts and the professions to those of the markets and corporate hierarchies (Hinnings and Greenwood 2002). According to research from the production-of-culture perspective, the effects of the corporate form on product choice and innovation in cultural and professional services industries warrants further study (Peterson and Berger 1996). How corporate strategies affect the welfare and careers of workers and their opportunities for creative expression remains relatively unexplored (Barley and Kunda 2001; Peterson 1999; Peiperl, Arthur, and Amand 2002). In addition, these industries have a significant impact on the economy—SIC codes list entertainment and the professions as the two largest dollar volume categories in the services sectors.

Although changes in institutional pressures encouraged publishers to become corporate divisions, research should examine whether firms that did so made the best strategic choice. Did corporate divisions have higher rates of survival than personal imprint publishers that remained true to the traditions of an editorial logic? Addressing such questions can extend ecological and institutional analyses and explore how multi-unit organizations affect the rate of founding and disbanding firms (Amburgey and Rao 1996; Land, Davis, and Blau 1994; Thornton 1999a).

I have examined the question of whether samples of only large firms may lead to biased results. This is an important inquiry because much of organization theory has been developed from research on samples of relatively large organizations (Aldrich 1999). My findings from a population-level analysis of both small and large firms are relatively consistent with sociological studies of large industrial firms (Fligstein 1985; Palmer, Jennings, and Zhou 1993), in that institutional effects hold, net of proxies for organization size and other social and economic structural variables. My findings suggest that while the particular effects attributed to culture may vary by industry, historical period, and nation-state; cultural effects on organizational decisions are universal, independent of size, but not of organization form.[1] Nonetheless, reconciling the implications of differences in industrial- versus craft- and profession-based firms for organization theory is an under-researched area.

The specific findings presented in this chapter may not be generalizable to other contexts. However, the theory that has been tested may apply to important industries that have been governed by the crafts, the professions, and personal capitalism and that are undergoing transformation under the influences of market capitalism. Such industries differ from the manufacturing industries because their products marry art, reputation, human welfare, culture, and commerce. These industries include, among others, architecture, film, education, and luxury brands (Jones et al. 1998; Djelic and Ainamo 1999; Mezias and Mezias 2000; Sperling 2000), as well as financial and accounting services (Zuckerman 1999). Acquisition editors for books have an analogous role to industry analysts in many respects; they both play gatekeeper roles in terms of using their personal expertise and professional reputation to influence what books are published and what stocks are recommended for purchase.

The conflict in the institutional logics of the professions and the markets is one of the most important issues in our professional services society—the conflict is between compliance with the profit seeking administrative procedures of the corporation and the adherence to professional standards in the performance of work. The differences in control are stunning and consequential. Professionals seek self-control through voluntary associations that they themselves organize. Self-control is supported by the external surveillance of conduct by peers, who are in positions to view the work, have the expertise to judge it, and themselves have the incentives to maintain the reputation of the profession. In this way the legitimacy of the institutions that support the profession are maintained. Professions lose legitimacy when individuals are more concerned with gaining the approval of administrative superiors inside the corporation than that of professional peers. The source of discipline within the corporation is typically not the professional peer group's ability to reward and negatively sanction, but the hierarchy of authority structures (Blau and Scott 1962). For those industries in which their products and institutions have public consequences, under market capitalism if the practices of the professions are weak inside and outside the corporation, in theory attention will focus on the bottom line and the share price. In this and the preceding chapters, I have examined how this shift in attention took place and its consequences for a change in the sources of organization structure.

I propose that the way in which institutional logics create pressures for organizational change is by structuring the attention of decision makers in organizations (Ocasio 1997). The findings suggest that conflict between institutional logics creates pressures for organizational change. Once an institutional logic becomes dominant, it affects a firm's strategy and structure by focusing the attention of decision makers toward those issues that are consistent with the logic and away from those issues that are not. Organizations are social structures that carry institutional models (Scott 2001). Those that are in conformity with the dominant institutional logic are more likely to be legitimate and competitive and immune from change pressures.

CHAPTER 7

Attention to the Sources of Strategy

In the late nineteenth and early twentieth centuries, a new
type of capitalism emerged. It differed from traditional
personal capitalism in that basic decisions concerning the
production and distribution of goods and services were
made by teams, or hierarchies, of salaried managers who
had little or no equity ownership in the enterprises they
operated. . . . In such industries as publishing and printing,
lumber, furniture, leather, and apparel and textiles, and
specialized instruments, the large integrated firm had
few competitive advantages. In these industries, the small,
single-function firm continued to prosper and to compete
vigorously.

—Alfred D. Chandler Jr. (1992), *The Emergence of
Managerial Capitalism*

RESEARCHERS HAVE generally focused on examining the large acquiring
firm from managerial and financial perspectives in terms of hubris (Roll
1986), diversification and growth (Marris 1964), increased synergies (Chatterjee 1986), enhanced market power (Stigler 1982), and scale-and-scope
economies (Chandler 1990). Others have focused on agency theories for
reasons of promotional gains (Beckenstein 1979), abnormal returns (Morck,
Shleifer, and Vishny 1989), and the market for corporate control (Jensen and
Ruback 1983). Other scholars examining acquisitions have focused on organization theories for reasons of power and resource dependence (Pfeffer
and Salancik 1978), board-and-bank interlocks (Fligstein and Brantley 1992),
managerial cognition and organizational routines (Amburgey and Miner
1992), and organizational learning (Haunschild 1993). Still others have examined the effects of regulatory activity, such as changes in tax and accounting laws (Golbe and White 1988), antitrust activity (Stigler 1966; Fligstein
1990; Dobbin and Dowd 2000), and a permission state (Stearns and Allan

1993). Macroeconomic forces have also been associated with acquisition activity, such as a decline in interest rates and the cost of capital (Steiner 1975), a rise in GNP and stock prices (Melicher, Ledolter, and D'Antonio 1983; Guerard 1985; Becketti 1986), and economic disturbances (Gort 1969).

However, this plethora of research has focused almost exclusively on the economic and strategic implications for the large acquiring firm, overlooking the population-level effects of small and large firms and the institutional and historical conditions that predict which firms are likely to be targets of acquisition (Golbe and White 1988). For both small and large firms, the identification of acquisition candidates on both sides of the fence is an important aspect of the entrepreneurial process. Whether in publishing or other industries, acquisitions enable firms to access new products (Arrow 1983; Hitt et al. 1996), provide a viable capitalization strategy for founders and entrepreneurs (Thornton 1999b), and assemble the building blocks to form new corporate divisions (Galunic and Eisenhardt 2001; Milliot 2000a). Indeed, it is the latter that offers an explanation for how the unlikely craft- and profession-based firms of publishing, with their typical human-asset intensity and slower growth rates, shifted more readily than expected to corporate-like structures (Chandler 1962).

In this chapter, I examine the process of corporate acquisition and its consequences to understand the fundamental means by which publishing firms gained access to expansion capital and corporate routines—the two central elements that led publishers to focus their attention on strategies consistent with a market logic. In publishing, acquisition is a particularly important strategy; it can help both parties to the transaction alter their capabilities (Mitchell 1994). The acquiring firm can save the target firm from market failure, by allowing it access to the resources of the parent firm (Capron and Mitchell 1998). At the same time, targets can provide essential combinations of resources that parent firms and their divisions cannot organically and easily create themselves.

Acquisitions are a particularly critical strategy in the publishing business in two respects. First, the learning curves are long—as the interviewees stated, it takes a long time to organically establish the name recognition of a publishing imprint. This is one reason that publishers list their founding dates in the LMP—heritage matters. Moreover, the knowledge necessary to develop a successful publishing imprint is not a commodity easily imitated; the expertise for successful contracts (books) is based in human capital (editors), not the routines inherent in hierarchical firms. However, hierarchies can readily acquire publishing imprints. Second, publishing, by its nature, is a difficult business in which to value, and hence leverage, the assets in exchange for expansion capital. Since retained earnings of private and smaller publishing firms on a year to year basis are often not sufficient to fund strategic growth, the advent of corporate sources of capital were a viable solution to meet in-creasing demand and a central reason for the transformation from an edito-rial to a market logic. The solution of corporate capital emerged en masse in the late 1960s from outside the industry, piggy-backing the trend of con-glomerate acquisitions. Although historians document that acquisitions were a strategy of economic survival in both the editorial and market periods—the data show that the meaning and consequences of acquisition are dra-matically different for publishing firms in the two periods.

To better understand how the shift from personal to market capitalism affected the strategy of acquisition in publishing, I build on existing agency and managerial history perspectives by examining how the risk of acquisi-tion is a consequence of capitalism selecting optimal organization structures (Manne 1965; Marris and Mueller 1980; Jensen and Ruback 1983). I de-velop the institutional aspects of this argument by exploring several ques-tions: How are the mechanisms of selection in capitalism historically and culturally contingent? What is an optimal organization structure? How does the historical contingency of such structures affect the identification of can-didates for acquisition? My theory and analysis build on resource depen-dence (Pfeffer and Salancik 1978) and economic and structural contingency perspectives (Burton and Obel 1998) by showing how the organization and market determinants of acquisition are moderated by the institutional log-ics of the prevailing form of capitalism.

This approach has one predecessor in Fligstein's (1990) research. Although not specifically focused on the acquired firm, his research is pertinent in il-lustrating an institutionalist revision of Chandler's economic contingency perspective for different variants of managerial capitalism. For example, Flig-stein showed that firms were more likely to grow by acquisition during the era of the finance conception of control, when their CEOs had backgrounds in finance, than during earlier eras of managerial capitalism, when CEOs typically had backgrounds in sales or manufacturing.

Building on these ideas, if capitalism selects optimal organization struc-tures and if forms of capitalism coevolve with forms of organization structure, it follows that we can test the consequences of such evolutionary changes for the rate of acquisition in publishing. Examining this proposition requires specifying the mechanisms that link shifts in the cognitive aspects of strategy to the evolution of the macroeconomic environment. I apply the theory of attention to understand how institutional logics mediate the attention of decision makers in organizations, and thereby moderate how structural and macroeconomic changes affect the rate of acquisition. To restate, according to this view, although economic forces impinge on organizations, how managers and entrepreneurs interpret the meaning and the consequences of those eco-nomic forces is contingent on higher-order institutional logics. Institutional logics define the norms, values, and beliefs that structure the cognition of actors in organizations, and provide a collective understanding of how strategic interests and decisions are formulated. Institutional logics are historically variant and are shaped by economic and social structural changes. With a shift in institutional logics, the perceived causes of an earlier occurrence of an acquisition may differ significantly from the perceived causes of a later one (Thornton 1995).

In this chapter, I show how a historical and cultural shift in the dominant institutional logic in the publishing industry—from the logic of personal capitalism to the logic of market capitalism—led to a transformation in the control of the firm and in the determinants of the risk of acquisition. Again using the ideal types and the theory developed in Chapters 2 and 3, I formulate hypotheses that relate those attributes—for example organization strategy, structure, and competition in the product market—to the risk of acquisition. Consistent with the theory of attention and the statistical findings presented in earlier chapters, overall the estimates of hazard rate models show a relative decrease in organizational and increase in market determinants of the risk of acquisition.

Hypotheses

ORGANIZATION DETERMINANTS OF ACQUISITION

Research on acquisition and the structural characteristics of organizations reveals mixed findings and is limited to a few studies of large corporations within a single time period. Palmer et al. (1995) found that larger organizations had a lower risk of acquisition in the 1960s. Davis and Stout (1992) found no relationship between organization size and acquisition, however firms that experienced workforce growth had a marginally lower rate of acquisition in the 1980s. Davis, Diekmann, and Tinsley (1994) found that diversified firms were more likely to be acquired in the 1980s. In contrast, Fligstein and Markowitz (1993) found that diversified firms did not have a significantly higher chance of acquisition for the period 1979–1987.

As previously noted, the number of imprints in a publishing firm is a measure of organization structure and differentiation that is parallel to the number of departments or divisions in an industrial firm. As predicted by the ideal-type attributes in Table 2.1, the number of imprints is also a measure of editorial control in the firm and in the market. Powell (1990) describes personal imprints in his research from the mid-1970s.

The book industry is, to a considerable extent, based on network relationships. One effort to recognize and profit from these linkages is the establishment of personal imprint lines within larger publishing houses. These extended networks allow an editor to rely on his or her own judgments and not have to appeal for higher-level approval. The large firm is able to keep top-flight editors' content and, at the same time, give them greater financial stake in the books they bring in. Personal imprint editors are on their own as far as acquiring and nurturing authors, yet retain corporate clout for financing, sales, and distribution.

However, since the mid-1970s, researchers have described how executives in publishing with backgrounds in marketing and finance gained power and control relative to editors and executives with editorial backgrounds (Powell 1985; Schiffrin 2000). This new breed of executives paid increasing attention to the influences of market forces by refocusing the strategies and structures of their firms to emphasize the development of formal hierarchies, to build market channels, and to grow by acquisition (Tebbel 1987; Greco 1997).

According to the theory of attention, a shift from personal to market capitalism is likely to create new selection pressures on firms to conform to the prevailing institutional logic. The organization strategy and structure of personal imprints conforms to an editorial logic, wherein authority was derived from the personal reputations of founders and editors who focused their attention on author–editor relationships to achieve organic growth. In the editorial period, firms with an imprint focus should be relatively immune to acquisition. However, firms that were organized as personal imprints did not enable the mission under market capitalism, that is growing by acquisition and building market channels; however imprints provided a supply of acquisition targets that could be easily integrated into the hierarchies of acquiring firms that conformed to a market logic. Hence, in the market period, organizations with an imprint strategy and structure should face increased risk of acquisition.

HYPOTHESIS I
The negative effects of the strategy and structure of personal-imprint publishing on the rate of acquisition will be greater in the editorial period than in the market period.

In the mid-1970s, publishers shifted their strategy from building personal imprints to building market channels, emphasizing the marketing and distribution of books as a key uncertainty (Asser 1989). Publishers' marketing and distribution choices can create resource dependence with consequences for the risk of acquisition (Pfeffer and Salancik 1978). Publishers have the choice of vertically integrating marketing and sales or contracting with other publishers and distributors that have established marketing and distribution resources.

The empirical findings on resource dependence and acquisition are difficult to interpret because of differences in the level of analysis and the lack of clarity in distinguishing the acquired from the acquiring firm. Pfeffer (1972) and Burt (1980) found at the industry level that resource dependence increased the risk of merger for acquiring firms. Contrary to theory, Palmer et al. (1995) discovered at the firm level that resource independence increased the risk of friendly acquisition.

The vertical integration of marketing should lead to economies of throughput, because producers are more likely to increase the flow of their products across existing markets if they have managerial control over those markets (Thompson 1967; Chandler 1977). Vertical integration may also have control benefits over alternative organization forms such as contractual relationships, because it reduces firms' resource-dependence on powerful organizations, particularly limited-source distributors (Pfeffer and Salancik 1978).

As previously described, the contracting of marketing, while ensuring broader distribution of current product, can inhibit the development of future product. Publishers without in-house marketing and sales representatives may find it difficult to keep in touch with market trends, to acquire cutting-edge new authors, and to develop best-selling titles (Hirsch 1972). Over the longer-term, this can weaken the acquisition editorial function of distribution-dependent publishers relative to publishers who choose to vertically integrate, making firms who rely on contractual forms of organization vulnerable to acquisition.

According to the attributes in Table 2.1, the expectation of the positive effects of resource dependence on the risk of acquisition is likely to be moderated by differences in publishers' cognitive interpretations of the meaning and appropriate use of distribution contracts in the two periods. Under the editorial logic, publishers' legitimacy was based on personal reputation and their organizational identity derived from the analogy of publishing as a profession—an identity in which acquisitions were not in the repertoire of growth strategies (Hirsch 1986). In theory, publishers would not be as likely to identify potential acquisition targets by taking advantage of information asymmetries. For example, a distributing publisher would not take advantage of proprietary knowledge of the sales and product lines of the distribution-dependent publisher. Powell's (1990) description supports this argument; he explains that traditional publishers' emphasis on trust and reciprocity should have a dampening effect on opportunistic behavior in the marketplace.

However, with a shift from personal to market capitalism, new selection pressures should come to bear on firms that failed to change their organization strategies and structures to conform to the prevailing institutional logic. While publishers with distribution contracts were attempting to build market channels, those with network forms of organization were less conforming to a market logic than publishers that were vertically integrating marketing and distribution. Moreover, the mitigating effects of personal reputation on opportunism should erode as the norms of trust transition from the institutional logics of the professions to those of the market. Thus, in the market period, publishers with distribution contracts should increasingly be subject to opportunistic behavior and the effects of the market for corporate control.

HYPOTHESIS 2

The positive effects of the strategy and structure of distribution via contractual relations on the rate of acquisition will be greater in the market period than in the editorial period.

MARKET DETERMINANTS OF ACQUISITION

Organization theories argue that competition is a universal constraint on the behavior of firms with consequences for acquisition (Pfeffer and Salancik 1978; Carroll and Hannan 2000, 45). However, previous research on the risk of acquisition has not examined the effects of competition in the product market on the risk of acquisition (Davis and Stout 1992; Palmer et al. 1995). Resource dependence and the ecological perspectives predict a positive effect: increasing competition is likely to increase acquisitions.

The historical research indicates that publishing was characterized as competitive in both the editorial and the market periods. John Tebbel (1987) illustrates this point by quoting a well-remembered speech in the 1960s by William Jovanovich Sr., then president of Harcourt Brace.

Editors are not votives who guard the truth against the black knights of capitalism. . . . Think not that publishing is the modern-day equivalent of the medieval monastery. It is a business. It is so purely a business that book publishing possesses all the characteristics of capitalism: central production, national distribution, routine wholesaling, retailing, price standardization, and unmitigated speculation.

The attributes in Table 2.1 indicate that in the editorial period, publishers' attention was focused on building the prestige of the *house* and growing the firm by increasing sales—missions well suited to publishers who derived their legitimacy from their relational networks and personal reputations. Powell (1990) argues that this organizational form suppresses the effects of competition.

Editorial research and evaluation relies extensively on personal networks, which are based on loyalty and friendship, cemented over time. Bonds of allegiance shape the processes of access and discovery. These personal relationships are also vital to economic success. While competition among firms does, to some extent, influence the success or failure of particular publishing houses, these selection pressures are dampened by the dense associational ties and personal relations that support all publishing transactions.

However, with the shift from personal to market capitalism, publishers refocused their mission—wherein the sources of legitimacy stemmed from increasing profits and building the market position of the firm. This shift required alternative organization forms with potentially different impacts on the effects of competition (Williamson 1991). These arguments imply that the universal effects of competition on the risk of acquisition are historically contingent and moderated by the prevailing institutional logic. Relational forms of organization lose their immunity to the effects of competition as the market logic prevails.

HYPOTHESIS 3
The positive effects of resource competition on the rate of acquisition will be greater in the market period than in the editorial period.

Results

Table 7.1 presents the mean values and the correlation coefficients for all variables in the models. Note that the mean values of all the independent variables are significantly different between the two periods. The mean values for the variables ln N Imprints (5) and D Distribution Contract (6) are higher in the market period than in the editorial period. In contrast, the mean value for Resource Competition (10) is higher in the editorial period than in the market period. The mean value for the dependent variable, D Acquired Firm (3), is not significantly different between the two periods. Moreover, using a constants-only piecewise exponential model with no covariates, the χ^2 contrast indicates that the base rate of acquisition is not significantly different between the two periods.

Table 7.2 presents the maximum likelihood (ML) estimates of piecewise exponential models on the rate of acquisition. To test for time variation in the effects of the variables, I compared two effects models: a time-invariant model (model A) and a time-varying model (model B). As I described in Chapters 5 and 6, model A has time-varying intercepts, listed under the historical covariates, and time-invariant effects of covariates, listed under the column labeled All Years. The pattern of effects in the All Years model is analogous to an average effect for the 1958–1990 period. Model B has time-varying intercepts and time-varying effects of covariates listed under the historical period for which they apply. The coefficients give the effect of the covariate on the log of the rate of acquisition. A relative interpretation of the scale of effects can be determined by taking the antilogs of the coefficients to provide the multiplier of the base rate. Two-tailed tests are used to interpret significance levels for the models as a whole. One-tailed tests are used to interpret the χ^2 tests of constraints that compare individual parameter estimates between the two time periods because the hypotheses are unidirectional.

TABLE 7.1

Means, Pearson Correlations, and F-tests for Covariates of Higher Education Publishing Firms

| | Time Period | | | | | | | | | | | | |
| | 1958–1972 Editorial | 1973–1990 Market | F-value | p-level | | | | | | | | | |
Covariate Means					1	2	3	4	5	6	7	8	9
1. D Acquired Firm (3)	0.03	0.03	0.04	0.834									
2. Founder Age Post 63 (14)	26.84	29.44	7.63	0.006	−0.04*								
3. Organization Age (15)	35.30	28.57	30.27	0.000	0.02	−0.42***							
4. N Division/Subsidiary (16)	0.46	0.59	4.09	0.043	−0.00	−0.19***	0.25***						
5. D Diversified Publisher (21)	0.70	0.74	8.84	0.003	0.01	−0.03*	−0.01	0.12***					
6. Percent Change in Interest Rates (23)	3.37	4.93	4.82	0.028	0.01	0.01	0.01	0.00	−0.00				
7. D Public/Private Ownership (8)	0.22	0.27	10.81	0.001	0.13***	−0.37***	0.24***	0.27***	−0.08***	−0.01			
8. ln N Imprints (5)	0.14	0.25	43.33	0.000	0.02	−0.16***	0.09***	0.62***	0.12***	−0.04*	0.23***		
9. D Distribution Contract (6)	0.26	0.34	23.76	0.000	0.07***	0.00	0.02	−0.05***	0.03	0.00	−0.06***	0.02	
10. Resource Competition (10)	1.67	1.59	72.48	0.000	0.01	−0.06***	0.04**	−0.06***	0.03*	−0.06***	−0.06***	−0.03	−0.05***

NOTES: N = number; D = dummy variable

* $p \leq 0.05$, two-tailed tests.

** $p \leq 0.01$

*** $p \leq 0.001$

TABLE 7.2

Maximum Likelihood Estimates of
Piecewise Exponential Models of the Rate of Acquisition

Covariates	All Years	Time Period 1958–1972 Editorial	Time Period 1973–1990 Market	χ^2 Test of Constraint
Intercept (model A)[a]		−4.198***	−4.275***	
Intercept (model B)[b]		−2.094*	−6.913***	
Control Variables				
Founder Age post 63 (14)	−0.007[+]	−0.013	−0.006	
Organization Age (15)	0.003	0.003	0.003	
N Division/Subsidiary (16)	−0.031	−0.352	0.001	
D Diversified Publisher (21)	−0.035	0.009	−0.189	
Percent Change in Interest Rates (23)	0.002	0.017	0.003	
D Public/Private Ownership (8)	0.225	0.092	0.264	
Theoretical Variables[c]				
ln N Imprints (5)	0.414[+]	−0.296	0.468*	3.27*
D Distribution Contract (6)	0.906***	0.495	1.104***	2.90*
Resource Competition (10)	1.25	−0.901*	1.727***	3.40*

NOTES: N = number, D = dummy variable, N of firms = 230, N of acquisition events = 106. Likelihood ratio χ^2 for model A = 35.63 *** (df = 9). For model B, χ^2 = 55.27*** (df = 18). For the difference between the models, χ^2 = 19.64* (df = 9).

[a] Model A has time-varying intercepts and time-invariant effects of covariates. Time-varying intercepts are shown under the historical period for which they apply. Time-invariant effects of covariates are listed under All Years.

[b] Model B has time-varying intercepts and time-varying effects of covariates. Time-varying effects of covariates are shown under the period for which they apply.

[c] Model B theoretical variables cannot be constrained to be equal across historical periods without significantly degrading its fit (χ^2 = 19.17; df = 3; $p \leq 0.001$).

[+] $p \leq 0.10$, one-tailed tests for χ^2 constraints, two-tailed tests for all other values.
* $p \leq 0.05$
** $p \leq 0.01$
*** $p \leq 0.001$

The nesting of model A within model B allows the use of a likelihood ratio χ^2 statistic to test the comparative fit of model A with model B. The likelihood ratio χ^2 test comparing model A against model B indicates that model B, with both time-varying intercepts and effects, significantly improves the fit of the model (χ^2 = 19.64; df = 9; p = 0.05). Thus, the model of time-invariant effects can be rejected when all covariates are considered simultaneously.

On the whole, the results strongly support the overall hypothesis that with a shift from an editorial to a market logic, the determinants of acquisition changed. A χ^2 contrast shows that the parameter estimates for all the theoretical variables as a group cannot be constrained to be equal across the two time periods without significantly degrading the fit of the model ($\chi^2 = 19.17$; $df = 3$; $p < 0.001$). The effects of the control variables are not noteworthy. There is a marginally significant retirement effect for founders in the All Years model.

I find support for Hypothesis 1, that the risk of acquisition will be greater for organizations with a strategy and structure of personal imprint publishing in the market period than in the editorial period. The estimate for the covariate ln N Imprints (5) is negative and nonsignificant in the editorial period and positive and significant in the market period, $p = 0.05$. This indicates that publishers who continued to build personal imprints, a strategy and structure consistent with the institutional logic of personal capitalism and an editorial logic, became vulnerable to acquisition when this strategy and structure fell out of favor in the market period. A χ^2 contrast shows that the two parameter estimates for ln N Imprints (5) cannot be constrained to be equal across the two time periods without significantly degrading the fit of the model ($\chi^2 = 3.27$; $df = 1$; $p = 0.04$). The effect of ln N Imprints (5) on the base rate is over twice as high in the market period as in the editorial period ($0.468 - (-)0.296 = 0.76$) ($e^{0.76} = 2.15$).

The results support Hypothesis 2, that the risk of acquisition will be greater for publishers with distribution contracts in the market period than in the editorial period. The estimate for the covariate D Distribution Contract (6) is large and highly significant in the market period, at $p = 0.001$, but not in the editorial period. The two-parameter estimates for D Distribution Contract (6) cannot be constrained to be equal across the two time periods without significantly degrading the fit of the model ($\chi^2 = 2.90$; $df = 1$; $p = 0.04$). The effect of D Distribution Contract (6) on the base rate of acquisition is over one and one half times as high in the market period as in the editorial period ($1.104 - 0.495 = 0.61$) ($e^{0.61} = 1.84$).

The findings support Hypothesis 3, that, because of the effects of Resource Competition (10), the risk of acquisition will be greater in the market period than in the editorial period. The estimate for the covariate Resource Competition (10) is negative and significant in the editorial period ($p = 0.05$), and positive and significant in the market period ($p = 0.001$). The two parameter estimates cannot be constrained to be equal across the two time periods without significantly degrading the fit of the model ($\chi^2 = 3.40$; $df = 1$; $p = 0.03$). The positive effect of Resource Competition (10) on the base rate of acquisition is over thirteen times as high in the market period as in the editorial period ($1.727 - (-0.901) = 2.63$) ($e^{2.63} = 13.85$).

As a diagnostic, I computed a 0/1 dummy variable set equal to 1 for firms that publish only college textbooks in any given year. Inclusion of this variable in the models does not change the effects of the theoretical and control variables. Further, χ^2 contrasts between the two periods for the theoretical variables, both individually and as a group, remain significant at the $p = 0.05$ level for a subsample analysis that excludes firms that produce only scholarly books.

Discussion and Conclusion

The findings support the overall hypothesis that the mechanisms of selection in capitalism are historically and culturally contingent. The sources of the risk of acquisition change as a consequence of the evolution of capitalism, and the extent to which an organization's strategy and structure are in conformity with the institutional logic of the prevailing form of capitalism. Overall, the findings suggest that the underlying processes that motivate strategic decisions, such as resource dependence and competition, are not universal—that the prevailing institutional logic moderates the effects of these processes on the risk of acquisition.

Publishing houses that were driven by an editorial logic, with their personal imprint and relational network strategies and structures and their values against vertical integration (Hirsch 1972), faced new selection pressures and an increased risk of acquisition if they did not transform themselves according to the prevailing logic—a market logic. The market logic focused publishers' attention away from building personal reputation and relational networks and toward the primacy of building market channels and the market position of the firm. However, those publishers who attempted to build market channels by distribution contracts fell prey to acquisition compared to those publishers who vertically integrated marketing and sales. The institutions of trust, cooperation, and reciprocity that made relational network forms of organization resistant in the editorial period eroded, and were no longer a defense against the downside of resource dependence—opportunistic behavior in the market period. The upside is that acquisitions allowed relational network forms of organization to survive and to prosper at a faster rate through increased access to the benefits of corporate hierarchy—benefits they would not have been able to otherwise achieve. The later is born out to a greater extent than the former in that most acquisitions resulted in growth, not death of the firm. Nonetheless, it does bear out an important scope condition of Powell's arguments—that network forms of organizations, such as relational networks in production and distribution in publishing flourish as independent forms under the logics of personal capitalism, but not under market capitalism.

Resource competition increased the risk of acquisition in the market period, but not in the editorial period. As was found in the two previous chapters in examining the sources of leadership power and organization structure, this suggests that also with respect to acquisition, attention to resource competition is dependent on the prevalence of a market logic rather than the actual level of resource competition.

The findings have implications for the analysis of structural alternatives, resource competition, and the market for corporate control. I have presented evidence to support Powell's (1990) claims that network forms of organization, which depend on trust and reciprocity, in such context may be more effective than hierarchy in controlling competition. However, Chandler (1962, 1977) argued explicitly that the rise of M-form hierarchy occurred because it was a superior alternative to dealing with the problems of growth, resource dependence, and market competition. One way to understand this contrast is that when the rules of the game changed from competing for authors to competing for market share, network forms were selected out of the population in favor of hierarchical forms of organization—the latter could more successfully employ the strategies of vertical integration and growth by acquisition. As the sources of legitimacy became increasingly tied to a firm's market position, the practice of acquisition fueled a market for corporate control wherein personal imprints, with their relative lack of structure and ease of integration, became easy targets for acquiring hierarchies. In sum, the selection of organization forms by acquisition is contingent on the prevailing institutional logic rather than on the actual level of resource competition in the product market.

There are caveats to consider. First, it may be that firms with distribution contracts were more likely to be acquired because they were weakened by the separation of the editorial and marketing functions. However, publishers that were distribution-dependent existed in both periods, yet in the editorial period, such publishers were not at an increased risk of acquisition.

Second, it could be that publishers with distribution contracts were smaller and economically weaker because of lesser scale economies and market power. However, the period effect of the variable, D Distribution Contract (6), holds after controlling for two measures of organization size, the number of imprints, and the number of divisions and subsidiaries.

Third, the lack of firm-level financial performance data may affect the interpretation of the results. I cannot determine if, in the editorial period, firms were relatively immune to acquisition because they could afford to sacrifice profits for prestige, or if, in the market period, firms were resistant to acquisition because they focused on profits and had the advantages of scale economies. However, note that I control for organization size and ownership form in the statistical models.

In addition, in other analyses, firm profits are shown to have declined with increasing size over time (Thornton 1999a). For example, in Appendix C the graphs of the historical trends in financial performance of firms reporting to the Association of American Publishers show astonishingly, the opposite of the economic and finance critique of my findings. In theory, larger firms, those more likely to achieve the benefits of scale and to be acquiring firms, should have increasing profits; but instead in the age of market capitalism, their profits on average declined relative to smaller firms. While this prediction fits Chandler's (1962) arguments of why the publishing industry should not develop large hierarchical firms, it obviously flies in the face of the empirical reality of the change in the market structure of the publishing industry. Moreover, it should be noted that the empirical findings on performance and the risk of acquisition are contradictory (Palmer et al. 1995; Davis and Stout 1992). Nonetheless, to rule out such questions, data are needed to test whether or not the effects of financial performance on acquisition are contingent on institutional logics.

The evidence in Table 7.1 shows that structural change did occur. Note the significant increase in the number of firms with an imprint and distribution contract strategy and structure. The nature of distribution contracts in the two periods also differed in material ways that may account for changes in the risk of acquisition. For example, Reid (1969, 15) notes in talking about the editorial period that contract sales representatives were sometimes independent, self-employed individuals. McCormick (1998), in discussing the market period, describes that distribution contracting was the domain of larger distributing or publishing organizations in which marketing executives elicited distribution contracts, particularly when they had warehouse and distribution capacity that was larger than their own product lines could employ.

However, my findings also suggest that there is not a one-to-one correspondence between changes in culture and social and economic structure and changes in the risk of acquisition. The mean value for resource competition was actually higher in the editorial period than in the market period. Moreover, there is not a statistically significant difference between the two periods in the *value* of the dependent variable—acquisition, both in the actual number and the rate within the population—but there is a change in the *effects* on the rate of acquisition between the two periods. The changing determinants of acquisition held independent of the control variables: Founder Age Post-63 (14), Organization Age (15), Organization Size, Diversification, Percent Change in Interest Rates (23), and D Public/Private Ownership (8).

Second, scholars have identified domains for new research on trust and reputation at multiple levels of analysis: trust as an inter-firm characteristic that affects the need for hierarchy in economic transactions (Gulati 1995; Gulati and Singh 1998), and trust as a characteristic of the institutional environment (Rousseau et al. 1998). My findings illustrate how cultural norms underlying trust were embodied in the institutional environment that was in transition from personal to market capitalism, where each form of capitalism carries different consequences for organizational forms and the practices of acquisition. Organizational structures that are less congruent with the institutional logic of the prevailing form of capitalism faced new selection pressures and were more likely to be at risk of acquisition. Acquisitions and network forms of organization, such as alliances and contracts, are increasingly used to access cutting edge research and technology innovations (Arrow 1983; Chesbrough and Teece 1996). We need to know more about how and why the norms of trust and reputation that affect such strategic choices emerge, become stable, and change.

CHAPTER 8

Meta-analysis

Interpretive activity is foundational for the commitments
and competitions that constitute economic action.
—Harrison C. White (2002, 306), *Markets from Networks:
Socioeconomic Models of Production*

TO DETERMINE THE precision of any theory one must assess its scope conditions. What phenomena are most susceptible to explanation by the theory and under which conditions? Is the theory contingent and particular in scope or does it produce robust and universal predictions across historical time and cultural contexts? Another important test of any theory is its power to explain interest and agency. Undoubtedly, any theory that cannot specify interest-driven behavior is limited in the range of problems and contexts to which it can be usefully applied (DiMaggio 1988).

In this final chapter, I compare the independent variables across the three studies of the decision making by higher education publishers to further understand the scope conditions of the theory of attention and to address the more general questions foreshadowed in the introductory chapter. To make this comparison I shift the focus of the analysis to a more abstract level—from the organization to the market. Rather than statistical analyses, I develop three ideal types of marketplaces—markets as economic exchanges, markets as relational structures, and markets as political–cultural arenas. These ideal types translate the findings on institutional logics and power, strategy, and structure presented in Chapters 5, 6, and 7 into a set of assumptions and predictions on the locus of agency—the logics of action.

For example, when are individual leaders, relational structures, and market institutions more or less likely to be the channels of influence? Which effects are more attributed to the influences of culture; which effects are more attributed to the influences of social and economic structure? How did the economic systems, both personal and market capitalism, differentially affect the sources of interest and agency in organization decisions? Of the organization and economic theories that I have employed in the previous analyses—agency, managerial, and resource dependence—which of these predictions were found to be universal? Which were found to be particular across history and culture?

Theories of the firm and the market have been proposed by different disciplines in the social sciences. Each discipline uses a different lens to understand the behavior of firms and markets. Mainstream economists and psychologists have largely neglected the influences of culture, arguing that the effects of culture on economy are not universal. In psychology for example, the assumption of universality is inherent in the earliest work—in the cognitive psychology of Piaget, as well as in the later psychology on learning theory and cognitive science.[1] Mainstream economic and psychological theories are also relatively clear in specifying their mechanisms for action—making utilitarian assumptions in which social phenomena can be reduced to the sum of individuals who optimize their self-interests.

Recent social psychological research departs from a focus on universalism and personal agency with new evidence and theories that are culturally variable. For example, the individualism of Americans makes them more prone to committing the fundamental attribution error compared to those of Chinese origin (Morris and Peng 1994). Personal agency and power among the ancient Greeks was located in the individual, whereas in the ancient Chinese, personal agency stemmed from a sense of reciprocal social obligations and group expectations for collective agency (Nisbett et al. 2001, 292).

In sociology, the productive school of relational networks makes clear both rational-actor and collective models of decision-making (Laumann, Knoke, and Kim 1985; Podolny and Page 1998). However, in other structural theories, the role of human interest and agency is less developed and understudied (Mizruchi and Fein 1999). This deficit is particularly notable in neo-institutional theories of organizations, wherein without a model of action, the theory cannot specify the conditions under which a particular social structure is or is not important to firms and to markets (Fligstein 2001, 13). While there have been calls to examine how individual and collective actors have access to the processes of construction and the channels of influence that transmit institutions (DiMaggio and Powell 1983, 148), research on the locus of agency has remained relatively understudied.

In Chapter 3 I argued for ways in which units of culture can operate somewhat independently of social structures, making cultural theories applicable to explaining strategic action and change in firms and markets. While the task of identifying the locus of agency and articulating culture from structure is daunting, several scholars offer guidance. DiMaggio (1992) traces these theoretical problems to Nadel's (1957) classic paradox in which he argues that an understanding of social structure requires discriminating cultural typifications from the relational aspects of role-related behavior. According to Nadel, roles have a duality; they are both mental representations and concrete social relations. Nadel posited that the qualities of organizations are related to the degrees of association between three variables: positions in the formal role system, positions in relational networks, and members' culturally embedded attributes outside the formal role system.[2] Drawing on Nadel's insights on culture and social structure, I group the independent variables for the meta-analysis by the positional, relational, and economic effects and develop a set of expectations for the locus of agency and the predictive power of the theories.

Conceptual Framework for Comparison

Each of the three studies examines how organizations made decisions in the context of a product market that was undergoing fundamental institutional change from one economic system to another. Markets coordinate many types of economic decisions; how this coordination occurs has been a subject of interest and debate among both economists and sociologists (Swedberg 1994). Drawing on this debate, I develop three stylized depictions of governance mechanisms that represent alternative models for the behavior of actors in markets: (1) markets as economic exchanges, (2) markets as relational structures, and (3) markets as political–cultural arenas (Granovetter 1985; Powell 1990; Williamson 1991; Fligstein 1996; White 2002).[3] These ideal types represent theoretical elements of a larger system—the economy (Powell 1990, 301).[4] First, I define the ideal types, then I use them to develop a set of assumptions and expectations with respect to my questions foreshadowed earlier on agency and structure, and universalism and particularism.

MARKETS AS ECONOMIC EXCHANGES

The view of markets as economic exchanges represents the stylized depiction of marketplaces governed by the "invisible hand" where faceless, atomistic exchanges occur and actors must be ever vigilant against guile and opportunistic behavior (Smith [1776] 1976).[5] In this neoclassical version of the marketplace actors are rational and self-interested. Assuming they know their preferences, actors have perfect information in the form of price signals that provide the basis on which they make decisions. Price mechanisms coordinate individual actors, not collective decision making or state controls. The individual actor is the locus of agency and the effects of the logics of action are expected to be universal across history and culture (Chancellor 1999).[6]

MARKETS AS RELATIONAL STRUCTURES

The relational-structures view is a response to the depiction of markets as economic exchanges; it has sociological (Granovetter 1985; Powell 1990) and economic (Williamson 1991) variants. The sociological view is in response to the problems of trust and opportunism in the neoclassical view and the observations that markets cannot be isolated from social relations. Relational structures are governance mechanisms that create an ethic of trust and cooperation enabling actors to protect themselves from the potential guile and opportunism of exchange partners. Powell (1990) further developed the sociological view by illustrating with case studies that relational structures are a distinct organizational form with their own ethical "logics" of governance. While this ethics view stresses quality advantages, it also places constraints on action.[7] Actors are rational; however actors may appear nonrational if viewed outside the particular situational context.[8] Actors do not have perfect information because the properties of information vary with location within the relational network (Burt 1992). The relations between actors are the locus of agency, and the logics of action are expected to be particular across history and culture.

According to the economic view (Williamson 1991), relational structures are motivated by the *universal* principle of transaction cost reduction through alliance capitalism. Networks are not a separate form of governance defined by an ethic of trusting or altruistic behavior, but instead are a hybrid form of capitalist organization on a continuum between markets and hierarchies. The sociological and economic approaches lead to contradictory expectations for the locus of agency and for the universality of the effects of the logics of action across history and culture.[9]

MARKETS AS POLITICAL–CULTURAL ARENAS

The view of markets as political–cultural arenas is a response to the earlier market views. While the view of markets as relational structures makes it clear that actors are not wholly self-interested and profit-maximizing; the view does not specify a theory of why actors are empirically tied—why do exchange partners seek to cooperate and shelter one another from opportunism, rather than compete (Fligstein 1995, 2001)? According to the political–cultural view, actors use culture in the form of managerial ideology to strategically interpret the politics of the firm, market environments (Bendix 1956; Fligstein 1990, 1996, 2001; Barley and Kunda 1992; Guillen 1994), and regulatory styles in public policy (Dobbin 1994).[10] Actors construct social reality (Searle 1995)—they use cognitive schemas and political organization to protect themselves against guile and to remedy the problem of incomplete information.[11]

TABLE 8.1

Assumptions of Ideal Types

		Markets As	
Scope Conditions	Economic Exchange	Relational Structure	Political–Cultural
Locus of agency	Individual actors	Relational networks	Individual actors, hierarchies, state
Power of prediction	Universal	Universal–particular	Particular

While power is created in the course of such actions (Stinchcombe 2002, 429), culture is more primitive in that it explains the incentives and the interpretations for political and economic interests and events.[12] In this view the locus of agency is difficult to partition (Barley and Kunda 1992). Net of economic interests, it is determined by multiple sources—the culture and power of entrepreneurial and governmental actors.[13] Therefore, the effects of the logics of action are expected to be particular across history and culture.

Each of the ideal types differs with respect to how, in theory, institutions and organizations constitute markets, with different implications for how market participants engage the institutional logics of action. Table 8.1 summarizes the assumptions of the ideal types.

Research Design

My comparative research design holds constant variation in the independent variables, industry, product market, data set, population and sampling methods, statistical modeling procedures, macroeconomic variables, and actions of the state. I vary the institutional logics, the two forms of capitalism, personal and market, to examine how industry-level culture affects strategic decision making—the dependent variables, the rates of executive succession, acquisition, and divisionalization. In the statistical models, the historical time periods interact with the values of each of the independent variables. For each of the independent variables, chi-square contrasts test for statistical differences between the values of the variables for the two time periods. Chapter 3 provided detailed information on the data and research methods.

Building on the concepts gleaned from the ideal types and on the insights of Nadel (1957), Table 8.2 specifies the independent variables of interest for comparison according to the effects of person roles, social relations, and economic structure. Specifically, I present the independent variables by the following categories—the positional (individuals), relational (organizations), and economic (markets) determinants of organizational decisions.

Positional variables (*D* Founder (4)) refer to attributes that involve an individual actor's role, reputation, or status position, such as founder or chief executive officer. Relational variables (ln *N* Imprints (5) and *D* Distribution Contract (6)) refer to attributes with respect to the structure of relationships among actors or groups of actors, such as author–editor relational networks in the acquisition of manuscripts or publisher–relational networks in the distribution and selling of books. Economic variables (Resource Competition (10), *D* Public/Private Ownership (8), and *D* Acquired Firm (3)) refer to influences that have consequences for firms in markets, such as resource competition in a product market and access to the capital markets, either through public equities or corporate capital.

TABLE 8.2

The Effects of Institutional Change on Three Organization Decisions
Classified by Universal and Particular Effects Compared Across Two Periods
of Industry Culture in the Higher Education Publishing Industry, 1958–1990

Organizational Decisions Dependent Variables	Organization Leadership Executive Succession	Organization Strategy Acquisition	Organization Structure Divisionalization
Independent Variables			
Positional			
Founder	Universal	N/S	N/S
Executive Succession	N/A	Not tested	Particular
Relational			
Production	Particular	Particular	Particular
Distribution	N/A	Particular	Particular
Economic			
Public Ownership	Universal	N/S	Universal
Resource Competition	Particular	Particular	Particular
Market for Corporate Control	Particular	N/A	Universal

NOTES: *Positional* = Sources of agency are attributed to an individual actor's role, professional reputation, positional status, and authority in a hierarchy, such as founder and chief executive officer.

Relational = Sources of agency are attributed to the structure of relationships among actors or groups of actors, such as author–editor networks in production and publisher–contractor networks in distribution.

Economic = Sources of agency are attributed to economic influences that have consequences for firms in markets such as resource competition, price setting, the markets for capital, products, and companies.

Universal = Effects are not contingent on a change in institutional logics (culture).

Particular = Effects are contingent on a change in institutional logics (culture).

Classification based on statistical tests at $p < 0.05$.

N/A = not applicable: N/S = not significant

Results

Table 8.2 reports the results of the comparison across the three studies. Overall, the findings show agency at each of the levels of analysis. The effects of positional (individual-level) variables are universal across different historical and cultural contexts. The effects of relational (network organization) variables are particular across different historical and cultural contexts. Finally, the effects of economic (market) variables are both universal and particular.

POSITIONAL EFFECTS

If the chief executive was the founder of the firm, there was a statistically significant negative effect suppressing executive succession. Although its strength diminished with the rise of a market logic, this effect was consistently *universal*. It remained highly significant across both historical periods representing different institutional logics, editorial and market. In both the All Years model and the Piecewise model, this founder variable was not significant in the analyses predicting the rates of acquisition and divisionalization. That is, it was not significant under an editorial or a market logic. For parsimony, I dropped the variable from the models presented in Chapters 6 and 7.[14]

RELATIONAL EFFECTS

If firms arranged their acquisition editing functions in an imprint organizational structure (network), net of organization age and other control variables, firms had significantly different rates of executive succession, acquisition, and divisionalization across historical periods representing different institutional logics. The combined effects of the relational network variables are consistently *particular*, exhibiting the predicted effects of the logics of action of the ideal type of marketplaces as relational structures.

In the case of succession, the effect of an imprint structure was positive and significant in the editorial period, but not in the market period, suggesting that the acquisition editorial subunit was the locus from which the top executive was more likely to rise. The effect suggests that those firms that had more imprints, that is, more editors, had higher rates of executive succession, implying not only a greater talent pool, but also increased competition for the top job. The effect is consistent with the theory—the rise of the top executive from the editorial ranks would have been the predicted chain of upward mobility in the editorial period, but not in the market period, where executives from other subunits, such as marketing and finance would be more likely to become CEO. This interpretation is consistent with Fligstein's (1987, 1990) research on Fortune 500 firms.

In the case of acquisition, the effect of an imprint structure was positive and statistically significant in the market period, but not in the editorial period. In the case of divisionalization, the effect of an imprint structure was negative and statistically significant in the editorial period, and positive and statistically significant in the market period.

If firms organized their marketing and distribution functions by a relational contract organizational structure (network)—for example as distinct from a vertically integrated structure (hierarchy)—net of organization age, size, and other control variables, firms had statistically significant different rates of acquisition and divisionalization across historical periods representing different institutional logics. The combined effects are consistently *particular* and in conformity with the theoretical predictions of the logics of action of marketplaces as social structures.

In the case of acquisition, the effect of a relational contract structure for marketing and distribution was positive and significant in the market period, but not in the editorial period. In the case of divisionalization, the effect of a relational contract structure for marketing and distribution, was positive and significant in the market period, but not in the editorial period.

ECONOMIC EFFECTS

The effects of resource competition are consistently *particular* for executive succession, acquisition, and divisionalization across different historical periods representing different institutional logics. This finding is robust for all three types of organizational decisions. The effects of corporate governance and access to public capital markets, as measured by public or private ownership, are *universal* across historical periods for both executive succession and divisionalization. This variable is not significant in either the editorial or market periods for the decision on acquisition. The effects of the market for corporate control and access to the corporate capital markets are *particular* for executive succession and *universal* for divisionalization. The effect of access to the corporate capital markets is positive and significant for executive succession in the market period, but not in the editorial period. The effect of access to the corporate capital markets is positive and significant for divisionalization in both the editorial and market periods.

Discussion and Conclusion

This analysis presents a test of the power and limits of the theory of attention, showing how institutional logics affect organizational decision making in markets. It sheds light on the agency–structure debate by comparing the multilevel effects of the independent variables across the three studies. The ideal types of markets suggest that the sources of agency should vary by level of analysis and be historically and culturally variant or invariant (Sewell 1992, 20). Following these assumptions, I partitioned the findings by the positional (individual roles), relational (network organizations), or economic (markets) conditions in which organizational decisions are situated.

Overall, the findings show that positional effects are universal across different historical and cultural contexts; relational effects are particular; and economic effects are both universal and particular across historical and cultural contexts. The findings show that the predictive power of the economic and organizational theories that I employed in the analyses—resource dependence, managerial, and agency—was not universal, but contingent on the prevailing institutional logic.[15]

INSTITUTIONAL LOGICS AND ORGANIZATION THEORIES

With respect to resource-dependence theory, this finding implies that an actor's power—that is ability to control and solve internal and external resource dependencies—is contingent on the ability to correctly interpret them within the prevailing institutional logic. Resource dependencies are shown to not just be technical in nature, but a perceived state that is socially constructed (Fligstein and Freeland 1995, 30–31; Aldrich 1999, 65).[16]

Agency theory assumes that capitalism selects on "optimal" organizational structures (Marris and Mueller 1980). My findings show that the interpretation of optimal is not a universal principle, but is contingent on how culture moderates the selection processes. According to agency theory, the market for corporate control is one of the mechanisms by which inferior structures are selected out from the population of firms (Manne 1965). Recently, Manne (2002) has drawn attention to his classic theory by arguing in a *Wall Street Journal* editorial that, if the state in the 1980s had not dismantled the ability of shareholders to accept takeover bids, the business climate of corporate fraud would be significantly diminished. My findings show that in addition to state regulation, culture is also a factor in modifying free-market processes. Recall, my data show that there was no significant difference in the number of acquisitions in the two periods of capitalism. However, note that the effects of those acquisitions produced significantly different decision outcomes. Net of the effects of the tightening or loosening of the state regulatory environment, my findings are quantitative evidence of the cultural contingency of acquisition practices (Hirsch 1986).[17] I am not aware of a prior test of the historical and cultural contingency of agency and resource-dependence theories applied in the context of management decision making in a population of firms in a product market.

POSITIONAL EFFECTS AS UNIVERSAL

The negative effect of the positional variable D Founder (4) across the two periods of family and market capitalism indicates that the locus of agency at the individual level is universal and historically and culturally invariant. Note that this effect holds after controlling for private ownership and lifecycle explanations such as founder and organization age (Carroll 1984; Greiner 1972). Scott (2001, 137) argues that in comparison the *traits* of individuals should be more stable across historical time and cultural context than the characteristics of organizations and environments. I unpack this proposition by discussing alternative explanations for the universalism of this effect, the first stems from personality psychology, the second from the work on identity and personhood in sociology.

Founders are identified as entrepreneurs with personalities that score high on the traits of commitment, control, and achievement compared to other members of the population (McClelland 1961; Brockhaus and Horwitz 1986). Personality theorists argue that personality traits are enduring and that if one can describe personal traits, one can predict how individuals will act across different situations. However, the question of whether individuals can be characterized on the basis of relatively enduring traits has been debated and is not well supported in experimental research (Bowers 1973; Funder and Colvin 1991; Mischel 1968).[18]

A second explanation for the universalism of the founder effect stems from the research on identity and personhood in sociology. According to this view, the founder effect is less about personality traits and behaviors associated with formal roles and more about how culture influences personal identity (Meyer 1986). Frank and Meyer (2002) argue that increasingly society is culturally rooted in the natural, historical, and spiritual world through the individual, rather than through corporate entities or groups. The traditional sources of personal identity, such as families, social classes, guilds, occupations, organizations, and nation–states have lessened in their influence on the individual. They argue the functions that these traditional entities play in identity formation are eroding due to the rise of democratic political, capitalist economic, and scientific cultural institutions that empower the individual as the locus of social membership and identity.[19]

This trend is argued to be a product of two countervailing forces—the rise of globalization and the weakening of the sovereignty of nation states.[20] According to Frank and Meyer (2002), the global spread of free-market capitalism diminishes the significance of the nation-state and its ability to serve as a base from which individuals derive identities, freeing individuals to adopt their own identities—for example, revolving around ethnic, religious, and gender subcultures. The outcome of these trends is that globalization empowers individuals under natural law and weakens the alternative for persons empowered under national law. The democratic underpinnings of this argument are evident in, for example, statements on equality in which one cannot validly claim, on the basis of spiritual, natural, or historical virtues, to be more of a person than others. Therefore the individual becomes the unit and measure of true equality for all of society (Frank and Meyer 2002, 93). Rather than the nation–state or hence, national identity, the relevant unit of analysis is personhood—the master identity from which an increasing number of new roles and specialized identities are spun off to explain and differentiate what individuals do in society. Applying this argument, the identity of a founder or an entrepreneur may signal personhood more than the obligations involved in highly institutionalized roles, the latter of which would explain entrepreneurial processes. This disconnection between personhood and formal roles may offer an explanation for why the traits approaches do not explain very much about the processes of entrepreneurial behavior. Further applying Frank and Meyer's (2002, 88) argument, the founder and the entrepreneur should be an identity empowered by the trends of the rise of personhood since WWII. In theory, family and market, but not managerial capitalism, should propel individual personhood. This argument is consistent with my findings in which the individual-level effects of the founder are a universal locus of agency under both editorial and market logics. My analysis, I believe, is the first quantitative test of the universalism and particularism of positional effects in a population-level analysis.[21]

RELATIONAL EFFECTS AS PARTICULAR

The findings show that the combined effects of the relational network variables as the locus of agency are particular and historically and culturally contingent in predicting change in organizational decisions. Overall, the findings show that the effects of relational networks in production and distribution immunized firms from change pressures in the editorial period, but not in the market period—when firms with relational network structures were at significantly higher risk of making decisions that resulted in acquisition and divisionalization. These findings support the ideal-typical predictions of markets as relational structures (Granovetter 1985; Powell 1990). If markets embody the logics of action in which there exist norms of trust and reciprocity, and if position and reputation are a salient focus of attention—as in the case of the editorial logic—then relational network forms of organization flourish and are the prevailing locus of agency. However, firms that decided on relational network forms of organization in markets consistent with the institutions of economic exchanges or political–cultural arenas—as in the case of a market logic—faced increased market selection pressures. These pressures led to adaptations in structure toward pure or hybrid forms of hierarchy.[22]

ECONOMIC EFFECTS AS UNIVERSAL AND PARTICULAR

It is of interest that the effects of the economic variables are mixed, in some cases exhibiting universal effects, but showing the particular effects characteristic of social structure in others. Ownership is the most universal—while at times it is nonsignificant, it never exhibits particular effects. The effects of access to the public capital markets appear as invariant to culture and to alternative forms of capitalism. One might argue that these universal findings are an artifact of the left censored data; the effects may have been particular if the observation period began earlier in the era of personal capitalism and an editorial logic. One response to this question is to draw on the international experience, which remains largely dominated by family capitalism. In the 1990s there were many examples of the hybrid coexistence of market and family institutions in the cross-national context. In these cases, capitalists in nation-states dominated by family capitalism competed for the opportunity to bring foreign companies public on the U.S. equities markets.

It is understandable that the effects of the market for companies were universal in predicting the rate of divisionalization. It was, after all, the primary and pragmatic way that hierarchies grew and is perhaps at the heart of why Chandler's (1962) prediction, that hierarchies should not arise in the craft of publishing, did not hold. The means of organic growth in publishing are slow and quixotic to capitalize by comparison to other industries. To meet the increase in market demand, acquisitions provided a central source of capital and organizational resources. However, the practices of acquisition are just that, not really fundamental market processes like resource competition, but culturally constructed practices (Hirsch 1986). These practices were not well seeded in the editorial period. They were in the market period, and the particularistic effects of the market for companies reflect this fact.

The finding that organizations' responses to resource competition is particular, and historically and culturally contingent, is consistent with the view of markets as relational structures and political–cultural arenas. This finding is especially noteworthy because organization and economic theories view competition as a universal material constraint (Williamson 1975; Hannan and Carroll 1992)—it is arguably the strongest test of a cultural theory of markets. My findings on resource competition are robust across the three different dependent variables, and, in combination, represent cross-validation of the contingent value of culture in interpreting the meaning of and differences in strategic responses to competition in product markets.

IMPLICATIONS FOR THE STUDY OF ORGANIZATIONS AND MARKETS

I have compared the consequences of relational networks in publishing market transactions under two different cultural and economic systems—the editorial and market logics (McLean and Padgett 1997, 232). My findings have implications for the prolific schools of research on relational networks (White 1981b, 2002; Granovetter 1985). These schools have had a dominant influence on the development of empirical studies in management science and economic sociology. First, the exercise of using ideal types to formalize the debate about markets as relational structures revealed equivocal assumptions. Are relational networks a hybrid organizational form between markets and hierarchies, motivated by lower transaction costs, implying universalism (Williamson 1991, 1994)? Or, are relational networks a distinct organizational form with their own logics of action, implying particularism (Powell 1990)? My findings support Powell's view that the network, a distinct organizational form, relies for its livelihood on a specific set of institutional logics that assume the values of trust, reputation, and cooperation. When these governance mechanisms are no longer dominant in the population of firms, network forms survived by evolving into other organizational forms consistent with the new prevailing logic.

Second, Podolny and Page (1998) argue that the belief in the stability and superiority of network forms of organization, for example in terms of information, learning, legitimacy, control, and cost, seems difficult to square with the journalistic accounts to the contrary. Whether firms that organized themselves as relational networks experienced positive outcomes or crippling dependencies is an unresolved question in the networks literature (Uzzi 1996; Ingram and Baum 1997; Greve 1999; Audia, Sorenson, and Hage 2001). My findings suggest that judgments about stability and superiority are socially constructed and, as Powell argues, need to be considered within the scope conditions of the particular industry or marketplace institutions. Institutions that support relational networks in one context may not in another, whether the case is trust in garment manufacturing (Uzzi 1996) or the collaborative norms of science in biotechnology (Owen-Smith and Powell 2002).

My findings offer a quantitative test of the cultural or nationality hypothesis, and address the two alternative hypotheses. In my analysis of organization structure, I tested the alternative argument that network forms of organization are a result of the particular features of the organization of work in craft- and profession-based industries. As presented in Chapter 6, the findings motivated by this argument were found to be contingent on the prevailing institutional logic. Consistent with the descriptions of publishing by Coser, Kadushin, and Powell (1982), under a market logic, network forms were under pressure to change, organically growing into hierarchies or morphing into existing hierarchies via acquisition. Also, I tested the alternative argument that with growth the powerful firms (hierarchies) had the capacity for vertical integration. Thus, alliances in distribution took on different meanings and consequences depending on the economic system—personal or market capitalism.[23]

Third, Fligstein (1995, 2001, 10–11), in his critique, argues that network studies emphasize description of concrete ties without adequate explanation of the motivation for those ties. When theory-driven, they are incomplete, focusing on one variable as a "stand-in" to the exclusion of other plausible explanations. He further argues that, rather than attempting to unify the various explanations, scholars have rigorously pursued partial theories such as resource dependence (Burt 1983), power and ownership (Mizruchi and Stearns 1988; Lincoln, Gerlach, and Takahasi 1992; Palmer et al. 1995), information (Davis and Stout 1992), trust (Uzzi 1996), and status (Podolny 1993). In my testing of the effects of the various attributes of the ideal types of institutional logics, I have attempted to integrate many of these variables into a theory of the behavior of firms in markets—including both network and hierarchical forms.

Fourth, I add emphasis to a relatively ignored critique of the networks literature by Podolny and Page (1998). In this view, markets are made up of diverse organizational forms and it is reasonable to expect that they affect each other's performance. Therefore, a sample of only relational network firms or of only large corporate hierarchies may not generalize to the majority of U.S. markets, which have both small and large firms (Aldrich 1999). For example, small manufacturers that have ties only among small firms are likely to have different probabilities of survival from small firms that may have ties to larger manufacturing hierarchies and to parent firms up or down the supply chain.[24] These critiques argue for future research that investigates the dynamic relationships in a population of firms bounded by a market in which there are strategic alliances among small firms and between small firms and large hierarchies, as well as firms that are themselves organized as relational network structures (Podolny and Page 1998, 74).[25]

The three empirical tests presented in this book show the comparative decision outcomes of firms as a consequence of two forms of national capitalism (Dobbin 1994; Whitley 1999). One could ask "Why study the effects of national capitalisms in the *age of globalization?*" While scholars are actively engaged in the study of globalization and its effects (Alderson 1999; Fligstein 2001; Guillen 2001), evidence indicates significant theoretical and empirical disagreements. The difficulty of assessing these disagreements is exacerbated by the fact that research findings vary substantially by levels of analysis and institutional sectors.[26] Historical evidence clearly shows that the largest firms have organized themselves on a world-wide basis for at least the last one hundred years (Chandler 1990). However, Guillen's (2001, 29) review and Fligstein's (2001) data and analysis lend a healthy skepticism to global arguments on globalization, making clear that national capitalisms are persistent and that the unique social, political, and organizational arrangements of nation–states are not disappearing or converging.[27] This research evidence supports recent managerial reassessments reported in the business press. Consider, for example, the case of the global media empires opining about not achieving anticipated synergies, profits, and globality, even after 25 years of efforts and the touted spread of "informationalism" (Orwall and Peers 2002; Castells 1996).

Biggart and Guillen (1999), in examining varieties of capitalism across nation–states, argue that research could be advanced by linking area studies of economic development to institutional theory in organization theory. I echo these proposals, but also add the need to draw on the research on U.S. business history in that it shows organizations have made, most dramatically, the transition from personal to market capitalism (Chandler 1962). Thus, it may offer analytical leverage in the analysis of descriptions of the evolution of family capitalism and globalization occurring in other nation-states. Aside from the United States, Japan, and Europe, this represents most of the world's economy.[28]

There is a tremendous need for theories of organizational design applicable to the multinational context. Admittedly, this need presents significant challenges to theorizing at higher and multiple levels of analysis. Economic sociology is experiencing a revival (Zelizer 1999); however, with the exception of a few scholars (Palmer, Jennings, and Zhou 1993; Ocasio 1997; Fligstein 1990, 2001), the role of the firm appears underemphasized, with individuals, institutions, and markets taking center stage (Swedberg 2003).[29] Yet, organizations arguably make the most consequential decisions in global markets.

Theories of organization have rarely been tested across societies. Hannan et al. (1995) is an exception, but at the population level, not firm level, of analysis. Some may argue that country differences are too large to make theories of organization and management useful. My response to this comment is to ask: What can be productively borrowed from any area that has formalization in theory and methods (Pfeffer 1994)? How would integration of areas move the production of ideas beyond description and ideology? Case in point, macro-organization theory emerged from cross-pollinations: consider the fruit derived from a change in levels of analysis. The development of resource-dependence theory (Pfeffer and Salancik 1978) morphed from the social–psychological work on power-dependence theory (Emerson 1962; Cook and Emerson 1978). Consider also the influences of population biology and event-history methods (Tuma and Hannan 1984).

In spite of the poor track record, managers have continued to try to generate profits by operating more globally. In publishing the seeds of this strategy have a history of resprouting in similar forms with the conglomerate wave of acquisitions in the 1960s, and again with the merger wave in the 1980s and the attempts to build global media empires (Greco 1997; Schiffrin 2000). However, managers engaging in global strategies face formidable obstacles in figuring out how to deal with the political and cultural differences. The largest challenge is to design organizational structures that funnel attention and resources to address two basic problems—fragmentation in markets and subunit interconnections. Resource-dependence theory (Pfeffer and Salancik 1978), theorized at a higher level of analysis, and Simon's

(1969) argument on nearly decomposable systems offer useful propositions to draw on in theorizing applications for these organizational design problems.[30] With respect to subunit interconnections, hazard rate models show, at least for higher education publishing, that the strategy of synergies across subunits that compete in the same market is a failed idea (Ocasio and Thornton 2002). Synergies across multiple markets, the central idea behind the global media empire, presents both of the above challenges and is best summarized by publishers at two different historical moments.

Most of the acquiring firms at the time (1960s) were considered outsiders to publishing, firms such as Litton Industries, Bro-Dart, Raytheon, Bell and Howell, IBM, ITT, Xerox, CBS, and RCA. Holt for example sold to CBS and their strategy was to have magazines, trade paperbacks, and educational materials all under one roof along with media and television. It was going to be wonderful—all synergy and we were going to all walk off into the sunset. But in reality, while we may have been with the same parent firm, no one talked to one another. We go to different conventions and belong to different networks. Besides, the film and trade people were always kind of snooty, thinking real authors write novels, not calculus books.[31] See, for example, the related theme in the recent case of Bertelsmann and the reported controversy over its strategy—to build a global empire or to return to a family-held firm that dominates local markets (Peers, Rose, and Karnitschnig 2002).

Although my analyses are a rudimentary effort to partition the effects of culture from social structure and markets; my approach is not meant as a critique of economic theories of organization and market structure. I am arguing like a few voices before me (DiMaggio 1994, 1997), that the study of culture is marginalized—in economics it is often viewed as uninteresting because it is exogenous or invariant (Stigler and Becker 1977) or concentrated in particular times and places.[32] One exception to this opinion is in the area of strategy, where economists have written about symbolic communication and cognitive maps (Porter 1980; Oster 1990) and organizational culture (Akerlof 1980; Kreps 1990; Casson 1991). In sociology, Swedberg (1994, 268) notes that sociologists in their research to delineate the characteristics of social structure through concrete network analysis have a deep "suspicion of psychological and cultural explanations." My intention in this book is to engage sociologists and economists in research that leads to a richer understanding of the interplay between culture, cognition, and economy in organizational decision making in markets.

CAVEATS AND CONTROLS

It is certainly possible that the results would be similar, but the jargon would be different, if the three studies were written by an economist, rather than a sociologist.[33] Undoubtedly disciplines are guilty of developing obscure and exclusive language—a practice that most in academia readily recognize as a way to define and expand the borders of a discipline (Abbott 1988). In spite of the language of my discipline, the effects are robust—they can stand alone on the basis of the data.

I have discussed the caveat that I do not have financial performance data at the organization level. Instead, I have relied on less direct indicators—interviews with publishers and investment bankers, aggregate population-level measures, such as resource competition in the product market, and trade association data on financial performance, which is based on a separate, voluntary, aggregate sample. I was able to cross-validate my interpretations using these multiple sources and am confident that the pattern of results represents the effects of the fundamental institutional changes represented by the shift from personal to market capitalism.

Meyer's (1994, 564) review points out that assessing firm-level performance in longitudinal research is problematic—he calls this a moving target because social processes account for the origin and diffusion of performance measures which themselves have been subject to change and controversy. Ironically, economic theory (Penrose 1952; Fama and Jensen 1983) assumes organizations that survive have the right form because firms seek to maximize their profits—arguing in a sense that longitudinal and population-level analyses are themselves a natural control for firm-level performance. Penrose (1952, 810) drawing on Alchian (1950) states, "To survive firms must make positive profits. Hence positive profits can be treated as the criterion of natural selection—firms that make profits are selected or adopted by the environment, others are rejected and disappear."

It is actually the sociologists who take issue with not having firm-level performance for at least three reasons. First, institutional theory argues that organizations can be permanently failing (Meyer and Zucker 1989), an idea partially stemming from the legacy of classic case studies of goal displacement in organizations with a social or public mission (Selznick 1949; Zald and Denton 1963). Second, ecological theory argues that survivor rates of organizations are age dependent (Hannan 1998). Third, mainstream structural sociology is empirically driven with an emphasis on demonstrating concrete relationships (Swedberg 1994). Of course, the other complicating factor that can defy economic relationships is family ownership—an alternative governance mechanism to the market and the public corporation. Nonetheless, the economic performance of firms under conditions of institutional change warrants more fine-grained investigation.

The results may simply reflect a movement from private to public equity and from small to large firms that are searching for scale economies in marketing and an alternative to organic growth. In my analyses, I am not arguing against economic theories that predict that large profitable firms must distribute cash by engaging in acquisitions—and that this is the real source of market restructuring. I am also not arguing against economic theory that private firms tend to carry lower valuations and therefore are more likely to be acquisition targets. Such patterns of transition in economic structure clearly gained momentum in the 1980s, particularly in industries that previously had been isolated from similar transitions that occurred decades earlier in corporate America (Berle and Means 1932; Chandler 1977; Jensen and Ruback 1983). By all accounts, such transitions indeed did take place in the higher education market during the period observed in this analysis. However, I did control for the effects of organization ownership and size in the hazard-rate models, and these measures were coded annually over the 32 years. Yet my findings hold net of these economic explanations.

It could be argued that by selecting publishing as a research context, I have stacked the deck toward finding effects that fit cultural rather than clean economic models (Hirsch, Michaels, and Friedland 1987). Chandler (1962) did argue that the publishing industry is fundamentally different from mass production industries in that it is a craft-based industry where scale economies are comparatively minimal on the production side. Hence, one would not expect as commonplace strategies the growth of hierarchies to control market competition and the development of acquiring firms. Yet, these practices did take hold and indeed eventually showed up on the front page of the business press (Dreazen, Ip, and Kulish 2002). It is precisely because these practices—based in the logics of market capitalism—were contrary to the logics of the professions and personal capitalism that I argue that the case history of publishing presents a more difficult test of the cultural argument.

MARKETS FROM CULTURE

Culture is not simply an artifact of noncommercial activity of the state, religion, and the family. It is at the center of the market sector more than ever in this age of the "attention economy" (Davenport and Beck 2001). In this book, I have presented a theory of attention and have empirically tested its limits. The empirical studies presented in Chapters 5, 6, and 7 show how management attention mediates the identification and meaning of problems and solutions perceived by organizational decision makers. I have theorized how mechanisms that carry culture such as cognitive schemas and organizational structures focus the attention of decision makers. I also have shown how these mechanisms are influenced by higher order institutional logics, moderating the meaning of social and economic forces that have consequences for organizational decision making in markets. I have attempted to tease apart the influences of culture from those of social and economic structure by identifying the locus of agency at different levels of analysis and by showing which of the influences are more universally agentive and which are more particular across different cultural contexts. The most important findings of this meta-analysis are that the effects of both relational networks and market competition on organizational decisions are robustly and consistently particular—that is, culturally contingent. When the editorial logic prevailed, the focus of attention was on the market for books that stemmed from relational networks with authors. When the market logic prevailed, the focus of attention was on the market for companies that stemmed from financial strategies and the growth of organizational hierarchies.

Finally, I have elaborated on the concept of institutional logics to show its application not only to theories of attention, organizational decision making, and institutional change, but also more broadly to corporate governance. The recent focus on corporate governance and fraud in the United States is but one example of the importance of studying the effects of culture on organizational decision making and market institutions. It can best be said in one sentence: The study of corporate decision making is not so much about the decisions made by good and bad individuals as it is about how the design of organizational structures and the larger business culture focuses the attention of decision makers on some strategies and structures at the expense of others.

I have developed a set of arguments that inform how the cultural units of analysis can operate somewhat independently of social structures, making cultural theories applicable to explaining strategic action and change in organizations and markets. I hope that this book will motivate others to embrace the study of culture in understanding the strategy and structure of organizations and other important relationships in markets. In developing the concept of institutional logics by linking cognitive theories of attention and the neoinstitutional perspective with applications to the strategy and structure of the firm, I have pushed the analysis of organizational decisions beyond the taken-for-granted category, advancing a cultural understanding of strategic action. In this process, hopefully, I have contributed to the few quantitative studies that examine the effects of culture on cognition and the economic decisions of organizations in markets.

Interview Methods and Procedures

PUBLISHERS REPRESENTING experience at both the editorial and executive levels in organizations of varying age, size, and structure were contacted by telephone and asked to suggest individuals they believed had broad experience and important reputations in the industry during the observation period. Publishers identified by their peers were invited to be interviewed. The chief executives in this sample often began their careers in entry-level sales and had worked in both sales and editorial positions for several publishing organizations.

A twenty-three question interview was administered to publishers from Boston, New York, and San Francisco. I asked publishers to describe how the higher education publishing industry changed from the 1960s to the end of the 1980s with respect to leadership, management strategy, market structure, products, technology, and legal changes. Many of the questions were open-ended and required recollections of past events. Respondents were asked to put themselves in the frame of reference of the particular historical time and to try not to use the benefit of hindsight. Similarly, a thirty-eight question interview was administered to three investment bankers who were identified by publishers as representing the key banking firms to the industry. In addition, two directors of well-known university presses were interviewed, one of whom was the president of the Association of American University Presses. Interview protocols were approved by the Human Research Subjects Committee at Stanford University. All respondents except one agreed to have their interviews tape recorded.

Quantitative Data Sources

Summary of Variables and Data Sources

Type	Level of Analysis	Variable	Data Source
Dependent	Individual	D Executive Succession (1)	Literary Market Place (LMP)
	Organization	D Acquired Firm (3)	LMP, Publishers Weekly, Wall Street Journal
		D Divisionalization (2)	LMP
Theoretical	Individual	D Founder (4)	LMP
	Organization	D Public/Private Ownership (8)	Standard & Poor's, Moody's Manual, Wards Business Directory
		D Division/Subsidiary (7)	LMP
		D Acquired Firm (3)	LMP
		D Acquiring Firm (9)	LMP
		ln N Imprints (5)	LMP
		D Distribution Contract (6)	LMP
	Environment	Resource Competition (10)	Digest of Education Statistics, LMP, Bowker's Annual
Control	Individual	D Executive Succession (1)	LMP
		Executive Age Post-63 (11)	Telephone survey
		D Estimated Age (12)	Telephone survey
		Founder Age Post-63 (14)	LMP, telephone survey
		Executive Tenure (13)	LMP
	Organization	Organization Age (15)	LMP
		N Division/Subsidiary (16)	LMP
		D Diversified Publisher (21)	LMP
		Related Diversification (20)	LMP
	Environment	Percent Change in Interest Rates (23)	
		Percent Change in College Enrollments (22)	Digest of Education Statistics
		Industry Proportion MDF (19)	LMP
		Industry Proportion Div/Sub (18)	LMP
		Industry Acquisition Activity (17)	LMP, Publishers Weekly

NOTE: N = number; D = dummy variable.

Financial Performance Data

THE GRAPHS ARE based on data from the Association of American Publishers (AAP) Statistics Reports for the years 1972 to 1995. These data are inclusive of all of the years data are reported. Higher education publishers who are members of AAP voluntarily report annual operating data, which are then summarized in aggregate form for use by the membership. Firm-level performance data include the following categories: cost of goods sold, book returns, total costs, and income from operations. The data in each of these categories are represented as a percentage of net sales. I include book returns because of the impact of the growth of the used-book market on the financial performance of publishers. These data are aggregated by organization size of publisher as determined by confidential sales figures. I relied on the definitions of size provided by AAP: small, medium, and large. AAP adjusted these definitions over the observation period to reflect the growth of firms and changes in the norms of organization size. It should be emphasized that these data are not a random sample. However, the self-report bias should advantage the discovery of scale economies. Note that these data indicate the opposite, the decline of financial performance of larger firms relative to smaller firms over time. Analyses were conducted to examine if organization size increased commensurately across all three categories. Statistical analyses using t-tests indicate that mean differences in costs and income, standardized as a percent of net sales, are not significantly different between small and medium and medium and large publishers, $p = 0.05$.

The recording of these data was discontinued in 1996 as a result of a decline in membership due to industry consolidation through mergers and acquisitions to a handful of parent firms. The Higher Education division of AAP itself was consolidated into other divisions as a result of this loss of membership.

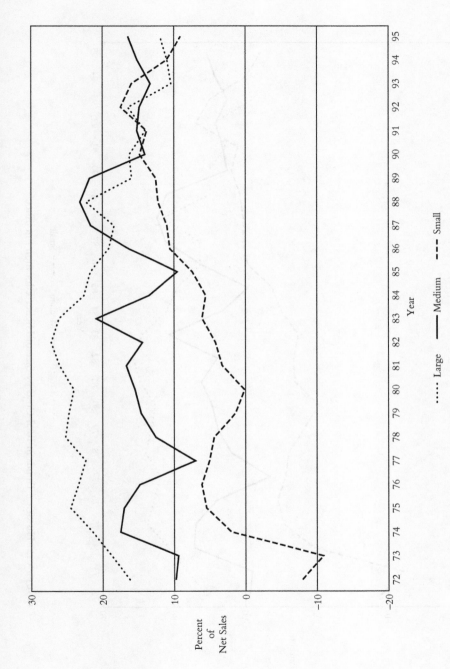

FIGURE C.I. Historical Trends in Cost of Goods by Size of Higher Education Publisher

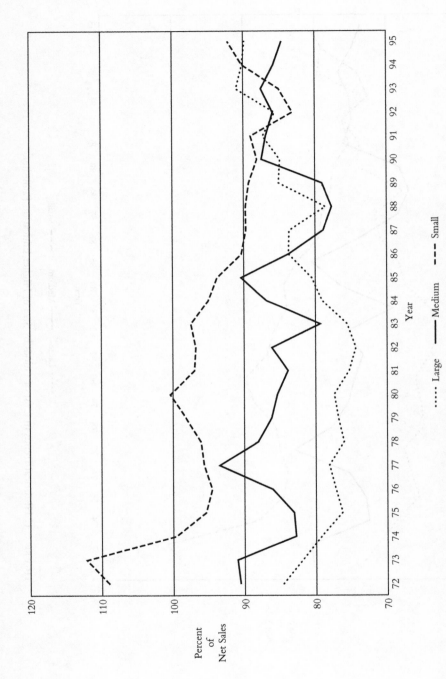

FIGURE C.2. Historical Trends in Total Costs by Size of Higher Education Publisher

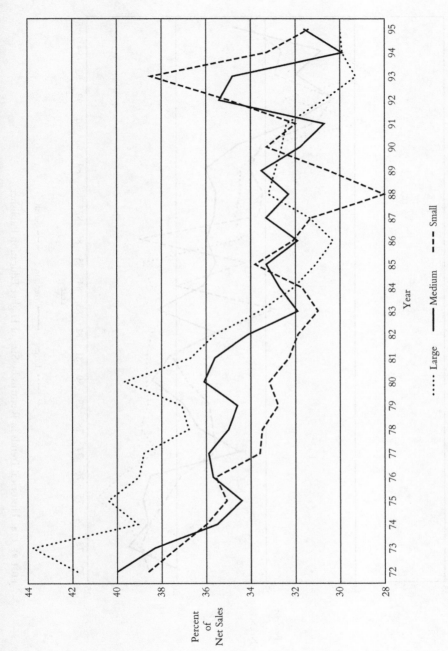

FIGURE C.3. Historical Trends in Income by Size of Higher Education Publisher

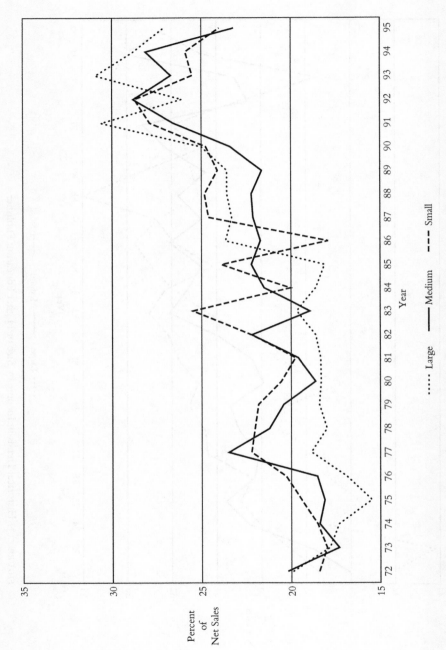

FIGURE C.4. Historical Trends in Returns by Size of Higher Education Publisher

Reference Matter

CHAPTER 1

1. The concept of rationality, while central to economic theory, is difficult to define, particularly when invoking comparisons across time and cultures. It is circular to define rationality as behavior intent on maximizing utility and then define utility as that which behavior tends to maximize.

2. Note, that Fligstein (1987) does not study executive succession directly but instead studies the functional background of executives at different periods of managerial capitalism. Furthermore, he focuses on how executive power and the strategy and structure of the American corporation are shaped by changes in state policies (Fligstein 1990). My approach differs from Fligstein's in that the emphasis is on the consequences of an empirical change in industry-level institutional logics—the shift from a professional to a market logic. Note that Fligstein's (1990) conceptions of control may be considered an alternative logic to either the professions or the markets—that of the corporation—with manufacturing, marketing, and financial conceptions as three distinct variants of managerial capitalism.

3. This makes a cultural explanation for a change in the period effects problematic. The period effects on the basis of state legislation are clear; consider for example the outlawing of horizontal mergers leading to conglomerate strategies.

4. According to Nelson and Winter (1982, 134) firms may be expected to behave in the future according to the routines they have employed in the past. The menu is not broad. It is built on the firm's routines, and most of the "choosing" is also accomplished automatically by those routines. Recent work is developing the dynamic aspects of the routine-based theory of the firm (Karim and Mitchell 2000).

5. I argue this while acknowledging that the analytic status of culture is pretty much a war zone in social and organization theory (Friedland and Alford 1991, 253; see Swedberg 1994 for a discussion).

6. Property rights in publishing were controlled as in ancient Greece by professors whose students carried on the literary work and in Rome by "wealthy men of literary taste who could afford valuable slaves who served as scribes." Publishing rights in the Middle Ages were controlled by the monopoly of the monasteries' writing rooms, by the libraries of kings and nobles, and by university supervision (particularly in 1150 in Paris and 1200 in Bologna). These entities prescribed the

preparation of textbooks and literary works and the rates at which they were sold or leased. In modern U.S. publishing, the passage of the Copyright Act of 1981 halted the pirating of English titles that had made up an important part of many U.S. publishers' lists. At the end of the nineteenth century, publishers relied on trade associations—the American Booksellers Association and the American Publishers Association (later the Association of American Publishers)—for rights protection. The publishing industry today relies on state enforcement of copyright laws.

The most recent and notable case with respect to higher education publishing involved Kinkos and the Association of American Publishers over the production of course-pack materials. Other publishing markets, such as children's, high school, and trade books, have been subject to court cases involving issues of political and moral censorship. For example, in the late 1970s, the Central Intelligence Agency acted to suppress or change books written by its former agents. School books, challenged on political, religious, and sexual grounds since the 1920s, were again under attack in the 1980s (Book Trade, Microsoft Encarta Encyclopedia 1997). These court cases generally involve individual authors and book titles, not firms with consequences for issues of pricing, control of competition, and other factors of strategic management. The Napster case may be an exception. Although not in book publishing, the Association of American Publishers did join the music industry in bringing suit to protect artists' labels, which also resulted in the protection of the strategic position of music firms.

7. It is reported that Gutenberg, inventor of the world's first printing press, walked away from his first two sets of venture-capital backers after they attempted to cut his ownership share in his fledgling printing venture. While Gutenberg refused, he eventually met his fate by forfeiting his set of moveable type to another backer when he was unable to repay a business loan.

8. The debates on the questions of interest and agency stem back to classic literature. For example, DiMaggio (1988, 9, 10) points out that Gouldner (1954) made a parallel argument in his critique of Weber (1904). Gouldner commented that Weber's sociological theories of bureaucracy "have been so completely stripped of people" (pp 17, 27, 237, 239), showing an obvious preference for structure over agency.

9. These expectations are also evidenced by differences in the styles of social science research between American and European scholars (Aldrich 1999, 14). American scholars believe there is greater professional prestige and scientific value attributed to the development of theories that are universal, hence generalizable to other contexts, whereas European scholars tend to assume their theories are nation-specific.

10. Barley and Kunda (2001) note how the study of workers in sociology got lost in this paradigm shift.

11. There was also a strong push to acquire into the American higher education marketplace by foreign publishers. One publisher explained why this was so advantageous to foreign firms, but not to the Americans.

Most European publishers, for instance the United Kingdom publishers, they do 20 to 30 percent of the sale of a given book in their home market and the rest of it has to come from outside with 50 percent or more of that sale having to come from the United States. . . . If the European publishers have strong currencies and of course tax advantages, and there are U.S. publishers for sale, it is very attractive for the Europeans to acquire. At the same time what you didn't find is many American publishers trying to acquire large European publishers in the same way the Europeans have done in the American marketplace. The markets are too small and the language and currency differences make it an unattractive business for the Americans.

12. Swedberg (1994), in his literature review, comments that network analysts have tended to be critical of psychological and cultural explanations.

13. One publisher stated: "Prentice Hall is the Ford Motor Company of publishing. It's black, its got four wheels, runs well, and they produce a lot of them. So they didn't talk about book development very much. They talked a lot about manuscript acquisitions, steady product flow, and heavy on marketing. They could get anything through the system—they could guarantee selling at least 3,000 copies because they had every system and procedure and market organized—just cram it through the Prentice Hall system. You turn on the tap in the morning and out come the books and the sales. This was unlike Harcourt, which was very flexible and author centered—polishing gems—the polar opposite of PH. PH was the first to key in on the Ford Motor company model. They brought big business to publishing. Though, Harcourt itself changed with diversifying into unrelated businesses such as insurance and theme parks such as Sea World—really the beginning of their downfall. Prentice Hall remained true to publishing—never engaging in unrelated diversification, and always knew its higher education sales were subsidizing its trade division."

CHAPTER 2

1. Weber defines authority as the probability that instructions from a given source will be obeyed by a given group of people. The group conforms because its members consider the instructions a legitimate source of control. The source of authority may be a person or it may be an impersonal institution, such as a system of laws (Blau and Scott 1962, 28).

2. This task is similar in some ways to identifying the mediating variables in a path analysis, except that the sequencing of variables is also longitudinal.

3. This is not to say that the elements of a typology—set of ideal types—should be connected as in a network analysis diagram. This statement will make more sense with Chapter 3's explanation of the theory of attention and institutional change. In short, the theory of institutional change is based in the idea that institutional entrepreneurs have random access to cognitive schemas and institutional logics (elements of the ideal types) and mix and match them in unexpected ways (Swidler 1986; DiMaggio 1997).

4. In the era dominated by personal capitalism, ownership of the firm and managerial control were integrated—owners made investment decisions (Chandler 1962). However, as corporations became larger and in need of professional management and new sources of capital, original owners sold shares of their companies to portfolio investors, separating asset ownership from managerial control (Chandler 1977). With this institutional change, from personal to managerial capitalism, the recruitment, training, and retention of professional managerial talent became central to the success of the large firm. To align professional managers' interests with stock-

holders' interests, stock options were adopted as a standard form of management compensation. The progression of such practices propelled the emergence of market capitalism and the development of a new tension for attention within the firm—focusing on the short-term performance of share price and de-emphasizing financial commitments for the longer-term growth of the company (Useem 1996). While this is an overly simple account, each era of capitalism embraced a different culture of business and a different set of locks and keys to structure the attention of organizational decision makers.

5. Acquisitions in the publishing industry should not be confused with hostile takeovers (Davis and Stout 1992). In examining all *Literary Market Place* and *Publishers Weekly* reports of acquisitions for the observation period, there were only three hostile takeover attempts in the 1980s, all of which failed. Furthermore, no hostile takeovers in the industry were found using Search Bank. When publishers were queried in interviews, they corroborated these findings that hostile takeovers are rare. As the president of the higher education division of one of the largest publishers put it, "Why would we have hostile takeovers? The assets in this business walk out the door every night."

6. The printer's mark symbolizes publishing as a profession, examples include the Tree of Knowledge of the Estiennes in the early history of publishing, and Wadsworth's motto, Education for Truth, in the 1960s and 1970s. The functional backgrounds of the founders of higher education publishers also evidence the connection to a profession. To name a few, George Bacon of Allyn & Bacon was a high school principal, Richard Prentice Ettinger of Prentice Hall was a college professor, and John Wiley was active in supporting church missions efforts (Tebbel 1972, 269; Wiley 1999).

7. One reviewer noted that committing capital to the firm rather than the editors is not exclusively the logic of the corporation; it is just as much the case with a law partnership (firm). The difference here is that the publishing contract is with the corporation, not the editor. While the publishing imprint may carry the editor's name as an incentive to retain the editor, and the editor can depart the corporation and steal away future author contracts, the existing investment (contract) remains with the corporate hierarchy. These characteristics have given publishing the description of a quasi- or accidental profession (Coser, Kadushin, and Powell 1982). It is not exactly the same case with law firms because the law firm does not own the attorney's license to practice and clients are not bound by contracts tied to law firms (partnerships). When attorneys leave firms, they often take their clients and the ongoing billable hours they represent (Phillips 2002).

CHAPTER 3

1. Attention is the taking possession by the mind, in clear and vivid form, of one out of what seem several simultaneously possible objects or trains of thought. Focalization, concentration of consciousness, is its essence. It implies withdrawal from some things in order to deal effectively with others (James 1890).

2. I build on process-based views of corporate strategy in which strategy represents the pattern of decisions made by firms based upon their objectives, purposes, goals, policies, and plans (Burgelman 1983, 1994). An attention-based view is meant

to augment other theories of strategic decision making, such as the routine-based and resource-based views of the firm (Nelson and Winter 1982; Wernerfelt 1984).

3. See DiMaggio and Powell (1991, 16–17) for a summary argument of how Parsons derived his emphasis on internalization of values from reading Freud. The result of Parsons' linking his theory of the social system to Freudian personality psychology was a view of culture that was not useful for explaining strategic behavior. Personality traits are relatively enduring and considering culture as an internalized element of the personality system, rather than an object of orientation outside the actor, stifled thinking that linked culture and decision making.

4. Socialization is a historical process in which culture and social and economic structures are inexorably linked. Institutionalized practices have inertia. Take for example the rise of business schools and the MBA, essential to the institutionalization of the finance conception of control (Fligstein 1990).

5. In a discussion of contingency theory, Donaldson (1996, 68) argues that with socialization as a causal mechanism, it is difficult to disentangle the effects of culture from those of social and economic structure. Donaldson (1996) points out that the functional background of the CEO is itself affected by the structure and, through the corporate strategy, by a contingency of structure. Thus, it is unclear that CEO background is a cause of structure or vice versa.

While developments in decision theory treat complex problems that arise from different kinds of information and available alternatives, the use of the more static notion of how values affect human behavior has implications for decision theory if values are taken as the inputs to the decision-making process.

6. Structural-hole theory, for example, explains how the structure of networks influences strategic decision making. While Burt's theory bridges the individual and organizational levels of analysis, it is unicultural in assuming that individuals are rational self-interested economic actors, some of which have better knowledge than others of how social structure can advantage and disadvantage their ability to discover and negotiate opportunities.

7. According to Simon (1962), hierarchical systems, which we can translate into organizational forms such as networks and hierarchies, vary in the level of decomposability of the system into its component subunits. The level of decomposability refers to two interrelated properties (1) the degree to which the operations and activities of the component subunits can be interrupted without affecting the other subunits of the hierarchical system, and (2) the degree to which interactions among component subunits are more limited. Simon (1962) expressly argued that nearly decomposable systems have evolutionary advantages over systems of comparable size because they have the flexibility of assembly and disassembly of parts without incurring interruption. For example, the multidivisional form of organization is more nearly decomposable than the functional form because the interactions between divisions are more limited than the interactions among departments of the functional form structure. Simon's argument suggests that the manipulation of structural attributes can have immediate consequences for the distribution of attention in organizations. One untested hypothesis is that structures that are more decomposable, for example because of limited interaction among component business units of the corporate hierarchy, lead to a distribution of attention characterized by greater specialization

of attention and information processing, both horizontally between component business units and vertically between the component business units and the central office of the parent firm (Ocasio and Thornton 2002).

8. Ocasio (1997, 192) develops this perspective stating how human cognition in general, and attentional processing in particular, is not a shared activity of a collective mind. Rather, it is distributed throughout the various concrete procedures and reflects both existing technology and the social structure of the organization.

9. Here, I am guilty of mixing different scholars' views of the analytic status of culture as a normative system of values or a cognitive system of classification.

10. According to attribution theory, individuals have at least two ways of understanding the causes of events (Kelley 1967, 1973). They can rely on the principle of covariation in which multiple behaviors and events are possible and observable; and they can rely on cognitive schemas.

11. An intriguing explanation for persistence of cultural elements such as scripts and schemas is theorized by Weeks and Galunic (2002). They apply an evolutionary theory of selection to social distributions of modes of thought and forms of expression (culture), which they define as memes. Memes reproduce by being replayed and memes that fit with other dominant memes are more likely to persist.

12. Using the concept of an organizational field as the boundary or unit of empirical analysis, where in theory there are strong pressures for isomorphism, is potentially tautological, and makes it difficult to understand the basis of conflict and innovation and change. Contradictions in the taxonomies of institutional logics, several of which may be prevalent to varying degrees in an organizational field, make clear the sources of conflict and change.

13. Some of the greatest conflicts between classes, organizations, and nations are about the appropriate relationship between institutions, which institutional logic (organizing principle) should regulate important activities, and to which categories of persons they apply (Friedland and Alford 1991).

14. There is a related argument at a higher level of analysis in the few studies that show how social and political movements have a cultural dimension in the reinforcing of attention of actors and in creating institutional change (Moore 1999; Hoffman and Ocasio 2001).

15. Sewell (1992) argues there are five key axioms that bear on an explanation of cultural change and that determine how structures can become transformed: the multiplicity of structures, the transportability of schemas, the unpredictability of resource accumulation, the multiplicity of resource meanings, and the structural intersections.

16. Other theories of cultural persistence argue that institutions live beyond their functional value because of structural inertia and transaction costs (Akerlof 1976; North 1990).

17. In early enterprise, a number of ways of signaling reputation and hence protection from guile in the marketplace were employed. Location, proximity to the cathedral was prime real estate, signaled the merchant's proximity to God, and thus his reputability.

18. These differences are not great according to Sewell's (1992) argument that the variance between the varieties of capitalism is not the point to emphasize as much as the fact that all forms of capitalism have commoditization as a goal. I tend to see the

similarities between the varieties of capitalism in a more Weberian sense of rationalization, which distinguishes the importance of the varieties of capitalism more clearly.

19. These ideas date back to classic concepts in sociology, such as role conflict, informal and formal systems of organization (Merton 1957), and loose coupling (Weick 1976; Meyer and Rowan 1977).

20. Gould (1995) argues that political protest networks did not create new collective identities, but rather activated identities that communards of the Paris commune already possessed. Bernstein (1975) demonstrates the impact of network structures on individuals' tendency to employ cognitive abstraction. DiMaggio (1997, 283) reviews other examples.

21. See DiMaggio (1997) for a more comprehensive discussion.

CHAPTER 4

1. Density (the number of organizations in the population) is an explanation for the failure rate of firms (Carroll and Hannan 2000). As a diagnostic, I entered the variables, Density and College Enrollments, into several models to examine the effects of density while controlling for market demand. Density is not significant in the All Years model, and the piecewise model is not a significant fit over this model. These variables correlate at 0.97, $p = 0.000$ and multicolinearity prevents their use as separate variables in the same model. When entered into the equation without a control for market demand, density is positive and significant in all the Years and Time Period models. I use the ratio measure of resource competition (N Organizations/College Enrollments) because it is not highly correlated with other variables in the models and because it measures the direct effects of competition while controlling for changes in market demand. Also see note on measures of market competition.

2. In 1958, 88 percent of the organizations in the risk set were independent; in 1975, 66 percent; and in 1990, 48 percent. In cross-tabulating independent (not being a division or subsidiary of a parent firm) and public or private ownership, I found that in 1958 only 3 percent of the organizations were both independent and public; in 1975, 4 percent; and in 1990, 2 percent. Given the small number of independent, publicly held firms, there are insufficient observations to analyze the subsample.

3. Although most contemporary studies of executive succession address these two factors, in our sample, these data could not be obtained for privately held firms or for firms that were divisions of publicly held corporations.

4. Economic studies of acquisition activity often control for differences in concentration because they are cross-industry studies and this is a conventional method of assessing market structure in economics. I do not control for concentration because this is a study of a population of firms in a market in an industry. McLean and Padgett (1997, 222–223) note that the most common way that economists evaluate market competitiveness is to measure industry concentration. They argue that this method is flawed for several reasons. Industry concentration measures only aggregate firm size distribution, not actual market behavior. Moreover, perfect competition theory does not provide a conceptual yardstick for deciding whether the observed level of concentration is too high or low; no probabilistic foundation exists for the concentration measures with which to assess statistical significance. My measure of

resource competition is a more direct measure of market competition with a probabilistic distribution.

5. The sensitivity analysis suggests that logics may have changed incrementally.
Incremental institutional change is likely if change involves the process of hybrid-
ization, where organizations eventually replace some features of their current logics
with those from one or more other logics (Zucker 1983; Haveman and Rao forthcoming). However, the objective of our analysis is not to determine whether the
transformation was discontinuous or incremental but to test whether a transformation in logics of control affected the determinants of succession, divisionalization,
and acquisition. Note also that an alternative modeling strategy of excluding a transition period could not be implemented, because it significantly reduces the sample
size and limits the power of the test.

CHAPTER 5

1. This chapter draws greatly from a article coauthored with William Ocasio in
the *American Journal of Sociology* 1999.

CHAPTER 6

1. Recall, I did not use organization size measures, such as the number of employees, that are unreliable in the publishing industry because of the use of contract
forms of organization (networks) (Coser, Kadushin, and Powell 1982).

CHAPTER 8

1. Nisbett et al. (2001, 291) traces this predisposition toward universal explanations in psychology to the British empiricist philosophers of the eighteenth and
nineteenth centuries, including Locke, Hume, and Mill who wrote about cognitive
processes as if they were the same for all normal adults.

2. Not surprisingly, Nadel's contemporary, Parsons, glossed over this duality as it
is inconsistent for grand and universal theories of social structure for which Parsons
(1951) is known.

3. White (2002, 310) argues that markets derived from agency are expressed
through social roles that are built in network relationships.

4. The ideal types do not exist in reality in pure form; they are theoretical models for purposes of comparison.

5. Smith assumed that individuals had an innate ability for "truck and barter"—
to successfully engage in self-interest. He considered this individual-level trait a natural motivation for competition. Allowing these attributes to flourish without constraint results in perfect competition and in aggregate the assurance of the public
good—hence the value of free markets.

6. The economic-exchange view stems from empirical observations of early markets as physical places to trade with no visible, system-wide governance that explained
their operation (Swedberg 1994). In theory, the invisible hand of market exchange
reconciled the pursuit of private interests with those of the general interests of soci-

ety as a whole (Smith [1776] 1976). Later views differed by introducing the idea of the market as an abstract process. In this view, markets were theorized as cognitive spaces, not physical places. Hayek (1945, 519), for example, argued that rational economic order is a result of spontaneous human actions, but not of human design; it is determined by the very fact that *knowledge* never exists in concentrated or integrated form, but instead is dispersed and exists in incomplete bits possessed by all the separate individuals.

7. In a critique of Williamson's (1975) treatise on markets and hierarchies, Granovetter (1985) argues that social relations emerge from incentives to pool resources and for repeated trading, and are superior to pure authority relations (hierarchy) in discouraging opportunism. Economists admit that explanations of relational structures are unresolved, but they argue that their positive effects of shelter from opportunism and their negative effects of power, restricted access, and path dependencies are simply background noise (Williamson 1994, 80). Podolny and Page (1998) point out that these assumptions are comparatively untested, and that although observed behavior of relational networks may seem unrelated to vertical integration and positional authority in hierarchies, quantitative research on relational networks does not control for the effects of hierarchies in markets.

8. Granovetter (1985, 506) notes that what may look to be nonrational behavior may in fact be quite reasonable when situational constraints, such as embeddedness are considered.

9. Several arguments cloud the question of whether or not the effects of relational networks are universal or particular. In spite of the findings on managerial ideologies, stemming in part from the study of Japanese firms, the scholarly evidence indicates that relational-network forms of organization are *universal* across societies and economies, and not more prevalent now than in earlier times both in the United States and in Europe (Clawson 1980; Granovetter 1985; Powell 1990; Laumann 1991). I find it interesting that those who study economic development outside the United States have not linked the study of relational network forms of organization to the earlier case studies of family (personal) capitalism in the United States (Chandler 1962). With Williamson taking up the argument that relational networks are a hybrid form without consideration for the elements of trust and altruism, he applies the *universal*, though cross-sectional, logics of transaction-cost theory. One argument that I have not seen explored is that relational networks, while an old form, now mean, in the economic sense, something different: the language of strategic alliances. This argument implies that while the prevalence of relational networks may be universal, their effects on organizational outcomes may be particular to history and culture.

10. Fligstein (1990; 2001, 35) defines "conceptions of control" as the rules of the game in markets. Conceptions are local knowledge in the anthropological sense (Geertz 1983). They are historical and cultural products specific to a certain industry or society. Empirical research shows that the curriculum in the top schools and the executive's experience in a subunit of the corporation (such as manufacturing, sales, and finance) socialize the individual to a managerial culture. Corporate actors create a set of understandings to control firms and markets, and then seek government legitimation and enforcement of those understandings (Fligstein 1996).

11. In addition to places, markets are cognitive spaces and market-making occurs because actors make and use culture; by storytelling they weave a web of meanings that are signaled and communicated through social relations of the participants, making valuation a product of cultural interpretation (White 1992, 2002). While this model assumes that culture is used changeably and strategically (Swidler 1986), DiMaggio (1994, 37) points out that for institutions to be effective, their instrumental function must be disguised, thus some actors are "cultural dopes" (Garfinkel 1967). The realism of this model is its strength, but also its weakness—it is problematic to empirically distinguish the influences of culture, power, and economy.

12. This view of markets differs in three respects from the work of Fligstein. First, this view differs in that imbibing culture is not necessarily based on socialization to values in concrete places, such as the subunit of a corporation or membership in an elite business school. Instead, it is an abstract cognitive process like Hayek's (1945) view of markets. This approach easily dovetails culture to action, not stasis, through the concepts of cognition and identity (DiMaggio 1997) as distinct from formal role structures. This view implies a response to the paradox of networks; culture can be shown to have a strategic effect, independent of concrete ties (Nadel 1957). Second, because power happens in the process, it may be a secondary, incomplete, mechanism to explain motivation and action. Third, the sources of legitimacy of practices are not necessarily state-dependent, but can occur under the influence of other authority structures, such as the family, the professions, and trade associations.

13. As Williamson (1994, 98) notes, the "symbolic construction of reality" to which Friedland and Alford refer thus has real consequences. It delimits the feasible set within which rationality operates: but rationality is fully operative thereafter.

14. Additionally, a related variable, Founder Age Post-63 (14), a control for the effects of the retirement of the founder, was not statistically significant at the $p < 0.05$ level in predicting the rates of acquisition and divisionalization.

15. This theoretical question stems from Fligstein's (1985, 377) analysis of the multidivisional form in which he expected different theories to come into play to explain relevant phenomena at varying historical moments.

16. The work of Pfeffer and Salancik (1978) was forward thinking in the early formulation of this argument and in the recognition of symbolic management's role. This symbolic role has been examined in subsequent empirical research (Westphal and Zajac 1994; Zajac and Westphal 2001).

17. The *linguistic framing* was necessary to transform what had been considered a marginal, deviant practice to a mainstream business strategy—prior to 1976, W. T. Grimm did not have a category for collecting data on hostile takeovers.

18. For example, social psychological research assessing the correlation between personality traits and behavior found that traits were not very helpful in predicting cross-situational consistency in behavior (Bem and Allen 1974; Bem and Funder 1978; Mischel and Peake 1982). Regardless of the social psychological findings, belief in the entrepreneurial personality and its assumptions of behavioral constancy across situations remains strong in popular thinking (Shaver 1995).

19. In pre-modern societies the sources of roles and personal identities came from above, from the kings and gods; note for example the entrepreneur of the fourteenth century was a person identified with managing the finances of the castle.

The sources of roles and identities in modern societies reach down and elaborate around the individual (Frank and Meyer 2002, 91).

20. I would add to the arguments of Frank and Meyer (2002) that the Internet is a technology, consistent with the "virtues" of a culture of democracy and science (Meyer 1994), which is propelling such identity formation among individuals. Take for example the identity of "suicide bomber" in the context of regions without nation–state sovereignty.

21. While the "traits" research on entrepreneurship from the perspectives of personality and social psychological may not have been very fruitful, the focus on individual-level effects should perhaps not be abandoned (Aldrich and Wiedenmayer 1993). Instead, this focus could be explored using the newer theories of personhood and identity.

22. A few large sample studies illustrate one or more of these points. Fligstein's (1990) analyses showed how CEOs in the finance subunit of the firm were socialized to financial conceptions of control in his comparison of three different variants of managerial capitalism, manufacturing, sales, and finance. Haveman and Rao (1997) showed how institutional logics are embedded in organizational forms—various thrift plans. However, their study is not about how logics of action cause forms to change, but instead about how forms were selected out (died) because they did not conform to the prevailing logic. In these studies, it is not clear whether the agency is due to individual action or the embedding of institutions in the routines and social structures of the firm (Nelson and Winter 1982).

23. Recall from the empirical chapters that the actual number of relational networks in production and distribution were increasing from the editorial to the market periods, but the effect was significantly different on strategic decision making.

24. Fligstein (2001, 136) found that hierarchies that are linked by networks, that is interlocked corporations, were actually less profitable in terms of returns on assets, sales, and equity, contradicting the bank control hypothesis that firms with interlocks were more profitable.

25. This critique needs to be placed in the context of the development of different branches of organization theory and economic sociology. Influential network studies in economic sociology were designed to ask a different question—"How do networks construct markets?" (Baker 1994; White 1993), not "What are the behaviors and outcomes of different types of organizations in markets?" Note also that these approaches undoubtedly motivate one of Fligstein's central questions—how hierarchies construct markets (Fligstein 1996).

26. Guillen's review explores six questions. Is it really happening? Does it produce convergence? Does it undermine the authority of the nation–state? Does it erode the viability of the welfare state? Is globality different from modernity? Is a global culture in the making?

27. Perhaps one way to reconcile these findings with the world society approach, which argues that we are experiencing a convergence to a global culture, is to distinguish those findings that have to do with economic development, governance of multinational corporations, and national law, from those that have to do with individual identity, nonprofit governmental organizations, and natural law.

28. My echoing of Fligstein's argument on the need for work on the differences in national capitalisms should not be viewed as inconsistent with my drawing on the work of Frank and Meyer (2002), who argue that the influences of nation–states (nationalism) on personhood is diminishing. The former argument has to do with corporate governance, which is still largely controlled by national law and the latter with the formation of personal identity under natural law.

29. A couple of observations underscore my comment. For one, as Meyer (1994) notes, the transaction-cost revolution placed firms and markets on an equal footing, shifting the focal unit of analysis to the transaction. Second, scholars (Baker 1984; White 1993) working to develop a structural approach to markets viewed markets as networks—tending to de-emphasize the role of hierarchies (firms) in markets. More recent work is examining how hierarchies are forms of networks (Burt 2000; Fuchs 2001).

30. Accordingly, as the level of system connectedness increases, so does the uncertainty and instability of an organization's environment. Simon argues that systems are more likely to survive if they are loosely connected. If each link in a system is effective, and the system is tightly connected, then any disturbance entering the system at any one point can affect every element. If on the other hand, the system is loosely coupled, then disturbances can be localized and positive changes can be absorbed into the system as a whole—making it very changeable, yet stable over time at least for the parent firm (Pfeffer and Salancik 1978, 69). However, for individual subunits, they are subject to operating on the interface "between market and hierarchy" (Williamson 1975).

31. Discussions with publishers revealed the irony in this comment. Higher education publishers argue that well-known trade houses have higher education divisions in order to stabilize their cash flows and increase their average margins—increasing trade publisher's survival rates. Moreover, they argue that the test of editorial acumen in higher education publishing is actually more difficult than in the case of trade publishing because trade can make better use of modern marketing methods. Trade publishers have the ability to presell and hype titles in the marketplace to a greater degree. The higher education publisher is less able to get away with this as professors are more astute consumers and the market is more restricted. If a higher education text doesn't reach an adequate level of sales in its first year, it has a high probability of being dead in future markets. This means that poor selling titles have no reprint or revision potential which is where profit margins are made.

32. With reference to this point, DiMaggio (1994, 29–30) notes that records referring to "culture" were more than eleven times as likely (15.7 percent) to contain the key word "organizations" than were others. The past apparently had more culture than the present: 38.3 present of "culture" references contained the keyword "history," more than four times the proportion of other records. Finally, less developed places have more culture than full-fledged market societies: "culture" records were more than twice as likely (33 percent) to contain the keyword "development" and more than three times a likely (10 percent) than others to contain the keywords "Africa," "Asia," "Latin America," and "South America."

33. I am grateful to Pete Kyle, Fuqua School of Business, Duke University, for his insightful and collegial comments in the development of the economic critique of the findings presented in this book.

Bibliography

Abbott, Andrew. 1988. *The system of professions: An essay on the division of expert labor.* Chicago: University of Chicago Press.

Abelson, R. F. 1982. Psychological status of the script concept. *American Psychologist* 36: 715–29.

Abrahamson, Eric, and Charles J. Fombrun. 1994. Macrocultures: Determinants and consequences. *Academy of Management Review* 19 (4): 728–55.

Akerlof, George. 1980. A theory of social custom, of which unemployment may be one consequence. *Quarterly Journal of Economics* 94: 749–75.

____. 1976. The economics of caste and the rat race and other woeful tales. *Quarterly Journal of Economics* 90:599–617.

Alchian, Armen A. 1950. Uncertainty, evolution, and economic theory. *Journal of Political Economy* June, LVIII.

Alderson, Arthur S. 1999. Explaining deindustrialization: Globalization, failure or success? *American Sociological Review* 64: 701–21.

Aldrich, Howard E. 1999. *Organizations evolving.* Newbury Park, CA: Sage.

Aldrich, Howard E., and C. M. Fiol. 1994. Fools rush in? The institution context of industry creation. *Academy of Management Review* 19 (4): 645–70.

Aldrich, Howard E., and G. Wiedenmayer. 1993. From traits to rates: An ecological perspective on organizational foundings. *Advances in Entrepreneurship, Firm Emergence and Growth* 1: 145–95.

Alexander, Jeffrey A., and Thomas A. D'Aunno. 1990. Transformation of institutional environments: Perspectives on the corporatization of U.S. health care. In *Innovations in health care delivery: Insights for organization theory,* ed. Stephen S. Mick, 53–85. San Francisco: Jossey-Bass.

Allen, Michael P., and Sharon K. Panian. 1982. Power, performance and succession in the large corporation. *Administrative Science Quarterly* 27: 538–47.

Altbach, Philip G. 1975. Publishing and the intellectual system. *Annals of the American Academy of Political and Social Science* 421: 1–13.

Amburgey, Terry L., and Tina Dacin. 1994. As the left foot follows the right? The dynamics of strategic and structural change. *Academy of Management Journal* 37: 1427–52.

Amburgey, Terry L., and Ann S. Miner. 1992. Strategic momentum: The effects of repetitive, positional, and contextual momentum on merger activity. *Strategic Management Journal* 13: 335–48.

Amburgey, Terry L., and Hayagreeva Rao. 1996. Organizational ecology: Past, present, and future directions. *Academy of Management Journal* 39: 1265–86.

Armour, Henry, and David Teece. 1978. Organizational structure and economic performance: A test of the multidivisional hypothesis. *Bell Journal of Economics* 9 (Spring): 106–22.

Arrow, Kenneth. 1983. Innovation in large and small firms. In *Entrepreneurship: Price Institute for Entrepreneurial Studies*, ed. J. Ronen, 15–27. Lexington, MA: Lexington.

Asser, Paul Nijhoff. 1989. Consolidation, internationalization, and the future of publishing: A scenario. *Book Research Quarterly* 5 (Fall): 51–59.

Audia, Pino G., Olav Sorenson, and Gerald Hage. 2001. Tradeoffs in the organization of production: Multiunits, geographical dispersion, and organizational learning. *Advances in Strategic Management* 18: 75–105.

Baker, DeWitt C., and James Hileman. 1987. Used books and the college textbook industry. *Book Research Quarterly* 3 (Fall): 8–17.

Baker, Wayne. 1984. The social structure of a national securities market. *American Journal of Sociology* 89: 775–811.

Barley, Stephen R., and Gideon Kunda. 1992. Design and devotion: Surges of rational and normative ideologies of control in managerial discourse. *Administrative Science Quarterly* 37: 363–99.

———. 2001. Bringing work back in. *Organizational Science* 12: 75–95.

Barnard, Chester I. 1938. *The functions of the executive*. Cambridge: Harvard University Press.

Barnett, William P., and Glenn R. Carroll. 1987. Competition and mutualism among early telephone companies. *Administrative Science Quarterly* 32: 400–21.

Barron, David N., Elizabeth West, and Michael T. Hannan. 1994. A time to grow and a time to die: Growth and mortality of credit unions in New York City, 1914–1990. *American Journal of Sociology* 100 (2): 381–421.

Baum, Joel A., and Christine Oliver. 1992. Institutional embeddedness and the dynamics of organizational populations. *American Sociological Review* 57: 540–59.

Baumol, William J. 1967. *Business behavior, value and growth*. New York: Macmillan.

Beatty, Randall P., and Edward J. Zajac. 1987. CEO change and firm performance in large corporations: Succession effects and manager effects. *Strategic Management Journal* 8: 305–17.

Beckenstein, Alan R. 1979. Merger activity and merger theories: An empirical investigation. *Antitrust Bulletin* 24: 105–28.

Becketti, Sean. 1986. Corporate mergers and the business cycle. *Economic Review, Federal Reserve Bank of Kansas City*, 13–26.

Bem, D. J., and A. Allen. 1974. On predicting some of the people some of the time: The search for cross-situational consistencies in behavior. *Psychological Review* 81: 506–20.

Bem, D. J., and D. C. Funder. 1978. Predicting more of the people more of the time: Assessing the personality of situations. *Psychological Review* 85: 485–500.

Bendix, Reinhard. 1956. *Work and authority in industry: Ideologies of management in the course of industrialization*. New York: John Wiley.

Berle, Adolf A., and Gardiner C. Means. [1932] 1968. *The modern corporation and private property*. New York: Harcourt, Brace, and World.

Bernstein, B. 1975. Social class, language, and socialization. In *Class, codes and control: Theoretical studies towards a sociology of language*, 2nd ed. pp. 170-189. New York: Schocken.

Bernstein Research. 1994. *The school publishing industry*. New York: Sanford C. Bernstein.

Biggart, Nicole Woolsey, and Maura F. Guillen. 1999. Developing difference: Social organization and the rise of the auto industries of South Korea, Taiwan, Spain, and Argentina. *American Sociological Review* 64: 722-47.

Blau, Peter M., and W. Richard Scott. 1962. *Formal organizations: A comparative approach*. San Francisco, CA: Chandler. (Reprinted 2003, Stanford University Press.)

Boeker, Warren. 1992. Power and managerial dismissal: Scapegoating at the top. *Administrative Science Quarterly* 37: 400-21.

Bowers, K. S. 1973. Situationalism in psychology: An analysis and a critique. *Psychological Review* 80: 307-36.

The Bowker Annual of Library and Book Trade Information sponsored by the Council of National Library Associations. Various years. New York: R. R. Bowker.

BP Report on the Business of Book Publishing. Wilton, CT: SIMBA Communication Trends.

Brint, Steven, and Jerome Karabel. 1991. Institutional origins and transformations: The case of American community colleges. In *The new institutionalism in organizational analysis*, ed. Walter W. Powell and Paul J. DiMaggio, 337-60. Chicago: University of Chicago Press.

Brockhaus, Robert H., and P. S. Horwitz. 1986. The psychology of the entrepreneur. In *The art and science of entrepreneurship*, ed. Donald L. Sexton and Raymond W. Smilor, 25-44. Cambridge, MA: Ballinger.

Brudderl, Josef, and Rudolf Schussler. 1990. Organizational mortality: The liabilities of newness and adolescence. *Administrative Science Quarterly* 35 (3): 530-47.

Burawoy, Michael. 2002 presidential candidate statement, American Sociological Association.

Burgelmann, Robert. 1983. A process model of internal corporate venturing in the diversified major firm. *Administrative Science Quarterly* 28: 223-62.

___. 1991. Intraorganizational ecology of strategy making and organizational adaptation: Theory and field research. *Organization Science* 2: 239-62.

___. 1994. Fading memories: A process theory of strategic business exit in dynamic environments. *Administrative Science Quarterly* 39: 24-56.

Burt, Ronald S. 1980. Autonomy in social topology. *American Journal of Sociology* 85: 892-925.

___. 1983. *Corporate profits and cooptation: Networks of market constraints and directorate ties in the American economy*. New York: Academic Press.

___. 1992. *Structural holes*. Cambridge: Harvard University Press.

___. 2000. The network structure of social capital. In *Research in organizational behavior*, ed. Robert Sutton and Barry M. Staw. Greenwich, CT: JAI Press.

Burton, Richard M., and Borge Obel. 1998. *Strategic organizational diagnosis and design*. 2nd ed. Boston/Dordrecht/London: Kluwer.

Capron, L., and W. Mitchell. 1998. The role of acquisitions in reshaping business capabilities in the international telecommunications industry. *Industry and Corporate Change*, 7: 715-30.

Carley, Kathleen. 1989. The value of cognitive foundations for dynamic social theory. *Journal of Mathematical Sociology* 14 (2–3): 171–208.

Carroll, Glenn R. 1984. Dynamics of publisher succession in newspaper organizations. *Administrative Science Quarterly* 29: 93–113.

———. 1985. Concentration and specialization: Dynamics of niche width in populations of organizations *American Journal of Sociology* 90: 1263–83.

Carroll, Glenn R., and Jacques Delacroix. 1982. Organizational mortality in the newspaper industries of Argentina and Ireland: An ecological approach. *Administrative Science Quarterly* 27: 169–98.

Carroll, Glenn R., and Michael T. Hannan. 2000. *The demography of corporations and industries.* Princeton, NJ: Princeton University Press.

Carroll, Glenn R., and Anand Swaminathan. 2000. Why the microbrewery movement? Organizational dynamics of resource partitioning in the American brewing industry after prohibition. *American Journal of Sociology* 106: 715–62.

Casson, Mark. 1991. *The economics of business culture: Game theory, transaction costs, and economic performance.* New York: Oxford University Press.

Castells, Manuel. 1996. *The information age: Economy, society, and culture.* Vol. 1, *The rise of the network society.* Oxford: Blackwell.

Caves, Richard E. 2000. *Creative industries: Contracts between art and commerce.* Cambridge: Harvard University Press.

Cerulo, Karen A. (ed.). 2002. *Culture in mind: Toward a sociology of culture and cognition.* New York: Routledge.

Chancellor, Edward. 1999. *Devil take the hindmost: A history of financial speculation.* New York: Plume.

Chandler, Alfred D. 1962. *Strategy and structure.* New York: Doubleday.

———. 1977. *The visible hand: The managerial revolution in American business.* Cambridge: Harvard University Press.

———. 1990. *Scale and scope: The dynamics of industrial capitalism.* Cambridge: Harvard University Press.

———. 1992. The emergence of managerial capitalism. In *The sociology of economic life,* ed. Mark Granovetter and Richard Swedberg, 131–58: San Francisco: Westview Press.

Chatterjee, Sayan. 1986. Types of synergy and economic value: The impact of acquisitions on merging and rival firms. *Strategic Management Journal* 7: 119–40.

Chesbrough, Henry W., and David J. Teece. 1996. When is virtual virtuous?: Organizing for innovation. *Harvard Business Review* (January/February): 65–73.

Chung, Kwang S., and J. Fred Weston. 1982. Diversification and mergers in a strategic long-range planning framework. In *Mergers and acquisitions: Current problems in perspective,* ed. Michael Keenam and Lawrence J. White, 315–47. Lexington, MA: D. C. Heath.

Clark, Burton R. 1956. *Adult education in transition.* Berkeley: University of California Press.

Clawson, D. 1980. *Bureaucracy and the labor process: The transformation of U.S. industry, 1860–1920.* New York: Monthly Review.

Clemens, Elizabeth S., and James M. Cook. 1999. Politics and institutionalism: Explaining durability and change. *Annual Review of Sociology* 25: 441–66.

Compaine, Benjamin M. 1978. *The book industry in transition: An economic study of book distribution and marketing*. White Plains, NY: Knowledge Industry.

Cook, K. S., and R. M. Emerson. 1978. Power, equity, and commitment in exchange networks. *American Sociological Review* 43: 712–39.

Coser, Lewis A. 1975. Publishers as gatekeepers of ideas. *The Annals of the American Academy of Political and Social Science: Perspectives on Publishing* 421: 14–22.

Coser, Lewis A., Charles Kadushin, and Walter W. Powell. 1982. *Books: The culture and commerce of publishing*. Chicago: University of Chicago Press.

Cyert, Richard M., and James G. March. 1963. *A behavioral theory of the firm*. Englewood Cliffs, NJ: Prentice Hall.

Dacin, Tina M. 1997. Isomorphism in context: The power and prescription of institutional norms. *Academy of Management Journal* 40 (1): 46–81.

Davenport, Thomas H., and John C. Beck. 2001. *The attention economy: Understanding the new currency of business*. Boston: Harvard Business School Press.

Davis, Gerald F. 1991. Agents without principles? The spread of the poison pill takeover defense through the intercorporate network. *Administrative Science Quarterly* 36: 583–613.

Davis, Gerald F., Kristina A. Diekmann, and Catherine H. Tinsley. 1994. The deinstitutionalization of conglomerate firms in the 1980s. *American Sociological Review* 59: 547–70.

Davis, Gerald F., and Henrich R. Greve. 1997. Corporate elite networks and governance changes in the 1980s. *American Journal of Sociology* 103 (1): 1–37.

Davis, Gerald F., and Suzanne K. Stout. 1992. Organization theory and the market for corporate control: A dynamic analysis of the characteristics of large takeover targets, 1980–1990. *Administrative Science Quarterly* 37: 605–33.

de Geus, Arie. 1997. The living company. *Harvard Business Review* (March/April): 51–59.

Delaney, Kevin J. 2000. A storied hotel in Paris plays "Inn-cubator." *The Wall Street Journal*, 17 August, B14.

DiMaggio, Paul J. 1983. State expansion and organizational field. In *Organizational theory and public policy*, ed. Richard H. Hall and Robert E. Quinn, 147–61. Beverly Hills, CA: Sage.

———. 1988. Interest and agency in institutional theory. In *Institutional patterns and organizations: Culture and environment*, ed. Lynne G. Zucker, 3–21. Cambridge, MA: Ballinger.

———. 1991. Constructing an organizational field as a professional project: U.S. art museums, 1920–1940. In *The new institutionalism in organizational analysis*, ed. Walter W. Powell and Paul J. DiMaggio. Chicago: University of Chicago Press.

———. 1992. Cultural boundaries and structural change: The extension of the high culture model to theater, opera, and the dance, 1900–1940. In *Cultivating differences: Symbolic boundaries and the making of inequality*, ed. Michèle Lamont and Marcel Fournier, 21–57. Chicago: University of Chicago Press.

———. 1994. Culture and economy. In *Handbook of economic sociology*, ed. Neil J. Smelser and Richard Swedberg, 27–57. Princeton, NJ: Princeton University Press.

———. 1997. Culture and cognition. *Annual Review of Sociology* 23: 263–87.

———. 1998. Discussant, Organizations, occupations and work session. *American Sociological Association*, August.

DiMaggio, Paul J., and Walter W. Powell. 1983. The iron cage revisited: Institutional isomorphism and collective rationality in organizational fields. *American Sociological Review*, 48: 147–60.

____. 1991. Introduction. In *The new institutionalism in organizational analysis*, ed. Walter W. Powell and Paul J. DiMaggio, Chicago: University of Chicago Press.

DiPrete, T. A., and J. D. Forristal. 1994. Multilevel models: Methods and substance. *Annual Review of Sociology* 20: 331–57.

Djelic, Marie-Laure, and Antti Ainamo. 1999. The co-evolution of new organizational forms in the fashion industry: A historical and comparative study of France, Italy, and the United States. *Organization Science* 10 (5): 622–37.

Dobbin, Frank. 1994. *Forging industrial policy: The United States, Britain, and France in the railway age*. New York: Cambridge University Press.

Dobbin, Frank, and Timothy J. Dowd. 1997. How policy shapes competition: Early railroad foundings in Massachusetts. *Administrative Science Quarterly* 42: 501–29.

____. 2000. The market that antitrust built: Public policy, private coercion, and railroad acquisitions. *American Sociological Review* 65: 631–57.

Donaldson, Lex. 1996. The normal science of structural contingency theory. In *Handbook of organization studies*, ed. Stewart R. Clegg,, Cynthia Hardy, and Walter Norg, 57–76. London: Sage.

Doty, D. Harold, and William H. Glick. 1994. Typologies as a unique form of theory building: Toward improved understanding and modeling. *Academy of Management Review* 19 (2): 230–51.

Dougherty, Peter. 1998. A random walk down Third Avenue. Paper presented in panel, The Crisis in University Press Publishing: Is It Real and How Will It Affect the Discipline? Annual meeting of the American Sociological Association, San Francisco.

Douglas, Mary. 1986. *How institutions think*. Syracuse, NY: Syracuse University Press.

Dreazen, Yochi J., Greg Ip, and Nicholas Kulish. 2002. Big business: Why the sudden rise in the urge to merge and form oligopolies? *The Wall Street Journal*, 25 February.

Dugan, Ianthe Jeanne. 2002. Before Enron, greed helped sink the respectability of accounting. *The Wall Street Journal*, 14 March.

Eccles, Robert G. 1981. The quasifirm in the construction industry. *Journal of Economic Behavior and Organization* 2 (December): 335–57.

Eccles, Robert G., and Harrison C. White. 1986. Firm and market interfaces of profit center control. In *Approaches to social theory*, ed. Siegwart Lindenberg, James S. Coleman, and Stefan Nowak, 203–20. New York: Russell Sage Foundation.

Edelman, Lauren B. 1990. Legal environments and organizational governance: The expansion of due process in the American workplace. *American Journal of Sociology* 95 (6): 1401–40.

____. 1992. Legal ambiguity and symbolic structure: Organizational mediation of civil rights law. *American Journal of Sociology* 97: 1531–76.

Educational Marketeer. Wilton: CT: SIMBA Communication Trends.

Eisenhardt, K. M. 1989. Building theories from case study research. *Academy of Management Review* 14: 532–50.

Emerson, R. M. 1962. Power-dependence relations. *American Sociological Review* 27: 31–40.

Epstein, Jason. 1998. Can the Bertelsmann deal take publishing back to its roots? *The New Yorker*, 6 April.

_____. 2001. *Book business: Past, present and future*. New York: Norton.

Fama, Eugene, and Michael E. Jensen. 1983. Separation of ownership and control. *Journal of Political Economy* 88: 288–307.

Fichman, Mark, and Daniel Levinthal. 1991. Honeymoons and the liability of adolescence: A new perspective on duration dependence in social and organizational relationships. *Academy of Management Review* 16 (2): 442–68.

Fiske, Susan T., and Patricia W. Linville. 1980. What does the schema concept buy us? *Personality and Social Psychology Bulletin* 6(4): 543–57.

Fizel, John L., Kenneth K. T. Louie, and March S. Mentzer. 1990. An economic, organizational and behavioral model of the determinants of CEO tenure. *Journal of Economic Behavior and Organization* 14: 363–79.

Fleck, L. [1935] 1979. *Genesis and development of a scientific fact*. Chicago: University of Chicago Press.

Fligstein, Neil. 1985. The spread of the multidivisional form among large firms, 1919–1979. *American Sociological Review* 50: 377–91.

_____. 1987. The Interorganizational power struggle: The rise of finance personnel to top leadership in large corporations, 1919–1979. *American Sociological Review* 52: 44–58.

_____. 1990. *The transformation of corporate control*. Cambridge: Harvard University Press.

_____. 1995. Networks of power or the finance conception of control? Comment on Palmer, Barber, Zhou, and Soysal. *American Sociological Review* 60 (4): 500–03.

_____. 1996. Market as politics: A political-cultural approach to market institutions. *American Sociological Review* 61 (4): 656–73.

_____. 2001. *The architecture of markets: An economic sociology of twenty-first-century capitalist societies*. Princeton, NJ: Princeton University Press.

Fligstein, Neil, and Peter Brantley. 1992. Bank control, owner control, or organizational dynamics: Who controls the large modern corporation? *American Journal of Sociology* 98 (2): 280–307.

Fligstein, Neil, and Kenneth Dauber. 1989. Structural change in corporate organization. *Annual Review of Sociology* 15: 73–96.

Fligstein, Neil, and R. Freeland. 1995. Theoretical and comparative perspectives on corporate organization. *Annual Review of Sociology* 21: 21–43.

Fligstein, Neil, and Linda Markowitz. 1993. Financial reorganization of American corporations in the 1980s. In *Sociology and the public agenda*, ed. William Julius Wilson, 185–206. Newbury Park, CA: Sage.

Florida, Richard. 2002. *The rise of the creative class*. New York: Basic Books.

Frank, David John, and John W. Meyer. 2002. The profusion of individual roles and identities in the postwar period. *Sociological Theory* 20: 1.

Frederickson, James W., Donald C. Hambrick, and Sara Baumrin. 1988. A model of CEO dismissal. *Academy of Management Review* 13: 255–71.

Freeman, John, Glenn R. Carroll, and Michael T. Hannan. 1983. The liability of newness: Age dependence in organizational death rates. *American Sociological Review* 48: 692–710.

Freidson, Eliot. 1986. *Professional powers: A study of the institutionalization of formal knowledge*. Chicago: University of Chicago Press.

___. 2001. Professionalism: The Third Logic. Chicago: University of Chicago Press.

___. 2002. *Professionalism: The third logic on the practice of knowledge*. Chicago: University of Chicago Press.

Friedland, Roger, and Robert Alford. 1991. Bringing society back in: Symbols, practices, and institutional contradictions. In *The new institutionalism in organizational analysis*, ed. Walter W. Powell and Paul J. DiMaggio, 232–63. Chicago: University of Chicago Press.

Fuchs, Stephan. 2001. *Against essentialism: A theory of culture and society*. Cambridge: Harvard University Press.

Fulcrum Information Services, Inc. 1998. Doing the right thing at the right time. Presented at the Second Annual Book Publishing Industry Mergers and Acquisitions Institute, December 7–8, New York.

Funder, D. C., and C. R. Colvin. 1991. Explorations in the behavioral consistence: Properties of persons, situations, and behaviors. *Journal of Personality and Social Psychology* 60: 773–94.

Galaskiewicz, J., and W. Bielefeld. 1998. *Nonprofit organizations in an age of uncertainty: A study of organizational change*, New York: Aldine De Gruyter.

Galunic, Charles. 1996. Recreating divisional domains: Intracorporate evolution and the multibusiness. Academy of Management Best Paper Proceedings.

Galunic, D. Charles, and Kathleen M. Eisenhardt, 2001. Architectural innovation and modular corporate forms. *Academy of Management Journal* 44 (6): 1229–49.

Garfinkel, Harold. 1967. *Studies in ethnomethodology*. Cambridge, MA: Polity Press.

Geertz, C. 1983. *Local knowledge: Further essays in interpretive sociology*. New York: Basic Books.

Golbe, Debra L., and Lawrence J. White. 1988. A time-series analysis of mergers and acquisitions in the U.S. economy. In *Corporate takeovers: Causes and consequences*, ed. Alan J. Auerbach, 265–303. Chicago: University of Chicago Press.

Goodstein, Jerry D. 1994. Institutional pressures and strategic responsiveness: Employer involvement in work/family issues. *Academy of Management Journal* 37: 350–82.

Gordon, G., and S. Becker. 1964. Organizational size and managerial succession: A reexamination. *American Journal of Sociology* 70: 215–33.

Gort, Michael. 1969. An economic disturbance theory of mergers. *Quarterly Journal of Economics* 83: 624–42.

Gould, Roger. 1995. *Insurgent identities: Class, community and protest in Paris 1848 to the commune*. Chicago: University of Chicago Press.

Gouldner, Alvin W. 1954. *Patterns of industrial bureaucracy*. Glencoe, IL: Free Press.

Graham, Gordon. 1994. *As I was saying: Essays on the international book industry*. London: Hans Zell.

Granovetter, Mark. 1985. Economic action and social structure: The problem of embeddedness. *American Journal of Sociology* 91: 481–510.

Greco, Albert N. 1989. Mergers and acquisitions in publishing, 1984–1988: Some public policy issues. *Book Research Quarterly* (Fall): 25–43.

___. 1996. Shaping the future: Mergers, acquisitions, and the U.S. publishing, communications, and mass media industries, 1990–1995. *Publishing Research Quarterly* (Fall): 5–15.

___. 1997. *The publishing industry*. Boston: Allyn & Bacon.

Greiner, Larry. 1972. Evolution and revolution as organizations grow. *Harvard Business Review* 50 (1): 37–46.

Greve, Henrich R. 1999. The effect of core change on performance: Inertia and regression toward the mean. *Administrative Science Quarterly* 44 (3): 590–614.

Grusky, Oscar. 1960. Administrative succession in formal organizations. *Social Forces* 39 (2): 105–15.

———. 1961. Corporate size, bureaucratization, and managerial succession. *American Journal of Sociology* 67: 263–69.

———. 1963. Managerial succession and organizational effectiveness. *American Journal of Sociology* 69: 297–317.

Guerard, John B. 1985. Mergers, stock prices, and industrial production: An empirical test of the Nelson hypothesis. In *Time series analysis: Theory and practice*, ed. O. D. Anderson, (7): 239–47. Amsterdam: Elsevier.

Guillen, Mauro. 1994. *Models of management: Work, authority, and organization in a comparative perspective*. Chicago: University of Chicago Press.

———. 2001. Is globalization civilizing, destructive, or feeble? A critique of six key debates in the social-science literature. *Annual Review of Sociology* 27: 235–60.

Gulati, Ranjay. 1995. Does familiarity breed trust? The implications of repeated ties for contractual choice in alliances. *Academy of Management Journal* 38 (1): 85–112.

Gulati, Ranjay, and M. Gargiulo. 1999. Where do networks come from? *American Journal of Sociology* 104 (5): 1439–93.

Gulati, Ranjay, and Habir Singh. 1998. The architecture of cooperation: Managing coordination costs and appropriation concerns in strategic alliances. *Administrative Science Quarterly* 43: 781–814.

Hannan, Michael T. 1998. Rethinking age dependence in organizational mortality: Logical formalizations. *American Journal of Sociology* 104, 126–64.

Hannan, Michael T., and Glenn R. Carroll. 1992. *Dynamics of organizational populations: Density, legitimation, and competition*. New York: Oxford University Press.

Hannan, Michael T., Glenn R. Carroll, E. A. Dundon, and J. C. Torres. 1995. Organization evolution in multinational context: Entries of automobile manufacturers in Belgium, Britain, France, Germany, and Italy. *American Sociological Review* 60: 509–28.

Hannan, Michael T., and John Freeman. 1977. The population ecology of organizations. *American Journal of Sociology* 82: 929–64.

———. 1984. Structural inertia and organizational change. *American Sociology Review* 49: 149–64.

Hannan, Michael T., and James Ranger-Moore. 1990. The ecology of organizational size distributions: A microsimulation approach. *Journal of Mathematical Sociology* 15: 67–89.

Harrison, Richard J., David L. Torres, and Sal Kukalis. 1988. The changing of the guard: Turnover and structural change in top-management positions. *Administrative Science Quarterly* 33: 211–32.

Haunschild, P. R. 1993. Interorganizational imitation: The impact of interlocks on corporate acquisition activity. *Administrative Science Quarterly* 38: 564–92.

———. 1994. How much is that company worth?: Interorganizational relationships, uncertainty and acquisition premiums. *Administrative Science Quarterly* 39 (3): 391–411.

Haveman, Heather A. 1993. Follow the leader: Mimetic isomorphism and entry into new markets. *Administrative Science Quarterly* 38: 593–627.

Haveman, Heather A., and Hayagreeva Rao. 1997. Structuring a theory of moral sentiments. *American Journal of Sociology* 102 (6): 1606–51.

——. Forthcoming. Hybrid forms and institutional change in the early California thrift industry. In *Bending the bars of the iron cage: Institutional dynamics and processes*, ed. Walter W. Powell and Daniel Jones. Chicago: University of Chicago Press.

Hayek, F. A. 1945. The use of knowledge. *The American Economic Review* 35 (4): 519–30.

Hinnings, C. R., and Royston Greenwood. 2002. Disconnects and consequences in organization theory. *Administrative Science Quarterly* 47 (3): 411–21.

Hirsch, Paul M. 1972. Processing fads and fashions: An organization-set analysis of cultural industry systems. *American Journal of Sociology* 77 (4): 639–59.

——. 1975. Organizational effectiveness and the institutional environment. *Administrative Science Quarterly* 20: 327–44.

——. 1986. From ambushes to golden parachutes: Corporate takeovers as an instance of cultural framing and institutional integration. *American Journal of Sociology* 91 (4): 800–37.

Hirsch, Paul M., and Michael Lounsbury. 1997. Ending the family quarrel: Towards a reconciliation of the "old" and "new" institutionalism. *American Behavioral Scientist* 40: 406–18.

Hirsch, Paul M., S. Michaels, and R. Friedman. 1987. "Dirty hands" versus "clean models": Is sociology in danger of being seduced by economists? *Theory and Society* 16: 317–36.

Hitt, M. A., R. E. Hoskisson, R. A. Johnson, and D. D. Moesel. 1996. The market for corporate control and firm innovation. *Academy of Management Journal* 39 (5): 1084–119.

Hochschild, Arlie Russell. 1983. *The managed heart: Commercialization of human feeling*. Berkeley: University of California Press.

Hoffman, Andrew, and William Ocasio. 2001. Not all events are attended equally: Toward a middle-range theory of industry attention to external events. *Organization Science* 12 (4): 414–34.

Hogarty, Thomas F. 1970. The profitability of corporate mergers. *The Journal of Business* 43 (3): 317–27.

Ingram, Paul, and Joel A. C. Baum. 1997. Chain affiliation and the failure of Manhattan hotels, 1898–1980. *Administrative Science Quarterly* 42: 68–102.

Jackall, Robert. 1988. *Moral mazes: The world of corporate managers*. New York: Oxford University Press.

James, William. 1890. *The principles of psychology*. Vol. 1: 403–4. New York: H. Holt.

Jensen, Michael C. 1993. The modern industrial revolution, exit, and the failure of internal control systems. *Journal of Finance* 48: 831–80.

Jensen, Michael C., and William H. Meckling. 1976. The theory of the firm: Managerial behavior and ownership structure. *Journal of Financial Analysis* 3: 305–60.

Jensen, Michael C., and Richard S. Ruback. 1983. The market for corporate control: The scientific evidence. *Journal of Financial Economics* 11: 5–50.

Jones, Candace, W. S. Hesterly, K. Fladmoe-Lindquist, and S. P. Borgatti. 1998. Constellations in professional services: How firm capabilities influence collaborative stability and change. *Organization Science* 9: 396–410.

Karim, Samina, and Will Mitchell. 2000. Path-dependent and path-breaking change: Reconfiguring business resources following acquisitions in the U.S. medical sector, 1978–1995. *Strategic Management Journal* 21: 1061–81.

Karnitschnig, Matthew, and Neal E. Boudette. 2002. Battle for Bertelsmann's Soul led to the ouster of its CEO. *The Wall Street Journal,* 30 July.

Kelley, H. H. 1967. Attribution processes in social psychology. In *Nebraska symposium on motivation,* ed. D. Levine, 192–38. Lincoln: University of Nebraska Press.

———. 1973. The processes of causal attribution. *American Psychologist* 28: 107–28.

Kraatz, Mathew S., and Edward J. Zajac. 1996. Exploring the limits of the new institutionalism: The causes and consequences of illegitimate organizational change. *American Sociological Review* 61 (5): 812–36.

Kreps, David M. 1990. Corporate culture and economic theory. In *Perspectives on positive political economy,* ed. James E. Alt and Kenneth A. Shepsie, 90–143. New York: Cambridge University Press.

Land, Kenneth, W. R. Davis, and Judith Blau. 1994. Organizing the boys of summer: The evolution of US minor-league baseball, 1883–1990. *American Journal of Sociology* 100 (3): 781–813.

Lane, Michael. 1975. Shapers of culture: The editor in book publishing. *The Annals of the American Academy of Political and Social Science* 421: 34–42.

Lane, Michael, and Jeremy Booth. 1970. *Books and publishers.* Lexington, MA: D. C. Heath.

Lant, Theresa K. 2002. Organizational cognition and interpretation. In *The Blackwell companion to organizations,* ed. Joel A. C. Baum, 344–62. Oxford, UK: Blackwell.

Lant, Theresa K., and Joel A. C. Baum. 1995. Cognitive sources of socially constructed competitive groups: Examples from the Manhattan hotel industry. In *The institutional construction of organizations: International and longitudinal studies,* ed. W. Richard Scott and Soren Christensen, 15–38. Thousand Oaks: Sage Publications.

Laumann, Edward O. 1991. Comment on "The future of bureaucracy and hierarchy in organization theory: A report from the field." In *Social theory for a changing society,* ed. Pierre Bourdieu and James Coleman, 90–93. Boulder, CO: Westview Press.

Laumann, Edward O., David Knoke, and Yong-Hak Kim. 1985. An organizational approach to state policy formation. *American Sociological Review* 50: 1–20.

Lawrence, Paul R., and Jay W. Lorsch. [1967] 1986. *Organization and environment: Managing differentiation and integration.* Boston: Harvard Business School Press.

Lazonick, William. 1992. Controlling the market for corporate control: The historical significance of managerial capitalism. *Industrial and Corporate Change* 1 (3): 445–88.

Levin, Martin P. 1996. The positive role of large corporations in U.S. book publishing. *Logos* 7: 127–37.

Lewin, Arie, Chris P. Long, and Timothy N. Carroll. 1999. The coevolution of new organizational forms. *Organization Science* 10 (5): 535–50.

Lincoln, J., M. Gerlach, and P. Takahasi. 1992. Keiretsu networks in the Japanese economy: A dyad analysis of intercorporate ties. *American Sociological Review* 57 (5): 561–85.

Literary Marketplace. Various issues. New York: R. R. Bowker.

Lopes, Paul D. 1992. Innovation and diversity in the popular music industry, 1969 to 1990. *American Sociological Review* 57: 56–71.

Manne, Henry G. 1965. Mergers and the market for corporate control. *Journal of Political Economy* 73: 110–20.

____. 2002. Bring back the hostile takeover. *The Wall Street Journal*, 26 June.

March, James G. 1994. *A primer on decision making: How decisions happen.* New York: Free Press.

March, James G., and Johan P. Olsen. 1976. *Ambiguity and choice in organizations.* Bergen, Norway: Universitetsforlaget.

____. 1989. *Rediscovering institutions: The organizational basis of politics.* New York: Free Press.

March, James G., and Herbert A. Simon. 1958. *Organizations.* New York: Wiley.

Marris, Robin. 1964. *The economic theory of managerial capitalism.* New York: Free Press.

Marris, Robin, and Dennis C. Mueller. 1980. The corporation, competition, and the invisible hand. *Journal of Economic Literature* 118, 32–63.

Martin, Joanne M. 1992. *Cultures in organizations.* New York: Oxford University Press.

Marwell, Gerald, and Ruth E. Ames. 1981. Economists free ride: Does anyone else? *Journal of Public Economies* 13: 295–310.

Mayhew, Bruce. 1980. Structuralism versus individualism: Part 1, shadowboxing in the dark. *Social Forces* 59 (2): 355–75.

McClelland, David C. 1961. *Achieving society.* New York: Irvington.

McCormick, Thomas. 1998. Bigger is confusinger. *Publishers Weekly*, 4 May 25.

McEachern, William A. 1975. *Managerial control and performance.* Lexington, MA: D. C. Heath.

McLean, Paul D., and John F. Padgett. 1997. Was Florence a perfectly competitive market? Transactional evidence from the renaissance. *Theory and Society* 26: 209–44, Apr.–Jun.

Melicher, Ronald W., Johannes Ledolter, and Louis J. D'Antonio. 1983. A time series analysis of aggregate merger activity. *Review of Economics and Statistics* 65: 423–30.

Merton, Robert K. 1949. *Social theory and social structure: Toward the codification of theory and research.* Glencoe, IL: Free Press.

____. 1957. *Social theory and social structure,* 2nd ed. Glencoe, IL: Free Press.

Meyer, J. 1986. Myths of socialization and of personality. In *Reconstructing individualism,* ed. T. Heller, M. Sosna, and D. Wellbery, 208–21. Stanford, CA: Stanford University Press.

Meyer, John W., John Boli, George M. Thomas, and Francisco O. Ramirez. 1997. World society and the nation-state. *American Journal of Sociology* 103 (1): 144–81.

Meyer, John W., and Brian Rowan. 1977. Institutional organizations: Formal structure as myth and ceremony. *American Journal of Sociology* 83: 340–63.

Meyer, Marshall W. 1994. Measuring performance in economic organizations. In *Handbook of economic sociology*, ed. Neil J. Smelser and Richard Swedberg, 556–78. Princeton, NJ: Princeton University Press.

Meyer, Marshall W., and Lynne G. Zucker. 1989. *Permanently failing organizations*. Newbury Park, CA: Sage.

Mezias, John M., and Stephen J. Mezias. 2000. Resource partitioning, the founding of specialist firms, and innovation: The American feature film industry. *Organization Science* 11 (3): 306–22.

Mezias, Stephen J. 1990. An institutional model of organizational practice: Financial reporting at the Fortune 200. *Administrative Science Quarterly* 35: 431–57.

Miller, E. J., and A. K. Rice. 1967. Systems of organizations. London: Tavistock.

Milliot, Jim. 2000a. Reed buys Harcourt, will sell parts to Thomson. *Publishers Weekly*, 20 October, 10.

———. 2000b. Two studies see healthy book market ahead. *Publishers Weekly*, 18 September.

———. 2002. Speculation mounts over Houghton Mifflin's future. *Publishers Weekly*, 15 July, 10.

Miner, Anne S., Terry L. Amburgey, and Timothy M. Stearns. 1990. Interorganizational linkages and population dynamics: Buffering and transformational shields. *Administrative Science Quarterly* 35: 689–713.

Mischel, Walter. 1968. *Personality and assessment*. New York: Wiley.

Mischel, Walter, and P. K. Peake. 1982. Beyond déjà vu in the search for cross-situational consistency. *Psychological Review* 89: 730–55.

Mitchell, Will. 1994. The dynamics of evolving markets: The effects of business sales and age on dissolutions and divestitures. *Administrative Science Quarterly* 39 (4): 575–602.

Mizruchi, Mark S. 1982. *The American corporate network, 1904–1974*. Beverly Hills, CA: Sage.

Mizruchi, Mark S., and Lisa C. Fein. 1999. The social construction of organizational knowledge: A study of the uses of coercive, mimetic, and normative isomorphism. *Administrative Science Quarterly* 44: 653–83.

Mizruchi, Mark S., and Linda B. Stearns. 1988. A longitudinal study of the formation of interlocking directorates. *Administrative Science Quarterly* 33: 194–210.

Moore, John Hammond. 1982. *Wiley: One hundred and seventy-five years of publishing*. New York: John Wiley and Sons.

Moore, Kelly. 1999. Political protest and institutional change: The anti-Vietnam war movement and American science. In *How social movements matter*, ed. Marco Giugni, Doug McAdams, and Charles Tilley, 97–118. Minneapolis: University of Minnesota Press.

Morck, Randall, Andrei Shleifer, and Robert Vishny. 1989. Alternative mechanisms for corporate control. *American Economic Review* 79 (4): 842–52.

Morris, Christopher. 1994. *A history of Harcourt Brace*. New York: Harcourt Brace.

Morris, M. W., and K. Peng. 1994. Culture and cause: American and Chinese attributions for social and physical events. *Journal of Personality and Social Psychology* 67 (6): 949–71.

Mueller, Dennis C. 1977. The effects of conglomerate mergers. *Journal of Banking and Finance* 1: 315–47.

Nadel, S. F. 1957. *A theory of social structure*. London: Cohen & West.

National Center for Education Statistics. 1993. *Digest of educational statistics*. Washington, DC: National Center for Education Statistics.

Nelson, Ralph L. 1959. *Merger movements in American industry, 1895–1956*. Princeton, NJ: Princeton University Press.

Nelson, Richard R., and Sidney G. Winter. 1982. *An evolutionary theory of economic change*. Cambridge: Belknap Press of Harvard University Press.

Nisbett, R., E. K. Peng, I. Choi, and A. Norenzayan. 2001. Culture and systems of thought: Holistic versus analytic cognition. *Psychological Review* 108: 291–310.

North, Douglass C. 1990. *Institutions, institutional change, and economic performance*. Cambridge: Cambridge University Press.

Ocasio, William. 1994. Political dynamics and the circulation of power: CEO succession in U.S. industrial corporations, 1960–1990. *Administrative Science Quarterly* 39: 285–312.

____. 1997. Toward an attention-based view of the firm. *Strategic Management Journal* 18: 187–206.

____. 1999. Institutionalized action and corporate governance: The reliance on rules of CEO succession. *Administrative Science Quarterly* 44:384–416.

Ocasio, William, and Hyosun Kim. 1999. The circulation of corporate control: Selection of functional backgrounds of new CEOs in large U.S. manufacturing firms, 1981–1992. *Administrative Science Quarterly* 44 (2): 384–416.

Ocasio, William, and Patricia H. Thornton. 2002. Markets with hierarchies: The effects of alternative strategies and structures on organizational survival, working paper, Kellogg Graduate School of Management, Northwestern University.

Oliver, Christine. 1991. Strategic responses to institutional processes. *Academy of Management Review* 16: 145–79.

Orwall, Bruce, and Martin Peers. 2002. Media megamergers aren't big hits as futuristic synergies prove elusive. *The Wall Street Journal*, 10 May.

Oster, Sharon M. 1990. *Modern competitive analysis*. New York: Oxford University Press.

Owen-Smith, Jason, and Walter W. Powell. 2002. Knowledge networks in the Boston biotechnology community, paper presented at conference on Science as an Institution and the Institutions of Science, University of Sienna, January 25–26.

Palmer, Donald, Brad M. Barber, Xueguang Zhou, and Yasemin Soysal. 1995. The acquisition of large U.S. corporations in the 1960s. *American Sociological Review* 60 (4): 469–99.

Palmer, Donald, Roger Friedland, P. Devereaux Jennings, and Melanie. E. Powers. 1987. The economics and politics of structure: The multidivisional form and the large U.S. corporation. *Administrative Science Quarterly* 32: 25–48.

Palmer, Donald, P. Devereaux Jennings, and Xueguang Zhou. 1993. Late adoption of the multidivisional form by large U.S. corporations: Institutional, political, and economic accounts. *Administrative Science Quarterly* 38: 100–131.

Parsons, Talcot. 1951. *The social system*. New York: Free Press.

Payne, John W., James R. Bettman, and Eric J. Johnson. 1992. Behavioral decision research: A constructive processing perspective. *Annual Review of Psychology* 43: 87–131.

Peers, Martin, Mathew Rose, and Mathew Karnitschnig. 2002. Bertelsmann chief's exit adds to the growing digital divide. *The Wall Street Journal*, 28 July.

Peiperl, Maury, Michael Arthur, and N. Anand. 2002. *Career creativity: Explorations in the remaking of work*. Oxford: Oxford University Press.

Penrose, Edith Tilton. 1952. Biological analogies in the theory of the firm. *American Economic Review* 42: 804–19.

———. 1959. *The theory of the growth of the firm*. New York: Wiley.

Perrow, Charles. 1967. A framework for the comparative analysis of organizations. *American Sociological Review* 32: 194–208.

———. 1986. *Complex organizations*. New York: Random House.

Peters, Tom J., and R. H. Waterman. 1982. *In search of excellence: Lessons from America's best-run companies*. New York: Harper and Row.

Peterson, Richard A. 1999. *Creating country music: Fabricating authenticity*. Chicago: University of Chicago Press.

Peterson, Richard A., and David G. Berger. 1996. Measuring industry concentration, diversity, and innovation in popular music. *American Sociological Review* 61: 175–78.

Pfeffer, Jeffrey. 1972. Mergers as a response to organizational interdependence. *Administrative Science Quarterly* 17 (3): 382–94.

———. 1981. *Power in organizations*. Marshfield, MA: Pitman.

———. 1992. *Managing with power: Politics and influence in organizations*. Boston: Harvard Business School Press.

———. 1993. Barriers to the advance of organizational science: Paradigm development as a dependent variable, *Academy of Management Review* 19: 599–620.

Pfeffer, Jeffrey, and Gerald Salancik. 1978. *The external control of organizations*. New York: Harper and Row. (Reprinted 2003, Stanford University Press.)

Phillips, Daemon. 2002. A genealogical approach to organizational life chances: The parent–progeny transfer and silicon valley law firms, 1946–1996. *Administrative Science Quarterly* 47: 474–506

Podolny, J. M. 1993. A status-based model of market competition. *American Journal of Sociology* 98: 829–72.

Podolny, J. M., and K. L. Page. 1998. Network forms of organization. *Annual Review of Sociology* 24 (1): 57–77.

Porac, Joseph F., Howard Thomas, Fiona Wilson, Douglas Paton, and Alaina Kanfer. 1995. Rivalry and the industry model of Scottish knitwear producers. *Administrative Science Quarterly* 40: 203–27.

Porter, Michael E. 1980. *Competitive strategy: Techniques for analyzing industries and competitors*. New York: Free Press.

Powell, Walter W. 1980. Competition versus concentration in the book trade. *Journal of Communication* 30 (2): 89–97.

———. 1985. *Getting into print: The decision-making process in scholarly publishing*. Chicago: University of Chicago Press.

———. 1990. Neither market nor hierarchy: Network forms of organization. In *Research in organizational behavior*. Vol. 12, ed. Barry M. Straw and L. L. Cummings, 295–336. Greenwich, CT: JAI Press.

___. 1991. Expanding the scope of institutional analysis. In *The new institutionalism in organizational analysis*, ed. Walter W. Powell, and Paul J. DiMaggio, 183–203. Chicago: University of Chicago Press.

Powell, Walter W., and Paul J. DiMaggio, eds. 2001. *The new institutionalism in organizational analysis.* Chicago: University of Chicago Press.

Powell, Walter W., K. W. Koput, and Laurel Smith-Doerr. 1996. Interorganizational collaboration and the locus of innovation: Networks of learning in biotechnology. *Administrative Science Quarterly* 42 (1): 116–45.

Powell, Walter W., and Laurel Smith-Doerr. 1994. Networks and economic life. In *The handbook of economic sociology*, ed. Neil Smelser and Richard Swedberg, 368–402. Princeton, NJ: Princeton University Press.

Puffer, Sheila M., and John B. Weintrop. 1991. Corporate performance and CEO turnover: The role of performance expectations. *Administrative Science Quarterly* 36 (1): 1–19.

Ramirez, Francisco O., Yasemin Soysal, and Suzanne Shanahan. 1997. The changing logic of political citizenship: Cross-national acquisition of women's suffrage rights, 1890–1990. *American Sociological Review* 62: 735–45.

Ravenscraft, David. 1987. The 1980s merger wave: An industrial organization perspective. In *The merger boom*, ed. L. Browne and E. Rosengren, 17–37. Boston: Federal Reserve Bank.

Reid, James M. 1969. *An adventure in textbooks.* New York: R. R. Bowker Company.

Reid, Samuel Richardson. 1968. *Mergers, managers and the economy.* New York: McGraw-Hill.

Roll, Richard. 1986. The hubris hypothesis of corporate takeovers. *Journal of Business* 59: 197–212.

Rousseau, Denise M., Sim B. Sitkin, Ronald S. Burt, and Colin Camerer. 1998. Not so different after all: A cross-discipline view of trust. *Academy of Management Review*, 23 (3): 393–404.

Roy, William G. 1997. *Socializing capital: The rise of the large industrial corporation in America.* Princeton, NJ: Princeton University Press.

Ruef, Martin, and W. Richard Scott. 1998. A multidimensional model of organizational legitimacy: Hospital survival in changing institutional environments. *Administrative Science Quarterly* 43 (4): 877–904.

Rumelt, Richard P. 1974. *Strategy and structure and economic performance.* Cambridge: Harvard University Press.

Salancik, Gerald R., and Jeffrey Pfeffer. 1980. Effects of ownership on executive tenure in U.S. corporations. *Academy of Management Journal* 23: 653–64.

Schiffrin, André. 2000. *The business of books: How international conglomerates took over publishing and changed the way we read.* New York: Verso.

Schneiberg, Marc. 1997. Associations and states versus markets and hierarchies: Contradictions and tradeoffs in property insurance governance. Paper presented at the meeting of the Western Political Science Association.

Schneiberg, Marc, and Timothy Bartley. 2001. Regulating American industries: Markets, politics, and the institutional determinants of fire insurance regulation. *American Journal of Sociology* 107: 101–46.

Schneiberg, Marc, and Elisabeth Clemens. Forthcoming. The typical tools for the job: Research strategies in institutional analysis. In *Bending the bars of the iron cage: institutional dynamics and processes*, ed. Walter W. Powell and Daniel Jones. Chicago: University of Chicago Press.

Scott, W. Richard. 1987. The adolescence of institutional theory. *Administrative Science Quarterly* 32: 493–511.

___. 2001. *Institutions and organizations*, 2nd ed. Thousand Oaks, CA: Sage.

___. 2003. *Organizations: Rational, natural, and open systems*, 5th ed. Upper Saddle River, NJ. Prentice Hall.

Scott, W. Richard, and John W. Meyer. 1983. The organization of societal sectors. In *Organizational environments: Rituals and rationality*, ed. John W. Meyer and W. Richard Scott. 129–53. Newbury Park, CA: Sage. (Revised version in *The new institutionalism in organizational analysis*, ed. Walter W. Powell and Paul J. DiMaggio, 108–40. Chicago: University of Chicago Press, 1991).

Scott, W. Richard, Martin Ruef, P. J. Mendel, and C. Caronna. 2000. *Institutional change and healthcare organizations: From professional dominance to managed care*. Chicago, University of Chicago Press.

Searle, John R. 1995. *The social construction of reality*. New York: The Free Press.

Selznick, Philip. 1949. *TVA and the grass roots*. Berkeley: University of California Press.

___. 1957. *Leadership in administration*. Berkeley: University of California Press.

Sewell, W. H., Jr. 1992. A theory of structure: Duality, agency, and transformation. *American Journal of Sociology* 98: 1–29.

Shatzkin, Leonard. 1982. *In cold type: Overcoming the book crisis*. Boston: Houghton Mifflin.

Shaver, K. G. 1995. The entrepreneurial personality myth, *Business & Economic Review* 41 (3), 20–23.

Shaver, Kelly G., and Linda R. Scott. 1991. Person, process, choice: The psychology of new venture creation. *Entrepreneurship Theory and Practice* 16: 23–45.

Simon, Herbert A. [1945] 1957. *Administrative behavior*, 2nd ed. New York: Macmillan.

___. 1962. The architecture of complexity. Proceedings of the American Philosophical Society, 106: 467–82.

___. 1969. *The sciences of the artificial*. Cambridge: Massachusetts Institute of Technology Press.

___. [1947] 1997. *Administrative behavior: A study of decision-making processes in administrative organizations*, 4th ed. New York: Free Press.

Simpson, Ida Harper. 1989. The sociology of work: Where have the workers gone? *Social Forces* 67 (3): 563–79.

Singh, Jitendra V., David J. Tucker, and Robert J. House. 1986. Organizational legitimacy and the liability of newness. *Administrative Science Quarterly* 31: 171–93.

Smith, A. [1776] 1976. *An inquiry into the nature and causes of the wealth of nations*. Vol. 1. Chicago: University of Chicago Press.

Smith, Joel. 1995. *Understanding the media: A sociology of mass communication*. Cresskill, NJ: Hampton Press.

Sperling, John G. 2000. *Rebel with a cause: The entrepreneur who created the university of phoenix and the non-profit revolution in higher education*. New York: John Wiley.

Spulber, Daniel P. 1999. *Market microstructure: Intermediaries and the theory of the firm.* Cambridge: Cambridge University Press.

Standard and Poor's. *Standard and Poor's Industry Surveys: Basic Analysis.* Various years. Standard and Poor's.

Starr, Paul. 1982. *The social transformation of American medicine.* New York: Basic Books.

Stearns, Linda Brewster, and Kenneth D. Allan. 1996. Economic behavior in institutional environments: The corporate merger wave of the 1980s. *American Sociological Review* 61: (4), 699–718.

Steiner. P. O. 1975. *Mergers: Motives, effects, policies.* Ann Arbor: University of Michigan Press.

Stigler, George J. 1966. The economic effects of the antitrust laws. *Journal of Law and Economics* 9: 225–58.

———. 1982. The economists and the problem of monopoly. *American Economic Review* 72 (2): 1–11.

———. 1983. Comments on "The Fire of Truth: A Remembrance of Law and Economics at Chicago, 1932–1970," edited by Edmund W. Kitch. *Journal of Law and Economics* 26:163–234.

Stigler, George, and Gary Becker. 1977. De gustibus non est disputandum. *American Economic Review* 67: 67–90.

Stinchcombe, Arthur L. 1959. Bureaucratic and craft administration of production: A comparative study. *Administrative Science Quarterly* 4: 168–87.

———. 1965. Social structure and organizations. In *Handbook of organizations*, ed. James G. March, 142–93. Chicago: Rand McNally.

———. 1987. *Constructing social theories.* Chicago: University of Chicago Press.

———. 1990. *Information and organizations.* Berkeley: University of California Press.

———. 1997. On the virtues of the old institutions. *Annual Review of Sociology* 23: 1–18.

———. 2002. New sociological microfoundations for organizational theory: A postscript. In *Social structures and organizations revisited.* Vol. 19, ed. M. Lounsbury and M. Ventresca, 415–33. Amsterdam: Elsevier Science.

Strang, David, and John W. Meyer. 1994. Institutional conditions for diffusion. In *Institutional environments and organizations: structural complexity and individualism*, ed. W. Richard Scott and John W. Meyer, 100–112. Thousand Oaks, CA: Sage.

Stuart, Toby, and Waverly Ding. 2002. Academic entrepreneurs. Talk presented at the Organizations & Markets Workshop, 5 March, at University of Chicago Graduate School of Business, Chicago.

Sutton, John R., and Frank Dobbin. 1996. The two faces of governance: Responses to legal uncertainty in U.S. firms, 1955 to 1985. *American Sociological Review* 61: 794–811.

Swedberg, Richard. 1994. Markets as social structures. In *The handbook of economic sociology*, ed. Neil J. Smelser and Richard Swedberg, 255–82. Princeton, NJ: Princeton University Press.

———. 2003. The case for an economic sociology of law. *Theory and Society* 32 (1): 1–37.

Swidler, Ann. 1986. Culture in action: Symbols and strategies. *American Sociological Review* 51: 273–86.

Tebbel, John. 1972. *A history of book publishing in the United States,* Vol. I, *The creation of an industry,* 1630–1865. New York: R. R. Bowker.

____. 1981. *A history of book publishing in the United States*, Vol. IV, *The great change 1940–1980*. New York: R. R. Bowker.

____. 1987. *Between covers: The rise and transformation of book publishing in America*. New York: Oxford University Press.

____. 1996. Book Trade. Entry in Microsoft Encarta 97 *Encyclopedia*. CD ROM.

Thompson, James D. 1967. *Organizations in action*. New York: McGraw-Hill.

Thornton, Patricia H. 1993. From craft house to corporate enterprise: Acquisition growth of college publishing 1958 to 1990. Ph.D. diss. Stanford University.

____. 1995. Accounting for acquisition waves: Evidence from the U.S. college publishing industry. In *The institutional construction of organizations: International and longitudinal studies*, ed. W. Richard Scott and Soren Christensen, 199–225. Thousand Oaks: Sage.

____. 1999a. Concentrated markets in cultural industries: Are economies of scale an entry barrier to new firms in the higher education publishing industry? Paper presented at Organizations: Regular Session, American Sociological Association, Chicago.

____. 1999b. The sociology of entrepreneurship. *Annual Review of Sociology* 25: 19–46.

____. 2001. Personal versus market logics of control: A historically contingent theory of the risk of acquisition. *Organization Science* 12: 294–311.

____. 2002. The rise of the corporation in a craft industry: Conflict and conformity in institutional logics. *Academy of Management Journal* 45: 81–101.

Thornton, Patricia H., and Nancy Brandon Tuma. 1995. The problem of boundaries in contemporary research on organizations. Best Paper Proceedings of the 1995 Academy of Management, 55th Annual meeting, Vancouver, Canada.

Thornton Patricia H., and William Ocasio. 1999. Institutional logics and the historical contingency of power in organizations: Executive succession in the higher education publishing industry, 1958–1990. *American Journal of Sociology* 105 (3): 801–43.

Tilly, Charles. 1997. History and sociological imagining. In *Sociological visions*, ed. K. Erickson, 67–82. Lanham, MD: Rowman & Littlefield.

Tolbert, Pamela S., and Lynne G. Zucker. 1983. Institutional sources of change in the formal structure of organizations: The diffusion of civil service reform, 1880–1935. *Administrative Science Quarterly* 30 (March), 22–39.

Tuma, Nancy Brandon. 1990. Event History Analysis. Seminar notes, Stanford University.

Tuma, Nancy Brandon. 1993. RATE software program, version 3.0A.

Tuma, Nancy Brandon, and Michael Hannan. 1984. *Social dynamics: Models and methods*. Orlando: Academic Press.

Tushman, Michael L., and Philip Anderson. 1986. Technological discontinuities and organizational environments. *Administrative Science Quarterly* 31: 439–65.

Tversky, Amos, and Daniel Kahneman. 1986. Rational choice and the framing of decisions. *Journal of Business* 59 (4): S251–78.

Useem, Michael. 1996. *Investor capitalism: How money managers are changing the face of corporate America*. New York: Basic Books.

Uzzi, Brian. 1996. The sources and consequences of embeddedness for the economic performance of organizations: The network effect. *American Sociological Review* 61: 674–98.

Ventresca, Marc J., and John W. Mohr. 2002. Archival research methods. In *The Blackwell companion to organizations*, ed. Joel A.C. Baum. Oxford, UK: Blackwell Publishers.

Vesper, Karl H. 1990. *New venture strategies*. Englewood Cliffs, NJ: Prentice Hall.

von Hippel, W., J. Jonides, J. L. Hilton, and S. Narayan. 1993. Inhibitory effect of schematic processing on perceptual encoding. *Journal of Personality and Social Psychology* 64: 921–35.

Walsh, James P. 1998. Top management turnover following mergers and acquisitions. *Strategic Management Journal* 9: 173–83.

Weber, Max. 1904. *The Protestant ethic and the spirit of capitalism*. Berkeley: University of California Press.

____. [1922] 1978. *Economy and society: An outline of interpretive sociology*, ed. Guenther Roth and Claus Wittich. Berkeley: University of California Press.

Weeks, John, and Charles Galunic. 2003. A theory of the cultural evolution of the firm: The intra-organizational ecology of memes. *Organization Studies* 24 (8): 1309–52.

Weick, Karl E. 1976. Educational organizations as loosely coupled systems. *Administrative Science Quarterly* 21: 1–19.

Weisbach, Michael S. 1988. Outside directors and CEO turnover. *Journal of Financial Economics* 20: 431–60.

Wernerfelt, Birger. 1984. A resource-based view of the firm. *Strategic Management Journal* 5: 171–80.

Westphal, James D., and Edward J. Zajac. 1994. Substance and symbolism in CEOs' long-term incentive plans. *Administrative Science Quarterly* 39: 367–90.

White, Harrison C. 1981a. Production markets as induced role structures. In *Sociological methodology*, ed. Samuel Leinhardt. San Francisco: Jossey-Bass.

____. 1981b. Where do markets come from? *American Journal of Sociology* 87: 517–47.

____. 1992. *Identity and control: A structural theory of social action*. Princeton, NJ: Princeton University Press.

____. 1993. Markets in production networks. In *Explorations in economic sociology*, ed. Richard Swedberg, 161–75. New York: Russell Sage Foundation.

____. 1997. *Identity and control: A structural theory of social action*. Princeton, NJ: Princeton University Press.

____. 2002. *Markets from networks: Socioeconomic models of production*. Princeton, NJ: Princeton University Press.

White, Harrison C., Scott A. Boorman, and Ronald L. Breiger. 1976. Social structures from multiple networks: Part I. Blockmodels of roles and positions. *American Journal of Sociology* 81: 730–80.

Whitley, Richard. 1999. *Divergent capitalisms: The social structuring and the change of business systems*. Oxford, UK: Oxford University Press.

Wiley, Peter. 1999. E-mail interview.

Williamson, Oliver E. 1975. *Markets and hierarchies*. New York: Free Press.

____. 1991. Comparative economic organization: The analysis of discrete structural alternatives. *Administrative Science Quarterly* 36: 269–96.

____. 1994. Transaction cost economics and organization theory. In *The handbook of economic sociology*, ed. Neil J. Smelser and Richard Swedberg, 77–107. Princeton, NJ: Princeton University Press.

Wrigley, Leonard. 1970. Divisional autonomy and diversification, Ph.D. diss., Harvard Business School.

Wuthnow, Robert. 1989. *Communities of discourse: Ideology and social structure in the reformation, the enlightenment, and European socialism.* Cambridge: Harvard University Press.

Zajac, Edward J., and James D. Westphal. 1996. Who shall succeed? How CEO/board preferences and power affect the choice of new CEOs. *Academy of Management Journal* 39: 64–90.

____. 2001. Explaining institutional decoupling: The case of the stock repurchase programs. *Administrative Science Quarterly* 46 (2): 202–28.

Zald, Mayer N., and Patricia Denton. 1963. From evangelism to general service: The transformation of the YMCA. *Administrative Science Quarterly* 8: 214–34.

Zelditch, M. 1971. Intelligible comparisons, In *Comparative methods in sociology*, ed. Ivan Vallier, 267–307. Berkeley: University of California Press.

Zelizer, Viviana A. 1999. Economic sociology. International encyclopedia of the social and behavioral sciences.

Zerubavel, Eviatar. 1998. *Social mindscapes: An invitation to cognitive sociology.* Cambridge: Harvard University Press.

Zey, Mary, and T. Swenson. 1998. Corporate tax laws, corporate restructuring, and subsidiarization of corporate form, 1981–1995. *The Sociological Quarterly* 39 (4): 555–82.

____. 1998. The transformation of corporate control to owners and the multisubsidiary form: 1981–1993. *Research in Organizational Change and Development* 11: 271–312.

Zhou, Xueguang. 1993. The dynamics of organizational rules. *American Journal of Sociology* 98 (5): 1134–66.

Zhou, Xueguang, Nancy Brandon Tuma, and Phyllis Moen. 1997. Institutional change and job shift patterns in urban China, 1949 to 1994. *American Sociological Review* 62: 339–65.

Zucker, Lynne G. 1977. The role of institutionalization in cultural persistence. *American Sociological Review* 42: 726–43.

____. 1983. Organizations as institutions. *Research in the Sociology of Organizations* 2: 1–47.

Zuckerman, Ezra W. 1999. The categorical imperative: Securities analyst and the illegitimacy discount. *American Journal of Sociology* 104: 1398–1438.

Printed and bound by CPI Group (UK) Ltd, Croydon, CR0 4YY

16/04/2025

14658401-0003